"Is it true, Mr. Chambers, that on August 26, 1986, you intended to cause serious physical injury to Jennifer Levin and thereby caused her death?"

—*Judge Howard E. Bell*

"YES, YOUR HONOR . . ."

—*Robert E. Chambers*

———————

With that confession to the charge of first-degree manslaughter, the most sensational trial of the decade ended. But haunting questions remain:

- Was the 6′ 4″ Chambers bound and sexually attacked by the 5′ 8″ Levin?
- Was it possible for her to have died quickly, as Chambers attested in his videotaped admission, or did she die slowly as a result of deliberate strangulation?
- Was the jury swayed by Chambers' attorney Jack Litman's practice of "putting the victim on trial," bringing up Jennifer's sexual past as an issue?
- Were the scratches on Chambers' face the fault of his cat, or did they represent Jennifer's desperate struggle to live?
- Who won the lawyers' duel which ended up in the plea bargain—Jack Litman or Assistant DA Linda Fairstein?

Veteran author and journalist Bryna Taubman delves into the mystery of what *really* happened in Central Park on that hot August night, takes you behind the scenes of a riveting murder trial and reveals the human side of this tale of murder, privilege and wasted lives among Manhattan's golden children.

THE PREPPY MURDER TRIAL

Bryna Taubman

ST. MARTIN'S PRESS/NEW YORK

THE PREPPY MURDER TRIAL

Copyright © 1988 by Bryna Taubman.

Cover photos by Sygma Photo News.

All rights reserved. No part of this book may be used or reproduced in any manner whatsoever without written permission except in the case of brief quotations embodied in critical articles or reviews. For information, address St. Martin's Press, 175 Fifth Avenue, New York, N.Y. 10010.

ISBN: 0-312-92205-1   Can. ISBN: 0312-99207-8

Printed in the United States of America

First St. Martin's Press mass market edition/August 1988

10 9 8 7 6 5

ACKNOWLEDGMENTS

I want to thank several busy people who took the time to answer my questions at length. Chambers' prosecutor Linda Fairstein and his defense counsel Jack Litman were most generous. So were jurors Elizabeth Bauch, Eliot Kornhauser, Gerard Mosconi, Robert Nickey and Cole Wallace.

Colleagues and friends who provided welcome support and information were Sam Maull of the Associated Press, Irene Cornell of WCBS News Radio, Mike Pearl of *The New York Post* and Tim Clifford of *New York Newsday*, Larry Sutton and Pat Clark of the *Daily News*, Kirk Johnson of *The New York Times*, Danny Meenan Jr. and the staff of WMCA's Barry Gray Show, Christine Cornell and Ellen Fleysher and Magee Hickey of WNBC-TV, Lou Young of WABC-TV, Jamie Zahn and Beverly Solochek of ABC-TV's "Good Morning America," Amy Rosenblum and Sue Wiggins of CBS "This Morning," and Randy Doughit of "Larry King Live!".

Important help came from Steve Marcus of the New

York Telephone Company, Sergeant Larry Engel and the Chambers trial court-officers crew, and Central Park tree coordinator Furman C. Horton 3d, who explained to me the difference between an American elm and a crabapple tree.

Special thanks to Bruno Butler for his constructive criticism and willingness to run errands—and to Ralph for everything.

To Ralph—
With all of my love, forever.

PROLOGUE

When Jennifer Levin was killed in Central Park, sometime between five and five-thirty in the morning of August 26, 1986, the vast park was as quiet as it always was just before dawn. The occasional sounds to be heard were muted—a lone automobile on the park roadway or the footfall of an early jogger. Of the thousands of New Yorkers asleep nearby, none heard Jennifer Levin's final gasp for breath.

But for all the silence, Jennifer Levin did not go quietly. The bruised and twisted body of the pretty eighteen-year-old was eloquent testimony to the violence of her death.

She was sprawled partly nude at the base of a large American elm tree off the park's winding East Drive, barely fifty yards behind the Metropolitan Museum of Art. She lay south to north, her arms and legs askew in all directions, her right fist tilted upward at the Manhattan sky.

The scoop-necked blouse and bra were pushed up to her throat, baring untanned breasts. The pink-and-

1

white skirt was hiked to her waist, with the belly and pubis exposed. Only the feet remained fully covered, in white canvas flat shoes.

The stark tableau, redolent of murder, was shielded from part of the East Drive by a sagging branch of the elm. Since death had occurred just before daybreak, the darkness provided even more cover.

Just one person was physically close enough to see how Jennifer Levin died. He was someone she had thought she knew very well. Too well, by some standards. Not nearly well enough, as it turned out.

Robert Chambers, nineteen, tall and handsome, had spent the last hour of Jennifer's life with her. He would stay close to her lifeless body for another ninety minutes, possibly never more than one hundred feet away.

An autopsy would indicate that Jennifer Levin had died of asphyxiation by strangulation, but exactly how she had been strangled remained a mystery.

For several hours Robert Chambers denied any knowledge of or responsibility for her death, then offered detectives a strange tale of kinky sex, anger, and reflexive action. His face and body bore wounds from an apparent struggle.

Despite a sixty-five-minute videotape in which Robert Chambers claimed that his actions accidentally caused Jennifer's death, his indictment on second-degree murder charges alleged that he intended to kill her.

Chambers' trial, beginning more than sixteen months after Jennifer Levin was killed, failed to clear up the confusion. Witnesses changed their accounts of what they had seen. The police confessed to a series of missed clues, misplaced evidence, misapplied procedures, and mistaken inferences that further clouded the case. Experts offered contradictory opinions about the causes and nature of the injuries to both

Robert and Jennifer. And the rules of evidence limited the information available to the jury about those fateful moments in the park.

Only Robert Chambers knew exactly what happened. To this day, only he knows the full truth.

The rest of the world, or the part of it that cares, knows only what emerged during his trial.

1

THE MORNING AFTER

Dr. Allen Garber was the first known witness at the scene. He was thirty-one years old, a bearded physician living with his pregnant wife a few blocks east of Central Park, and he often awoke early to go jogging.

On that August morning, the digital clock on the microwave oven in the kitchen read 5:00. Garber remembered glancing at it on his way to the apartment door.

Five minutes later he entered the park at East 72nd Street and Fifth Avenue, Garber testified at Robert Chambers' trial. The streetlights were off in that part of Manhattan, and the sun was not up yet, but the sky was getting lighter.

Inside the park, Garber headed north on the one-way East Drive, jogging beside the few automobiles out at that hour. He ran in the bike lane three feet off the left curb. At the south end of the Metropolitan Museum of Art he climbed a gentle rise crowned with the three-thousand-year-old Egyptian obelisk known as Cleopatra's Needle.

After rounding the curve at the obelisk, Garber said, he dimly glimpsed two people on the grass in a grove of trees off to the left about ten yards ahead of him. One person was kneeling, straddling the other person. They faced each other, their shoulders parallel.

The bespectacled Garber slowed his pace slightly and peered at them. He told police the next day that the straddler was "rocking," and that he thought "something sexual" was going on.

A reasonable assumption on any summer night in Central Park.

But in court months later Garber changed some details. He said he had since measured the site. He placed it about two hundred feet northeast of where the body was found an hour later.

"I saw one person shaking another person," Garber said on the witness stand. "One person leaning over the other. The person on top was shaking the person on the bottom, what appeared to be [by] the shoulders."

He could not see their faces. "The person on top was facing northwest, away from me." And the second person? Garber, an internist at Bronx Lebanon Hospital, replied:

"The second person appeared lifeless."

Garber said he had first told the police he thought "something sexual" was going on because "at that time, I wanted to minimize what I had seen."

Now, seventeen months later, he recalled more details.

The person on top was a broad-shouldered man in a white shirt, Garber said. "He had hair that looked like Caucasian hair . . . a little longer than mine." Both persons were white, Garber thought, but he was thirty feet away and in the murky light at five-fifteen or so he could only distinguish an "outline" of the person on the bottom. He couldn't tell if it was a woman.

Garber remembered pausing uncertainly in the empty roadway. The silence seemed absolute. He testified that he heard no sound from the pair on the grass.

He watched them for "ten or fifteen seconds" before running footsteps came up behind him, said Garber, and he turned around. Another jogger. He stopped him and pointed at the pair. The man laughed, made an obscene comment, shook his head, and kept running.

Garber said he also jogged on, but slowly. He thought of his wife alone at home. He weighed his own vulnerability, alone with two dim figures in the grove. He glanced backward once as he ran north. Now he could barely see them, but their positions had not changed.

As Garber jogged around the huge Central Park reservoir on the cinder path that circled the water, two or three other runners were also on the path. Completing the loop in "fifteen or sixteen minutes," testified Garber, he regained the East Drive, heading south.

As he approached the spot behind the museum, it had gotten "a little lighter," said Garber. He glanced again toward the grove of magnolias and flowering crabapple trees—a stage with two players.

They were still there, Garber said, and they still hadn't changed position. After fifteen or sixteen minutes? "Yes," Garber testified. "I saw the two people in the same position. The top person shaking the bottom person."

It had to be about five-thirty by then. Was Garber sure? "I'm absolutely sure," he said on the stand.

This time, recalled Garber, he made a decision quickly. He wanted no part of it. To intrude on strangers in the park at that hour did not seem like a good idea.

He jogged south and left the park at East 72d Street,

his normal exit. "I ran home, stopping at the usual deli for breakfast." It was 5:45 A.M. by the clock on the deli wall.

Garber soon departed for the health center where he worked. Not until the following day, after reading in *The New York Times* about the strangulation of a young woman in Central Park, did he call the police.

In court he was challenged with a question:

"You were a doctor at that time. You saw what appeared to be a lifeless body, and you did not stop to help?"

"No. I don't know why I didn't do anything about it," Garber said, "but I didn't."

When he phoned the police, he said. "I just wanted to report that I'd seen something."

Why not the whole truth?

"I minimized what I saw because of fear," he said. "My wife was pregnant and was about to have a baby. . . . I don't know why else."

In time, his report that he had seen "something sexual" going on would be described in court as "the closest thing we have to an eyewitness in this case."

But Allen Garber had also told the jury that he had seen a broad-shouldered man in a white shirt at the homicide scene. And that he had twice seen the man shaking what looked like a lifeless body.

Christopher C. Ferrer, a lanky forty-four-year-old multinational trade consultant, testified that he'd jogged behind the museum that same morning, slightly later. It was nearly 5:40 A.M. when Ferrer completed his stretching exercises, he said. His wife tended their child in their Upper East Side apartment while Ferrer was in the park. Then he baby-sat, and she jogged.

He entered the park at East 96th Street, eleven blocks north of the museum, and jogged down the East Drive. He preferred the lane next to the curb,

reserved for runners. The sun still hadn't appeared as
Ferrer enjoyed the dawn's quiet beauty.

On a slight hill near some small fruit trees, something caught his attention. Ferrer said it was about
sixty feet from where Jennifer Levin's body was
found.

"I saw a white shirt in the trees next to the roadway," Ferrer testified. "You develop a sixth sense
when you run alone early in the morning, and I noticed
an individual standing under a canopy of trees just off
the roadway. He appeared to be rummaging through
the leaves . . . with his toe brushing the leaves aside.

"It occurred to me that this was very unusual conduct," said Ferrer. "I slowed down to ask if I could
help find what was lost—and then I decided not to."

Ferrer was a slender five feet eleven. He said the
individual he saw was a "large" and younger white
man. The man wore a clean Oxford-style shirt with
the sleeves rolled up. Its shirttails were hanging out at
the beltline. He wore "tan or gray" casual slacks.

"Disheveled" was the description Ferrer gave the
police the next day, "as though he might have slept in
the park." He thought the man was in his thirties.

Did they make eye contact?

"He never raised his eyes from looking at the
leaves," said Ferrer.

At one point they were twenty feet apart, the distance from the curb to the man. "I later paced if off,"
Ferrer said. But he could not identify the man again.
"I had only a three-quarter rear view," Ferrer testified. "I only saw him from the back."

Jogging slowly, he watched the white-shirted man
for "twenty or thirty seconds," said Ferrer, "about
five-forty-five or five-fifty A.M." He looked for other
joggers. "I did quite a scan, but I didn't see anyone. I
was very apprehensive."

But Ferrer did not cut short his exercise. He took

his usual route home. He didn't say whether he mentioned the episode to his wife before she left to jog a half hour or so later. It was broad daylight by then, with a lot more people around.

"She returned about seven-ten or seven-fifteen," Ferrer said, "and told me about the police and the ambulance in the park."

He picked up the phone and called the Central Park police precinct.

Patricia Reilly was on her bicycle at 6:06 A.M., riding past St. Patrick's, the big cathedral on Fifth Avenue at 50th Street.

The time was on the clock next to the speedometer and odometer on her handlebars. She had checked the clock because she bicycled four or five times a week, Pat Reilly testified, and the traffic seemed heavier than normal that day.

Reilly worked as a mutual fund trader. She wore a suit, blouse, and pearls on the witness stand, a confident thirty-four-year-old woman with shoulder-length brown hair.

She was a serious cyclist, and that Tuesday she was taking her customary "loop" route into midtown and back, Reilly testified. From St. Patrick's, she headed west to Sixth Avenue and pedaled north into Central Park about 6:10 A.M. . . . "maybe six-o-nine." The sky was "light enough for me to know I can go into the park and feel safe."

On the East Drive she was alone in the left bike lane riding past the park boathouse, up a slight hill. At the top the road curves left, around Cleopatra's Needle.

That's where Pat Reilly got her first jolt of what would be a very long day.

Suddenly, she testified, a brown car with New York plates and headlights on came around the curve and down the hill toward her—going "very fast" . . . and going the wrong way. That's something "which is not done," Reilly declared, at any hour in Central Park.

"It was a definite surprise. The car was close enough to the lane to scare me, but I didn't fall off my bike or anything. I looked at the car to see if I could see who was driving, because I like to give them a look. The windows were tinted. . . ."

She saw a lone woman jogger with a headset trailing the speeding car around the curve. Neither woman stopped—but they communicated, New York style. "We exchanged looks, like, who is this lunatic?"

Reilly kept her eyes open as she proceeded north. "A cyclist is less safe in Central Park than a runner, because the bike is worth stealing. The runner has nothing but shorts," she said.

"I am looking left and right," testified Reilly—she was now about fifty yards past the obelisk—"and then I saw, in the distance on an angle, what looked to me like a bag lady on the grass.

"But as I rode past I did a double take."

She rode slowly for several more yards, staring, "like doing a double take the entire time." Finally stopping, she switched off the odometer and turned her bike around.

"I realized that this was not a bag lady—that something was definitely wrong."

Reilly rode back until she was parallel to the trunk of the large elm tree next to which the body lay. She was one-hundred feet away, too far to see clearly. She had to get closer.

It took courage. Reilly went over the curb on her bike so she could dismount on the grass. "I was wearing cycling cleats, and you can't walk on pavement with them." She walked her bike toward the elm, within thirty or forty feet of the body.

"I got close enough to realize that it was a woman. That this woman was, for all intents and purposes, naked. Her clothes were around her waist and . . . around her neck, but I knew that I was looking at the front part of a naked woman. . . . Her body was in disarray.''

At first, ''I assumed she was a runner,'' Reilly said. The legs were bare. The woman was lying on her back, facing away from the road. ''Her head was to the tree, so I didn't see her face, but I knew she had dark hair.''

As Reilly's shock subsided, the body came into clear focus. The blouse and bra had been pushed up so the breasts were exposed. The skirt was up above the thighs, with no underpants.

''Her right leg was slightly bent. Her left leg was a little more so. Her right arm was bent back at a ninety-degree angle and lying back with her fist facing upward. It was sort of a twist, like a body twist,'' Reilly testified.

''It's something I will never forget.''

The biker had just discovered the body of eighteen-year-old Jennifer Levin. But at that moment Pat Reilly couldn't know who Levin was and didn't know if she was alive or dead.

''I didn't want to get closer to see if she was dead, because if so, I didn't want to know, and if she wasn't, I couldn't help her anyway,'' Reilly said in court. ''So I went for the police.''

Her quest took time. While no exact moment of the body's discovery was established, it was about 6:15 A.M. And for Reilly, the next quarter hour was a nightmare.

Behind the boathouse she had spotted a police jeep, and now she biked south to it, Reilly testified. The jeep wasn't there. An Emergency Medical Services truck was there, though . . . ''with his engine running and the doors locked,'' she said.

''I knocked on the window. There was no answer. I

then went to the phones that are in front of the
boathouse. They had all been ripped out."

On her morning rides, Reilly remembered, there was
often a police officer parked at 90th and Fifth. She
rode north again, past the body. "I looked to make
sure that she was still there, and she was."

Now there was someone else nearby, too—a tall
man walking on a path about forty yards west of the
body. Reilly thought he wore khaki pants—"I mean
the cut. Don't ask the color. A straight leg as opposed
to sweatpants or jeans." He was not walking a dog or
carrying a briefcase, Reilly remembered.

Some scraggly trees were between him and the elm
tree, but it puzzled Reilly that he didn't notice the
body.

"I was surprised that whoever it was couldn't see
her and if so, didn't stop. I just—she was clearly—I
mean it was in plain view."

No police car was at 90th and Fifth. A block east, at
Madison Avenue, there was a pay phone that worked.
Reilly dialed 911, the emergency police number.

Many New Yorkers in urgent circumstances have
had reason to believe that 911 is Kafka's phone number. For Pat Reilly, reporting a body in Central Park,
it was no different.

The 911 operator wanted the body's precise location. Few park regulars, however, and fewer bikers,
are aware that each lamppost bears a small metal tag
with four digits—and that the first two indicate the
nearest cross-street latitude. Reilly knew only that the
body was behind the museum.

"I couldn't make it clear to her where it was. She
wanted the street. There are streets in Central Park? I
told her I would wait at the scene."

She rode back to the museum. There were more
runners now. The sky was lighter. But coming south,

with a slight roll in the hill near the elm tree, Reilly couldn't see the body.

"That made me very nervous. I was afraid I'd just made a false phone call to the police, and now I'm really in trouble." But the elm's drooping branch obscured her view only briefly, and Reilly soon saw that the body was in the same place.

She propped her bike against the nearest lamp post, its unnoticed metal tag reading E8201.

"There are more runners now," she recalled in court. "I just watch them go by. We made eye contract, but nothing stopped."

She couldn't look at the corpse. "I sat down on the curb with my back to her, and just waited for the cops."

They arrived five or ten minutes later.

Sergeant Anthony E. Michalek, eighteen years on the force, was now midnight tour supervisor for the Central park precinct. He was riding with Officer James McCreary at 6:25 A.M. when the radio crackled with its first report: "Woman down" behind the museum.

Michalek knew the patrol car assigned to that area would respond, but with his emergency first-aid training he thought he could help if someone was hurt. McCreary, off the East Drive about 87th Street, drove south with beacon flashing to signal his wrong-way approach.

A woman sat on the curb at Lampost E8201, pointing behind her. McCreary turned onto the grass, parking perpendicular to the road. Michalek got out and saw the woman under the elm tree. He checked her pulse—and turned his attention to Pat Reilly.

Minutes later two unmarked cars arrived with plainclothes detectives. One listened to Reilly's story. Then, for the next half hour, she waited.

"Runners would stop and ask what was going on," she testified, "and they would move on . . . in a hurry because they have to go to work. They don't have time, so they would stay briefly, for two seconds."

But not every spectator moved on.

About 7:10 A.M., Reilly testified, she became aware of a figure perched on a low stone wall across the road, directly behind the museum. It was a man in khaki-cut pants. He sat with his legs drawn up, arms clasped around his knees, watching the activity. By now there were four police cars at the scene and nearly a dozen cops.

The stone wall was shadowed by three mulberry bushes, "so I couldn't have identified whoever was sitting there," Reilly testified. She knew only that "the clothing was . . . it was like khaki pants. But recognize, no."

Was it possible the man had been there a half hour earlier as she awaited the police? "Definitely not," she said. "I would have known it. I was sitting right there."

Could he have been the same tall man she saw on the path west of the body?

"Could be," Reilly said.

Her strongest impression was of his idle demeanor amid the increasing crowd of spectators who kept moving.

"You know, he was relaxed," she said. "This person was there for a while. This person wasn't just stopping and looking . . . this person had time."

For over five minutes, Reilly watched him on and off. He stayed on the stone wall. He was still there when a television crew showed up about 7:15 A.M., she testified.

"I wanted no part of that, so I asked if I could leave." The answer was no, but McCreary drove her to the station house on the 86th Street transverse.

Later, the cops brought Reilly's bike there.

That Tuesday also had begun early for real estate broker Susan Willett Bird—also an Upper East Side high-rise dweller, also a jogger. She and a buddy—his name was Mason Buddy—finished circling the reservoir at about 6:45 A.M. Hearing sirens, Buddy went home. Bird stopped to watch.

"I saw a police car. I saw a police officer and a woman with a bike. There was a commotion about something in the park, something on the ground had been covered."

She stayed on the other side of the road, testified Bird, a thin woman in her forties.

"There was a young man sitting on the wall next to me, a foot or two away. He was a young man in his early twenties with dark hair, well built, an attractive young man. I couldn't tell how tall he was. I noticed severe scratches on his face. It looked as if he'd been in an industrial accident."

He sat with one leg dangling over the wall, partially concealed from the police by mulberry bushes, "but not from me," Bird testified. She said she spoke to him first.

"I asked, 'What's going on?' or something like that. I believe he said something like 'I think they found a body.'

"I said something like, 'Well, have you gone over there, are you going to do something?'

"He said 'No.'

"I said, 'Why not?'

"He said, 'Because the police would make me leave.' "

His answers were responsive but "indifferent," Bird thought.

Was he in a daze?

"Not at all. . . . He was glued on the scene—he was intently watching it," Bird testified.

Intent, but indifferent? "His answers to me were indifferent," she explained.

Bird stayed at the wall ten to fifteen minutes. More cops arrived. Other joggers stopped briefly, then ran on. Bird finally went home.

Did she see the attractive young man again?

"Only in the newspapers."

Did she see him in court now?

"Yes," testified Susan Bird.

She pointed at Robert Chambers.

2

THE NIGHT BEFORE

He was nineteen years old. She was barely eighteen. What brought them to a deserted park in the dark of the night?

Sex. That was the first thought. A teenage male like Robert Chambers would gravitate by nature toward sexual opportunity. And many would conclude that her presence in the park surely meant that Jennifer Levin was drawn there for the same reason. Both of those assumptions remained in dispute.

Many believed that the perils of Central Park after midnight would make it off limits for any sober teenager, so drugs or liquor had to be a factor. "What was the amount of alcohol these kids had that night?" asked one elderly spectator at Chambers's trial. "And why would they go to the park unless they were bombed?"

Exploring the "why" factor seemed futile at that point. It was much easier to trace the separate paths that brought the two of them together there at 4:30 A.M. on August 26, 1986.

17

One recurring surmise was that Robert Chambers had gotten there on his looks. A six-foot-four and 220-pound frame with a moviesque face defined him to admirers as a successful player—someone who could do no wrong. There was a certain shy and secretive charm, too, though several acquaintances seemed to perceive him as weak. One dismissed him as a "pretty boy."

Any dossier on Robert Chambers among acquaintances that summer probably included mere basics.

His prestige address on East 90th Street between Madison and Fifth provided only a veneer of glitter. He lived with his Irish-born Catholic mother, a registered nurse who worked nights. His absent father, of middle-class WASP stock, was a recovering alcoholic with a modest job. Money was tight all around.

Robert, an only child, had been bounced from two upper-crust prep schools for poor grades, drug abuse, and possibly petty theft. After finally graduating from York Prep, a last-chance Upper East Side school, he had flunked out of Boston University after one semester.

Some girls liked his moody ways and seductive smile, but Rob's self-esteem was low and his prospects bleak. He had had summer jobs as a schoolboy and had done odd jobs for neighbors, but adulthood required folding money. He allegedly turned to serious burglary, then credit card fraud, but his budget was severely strained by a taste both for cocaine and tequila. In March of 1986 he had landed in Minnesota's chic Hazelden drug tank for about five weeks of treatment. It didn't take.

Now, with drink in hand, Robert Chambers was spending many nights at Dorrian's Red Hand, an old-fashioned saloon restaurant on Second Avenue at East 84th Street, currently a hotspot for Upper East Side college kids and preppies.

Picture a long rectangular room of perhaps twenty tables with red- or blue-checkered cloths. A third of the floor, in the rear, was platformed alongside a hallway to the kitchen. There was a massively carved twenty-foot bar with mirrored backdrop, an ancient fireplace, and a pressed-tin ceiling that suggested its origins as a neighborhood Irish pub, but hanging plants had been added, along with a glass-enclosed sidewalk cafe. Red Dorrian, then eighty-three but still presiding at times, had opened the place in 1961. Red's son Jack, fifty-five, ran it now with the help of grandsons Jack Jr. and Michael. They attracted old chums and acquaintances, who in turn drew more friends—and then friends of friends. It was clubby.

Many of those who were not yet twenty-one years old put Dorrian's on the circuit of bars, clubs, and discos they patronized mainly because ID cards were examined only cursorily at the door, if at all. A fake ID card was easy to come by in New York, but it was pleasanter still not to be asked for it at all. Some nights, anyone who came into Dorrian's could get served.

They were, for the most part, children of divorce, half-worldly teenagers accustomed to hearing about sexual flings and drug abuse among the adults they knew. Money made many of their lives simpler—providing luxury apartments, beach houses, servants, and prep school education—even if divorce meant less time spent with a father or mother.

Robert Chambers, scuffling for cash and equilibrium, was among them. Much of his tangled history was known, including suspicion that he had rifled the wallets of several girls in and out of Dorrian's. Yet Chambers was accepted. Dorrian's was home.

That night Chambers got there at 11:30 P.M., approximately six hours before Jennifer Levin died. He was sitting at a rear table with friends when Jennifer walked into Dorrian's for her last party. It was just past midnight.

Inside, with nearly one hundred of her peers packing the place on a summer Monday night, it seemed as if everyone Jennifer knew was in Dorrian's. It was a joyful reunion for many who hadn't seen each other all summer, and soon most would part again, bound for college. Jennifer was to leave the following week for Chamberlayne Junior College in Boston. Now she made her way through the crowd, greeting friends with a hug and kiss, bubbling with excitement and, by all accounts, eager anticipation.

Jennifer had a major crush on Robert Chambers, the troubled young man she first had met at a winter party. Her friends said she boasted of sleeping with him at least twice during the summer, and she had chattered earlier that evening about the prospect of seeing Chambers again. While the depth of her feeling remains unclear, Jennifer was clearly interested.

Jennifer Dawn Levin at eighteen was still a young girl in terms of judgment and wisdom, but womanhood was upon her. Lithe and shapely at five-eight and 135 pounds, the lively brunette had been voted "Best Looking" in the Baldwin School's graduating class that June. By August she had a deep and striking tan, the universal badge of the leisure class.

But like Chambers, she had begun life as an outlander, by Upper East Side standards. Born May 21, 1968, Jennifer grew up in Port Washington, Long Island. She was five when her parents divorced and remained with her mother, Ellen, and older sister, Danielle, on the island's north shore until junior high.

At fourteen Jennifer joined her father, Steven Levin, and his second wife, Arlene, in their loft apartment in Manhattan's SoHo section, near his realty firm's offices. She remained close to each parent, both now in their early forties. Ellen Levin had moved to lower Manhattan, too.

A beloved child amid what were now several sets of grandparents, Jennifer was thought of as affectionate but independent.

"She made people smile just by walking into a room," Ellen said. And she had a habit of leaving small notes of love and thanks for family members. But even though the Levins were well-to-do, Jennifer found ways to fill some needs on her own. She talked a Manhattan cabbie into giving her parking lessons before her driver's license test. "She'd come home and say, 'I'd like a Sony Walkman. I think I can get enough money if I work four days next week,'" Arlene Levin recalled. "Her first thought was 'How can I make the money to get it?'—not 'Buy it for me.'"

Her four years at the expensive Baldwin School on the Upper West Side, where her senior-year tuition was $7,800, meant no apparent financial hardship. But Arlene Levin thought it tragically ironic that Jennifer's desire to attend prep school was based partly on fear of potential danger at almost any public school. "They'll kill me if I go there," Jennifer had said.

Not one for reading books, she also tended to ignore television, preferring to hang out with her friends. Musically, she listened to soft-rock singer Elton John or reggae. When she was alone she liked to work out, doing exercises for an hour at a time in her room. She was a vegetarian concerned about keeping her body strong and healthy.

Her crush on Chambers did not end a long relationship with another York Prep student, Brock Pernice, who was Levin's steady through most of the eleventh grade. She then began dating other men she met at Dorrian's but had been seeing Brock again that spring before he went to Europe.

In previous summers Jennifer had worked for extra spending money, and after graduating Baldwin she served as a hostess at Fluties, a bar-restaurant jammed with college kids at the South Street Seaport in lower Manhattan. "Never once did I ever see her come to work with anything but a smile," Fluties' manager said. He recalled her as a willing worker who, when the Fourth of July came, helped unload a tractor-trailer of food and beer for the huge holiday crowd.

Jennifer stopped working at Fluties in mid August to fly to California for a week with her friend Laura Robertson. Another close friend, Alexandra LaGatta, then invited Jennifer for a beach weekend at her family's house in Southampton. The following Monday, August 25, they "impulsively" decided to take a train back to the city, recalled Alex LaGatta in court.

Among the four good friends of Levin who would testify for the prosecution at Chambers' trial (and subsequently face his lawyer's cross-examination), LaGatta was in closest proximity on that last day. A Spence graduate, now a college sophomore in California, LaGatta wore a black-and-white-checked miniskirt with black stockings on the witness stand. A black jacket and white blouse set off her long, light brown hair.

At about six P.M. that Monday night they had dressed up for dinner with Alex's father at Marcello's, a First Avenue restaurant, then returned to the LaGatta apartment to change into "clothes we would wear with our friends," Alex said, "more casual clothes."

What Levin wore that night—except for her bra and a faded oversize men's denim jacket she loved—was borrowed entirely from Alex. Everything from the shoes on up was new "and hadn't been worn yet,"

LaGatta said on the witness stand, examining each item, no longer new.

The white camisole blouse. "This is the blouse she was wearing. It is dirty, ripped, wrinkled, and torn. It was perfectly white when I had it."

The pink-and-white miniskirt. "Yes, I bought it at a street fair in France. It was in perfect condition, never worn."

The canvas Kenneth Cole flats, shoes "I just bought and never wore. They were new. Now they're very dirty, not very, just dirty. They were white. That's her jean jacket. She had worn it all weekend. That's my lipstick. I know the name and color, a dark reddish brown I rarely wore. I gave it to Jen that night.

"That's a pair of my underwear. Underwear is a personal thing. They were perfectly white and clean."

At ten P.M. on that fateful evening, Alex and Jennifer left the LaGatta apartment to meet Larissa Thomson and Laura Robertson by prearrangement at Juanita's, a Mexican restaurant on Third Avenue, within walking distance. "A fun place, the crowd is young," said Alex, who was then seventeen. "We ordered margaritas"—tequila and lime juice—"and got served without a problem."

They talked about their next stop: Dorrian's. When Chambers' name came up, Alex remembered no mention of sex, but "Jennifer was excited about seeing him. She was hoping he would be there later."

Larissa and Laura arrived at Juanita's. A man they didn't know sent a bottle of champagne to their table, "with a compliment," LaGatta recalled. Jennifer smilingly bowed thanks to him. A waiter opened the bottle for them. She and Alex had a few sips of champagne—on top of two Margaritas apiece, LaGatta testified—and nibbled at the chips and sauce on the table. Larissa had two vodka collinses. At about midnight the four young women rode up to Dorrian's by cab, as

Jennifer laughingly clutched the half-empty bottle of champagne.

Alex LaGatta remembered the Dorrian's scene vividly, seventeen months later.

"We walked in and immediately went to the back. Dorrian's is the kind of place where you know so many people, twenty or fifty, it's just like a big party with a lot of friends. We went in separate directions, then hung out together. Then we'd see someone else and separate again. We mingled."

Larissa Thomson said that when Jennifer spotted Robert Chambers sitting with two other people, she "immediately" made a beeline for his table and "started speaking with him." Chambers would later complain that Jennifer had talked only about her California trip and her tan—and that he wasn't interested in seeing her. He made that clear. As soon as Jennifer's friend Betsy Shankin came up to the table, Chambers took the opportunity to leave.

Betsy, a petite, curly-haired graduate of McBurney School who was also bound for college in Boston, testified to her closeness with Jennifer.

"She was one of my best friends. We spoke together every day." They had jobs near each other at the Seaport. "I saw her on her breaks, my breaks, she brought me lunch, and I would annoy her while she was working. We took the train [subway] home together at night."

That evening they had hoped to join up at Juanita's, but Betsy landed instead with mutual friend Edwina Early, and they didn't reach Dorrian's until shortly after midnight. Betsy couldn't locate Jennifer in the mob scene for about fifteen minutes, she said, at a table farthest from the front door.

"She was sitting with Robert and two others. I went up and said hello. He got up as I approached, said 'hi,' and walked away."

If it seemed awkward, the interruption apparently didn't bother Jennifer. The two friends hugged and kissed hello, then sat down to catch up. Both were drinking bay breezes—cranberry and pineapple juice laced with vodka, said Betsy. "I spent about twenty minutes with Jennifer at that table," she testified. "We were alone and talked, but not about Chambers."

The omission apparently was rare. Shankin had been instrumental in bringing Robert and Jennifer together two months earlier—purely at his initiative, Betsy told the jury. She recalled the first time she ever spoke to the tall young man whose looks attracted so much attention.

"Sitting in Dorrian's one night, when it was almost empty, I saw him looking at me. I smiled, he smiled back. He motioned for me to come over, I motioned to him. I met him at a table halfway," said Betsy. But Chambers' interest was not in Betsy.

"He said, 'Your friend Jennifer is the most beautiful girl I've ever seen. I can't talk to her in here because some of my girlfriend's friends are here.' He wanted to meet Jennifer outside."

Betsy had conveyed the message that June night. And Jennifer had gone outside, joining Chambers on the corner of 84th and Second to talk for some time. As Betsy watched through the wide window, she told Michael Stone of *New York* magazine, something "clicked" between Jennifer and Robert. "I remember her face turned a different color," she said, "and how he turned his head to the side, his hands in his pockets, almost smiling—trying to maintain his coolness."

In court Betsy testified that when Jennifer came back inside after that first approach by Chambers, "she was glowing. She was very happy. They talked. She said he was a nice guy."

But two months later, in that first hour after midnight of August 26, something was going wrong.

Chambers reportedly told someone he was depressed that night over the suicide of an acquaintance. But a friend said he was morose about doing cocaine again and was arguing with his current lovely, Alex Kapp.

"She was in the bar that night," said Shankin. And Kapp was described as steaming over Chambers' inattention.

"Friends say she threw a bag containing packages of condoms in his face," wrote Michael Stone in *New York* magazine, "and people heard her say, 'Use these with someone else, because you're not going to get a chance to use them with me.'"

Teenage passions were running high on a hot summer night. Where would it lead? One major issue at Chambers' murder trial seventeen months later would be the amount of liquor Levin drank that night—margaritas, champagne, bay breezes—and the degree of its cumulative effect on her.

Filling in as a bartender for ten days that August, as a favor to Jack Dorrian, Jr., was his lifelong pal John Zaccaro, Jr., twenty-three-year-old son of Geraldine Ferraro, the 1984 Democratic vice presidential candidate.

Zaccaro, then facing conviction for dealing cocaine as a student at Middlebury College in Vermont, had known Robert Chambers long ago at St. David's Grammar School. But since they were four years apart in age, their only contact had been at Dorrian's, Zaccaro testified. He said he had seen Chambers there twice that night—talking with friends at midnight and later to two girls at the bar. "He had a drink in his hand, a highball glass with tequila in it. I didn't serve him anything, and I don't know how much or what he drank."

Zaccaro had met Levin ten or fifteen times over six months at Dorrian's. When she arrived that night she came over to him. "She asked if she could put her jacket behind the bar and asked for a glass of water. I took the jacket by the neck, handed it to another bartender to put away. She asked for a glass of water. She said, 'Fill it with ice cubes, then add water.'

"She seemed upbeat and friendly," said Zaccaro, poised and self-assured on the witness stand, in suit and tie. "She did not display any of the characteristics I associate with intoxication. She seemed focused and was not slurring her words. I didn't serve her a drink. I didn't see Nick [the other bartender] serve her, but I have no knowledge if she ordered one from a waiter or when I wasn't around."

Zaccaro did not recall seeing Levin again after he took her denim jacket; neither did he recall seeing her talk to Chambers or know whether either one had anything further to drink. Someone in the press room quipped: "The perfect bartender—unable to remember anything about anyone."

Edwina Early was now a nineteen-year-old college sophomore in Ohio, tall and swan-necked, wearing pearls on the witness stand. She remembered Levin that night as "happy and high-spirited, very excited about going away to school." They had met through Brock Pernice, but that night Levin played the flirtatious coquette with several young men, Edwina testified.

"We were running around talking to guys in the bar. If we didn't want to see them, we gave them a different name and phone number. We were just talking to all of the good-looking guys in the bar."

For all the hilarity, Edwina said the only time she saw Jennifer with a glass in her hand, it was water.

"I had had a wallet stolen at Dorrian's before, and Jennifer wanted to teach me a lesson. She took all the credit cards out—she left the money. When I went to get the wallet, I saw the cards were missing. Then I saw Jennifer, standing at the bar, talking to John Zaccaro, and she had the cards in her hand. She lectured me the way my mother would.

"She had a large glass in her hand, the kind of glass that at Dorrian's you get for either tap beer or water. She didn't have beer, so I assume it was water," Early said.

"She was acting drunk, but it was just her giddiness. She wasn't acting any different than I was that night, and I wasn't drunk."

Larissa Thomson, who had drawn close to Jennifer over the past few months, spent most of her two hours in Dorrian's that night with her boyfriend. But at some point Jennifer stopped by to confide her feelings about Chambers, said Larissa. "She said he was the best sex she ever had and she wanted to go home with him that night," said Larissa, now a twenty-year-old college sophomore in Philadelphia, round-faced with bangs and long brown hair.

Thomson had brought a camera and took pictures of many of the people at the bar that evening, including Jennifer. "She asked to borrow my camera for about fifteen minutes," Larissa testified. Jennifer wanted to take a picture of Robert. "After a while, I went to look for her when she didn't return with it."

Jennifer was "very excited, bubbly, flying around, with a lot of people," said Thomson, who had decided to leave by about two A.M. and looked around for Levin, to say good-bye. She saw her "in the back of the bar, having a heavy discussion with Betsy Shankin."

Shankin remembered it—her last private conversation with Jennifer at Dorrian's, in the "middle of the night, one-thirty or two." It was intense. The subject was Robert Chambers.

"I was sitting at a round table. Jennifer came up, took my hand, and said she had to talk with me about something very important. We went to the hallway near the kitchen to talk alone together," Betsy testified.

"She told me she went up to Rob and said: 'I just want you to know that the sex I had with you was the best sex I ever had in my life. I just wanted you to know that.' He looked down at her and said: 'Jennifer, you shouldn't have said that.'

"She wanted me to tell him that she wanted to talk to him and ask him to meet her outside in twenty minutes," said Shankin, who at first tried to beg off playing emissary again. "I didn't think it was right. . . ." But finally Betsy relented.

"I told her I would do it," she testified. "I left her and walked several feet to where Rob was standing near an ice machine. He was alone. I walked up to him and said, 'Jennifer wants to talk to you outside.'

"He looked at me strangely," said Shankin, who outside of court would describe Chambers as "creepy—with a green aura of strangeness." She said he asked her, "Why, what does she want?"

"I don't know what she wants," Shankin remembered saying.

"He said he couldn't. I asked him why. He said Michael Dorrian wouldn't let him go in and out. I said, 'You know that's not true. Look, do what you want to do.' "

The problem Jennifer was having with Chambers upset her enough to confide it to Alex LaGatta, too.

"She was really upset and pulled me to the back," LaGatta recalled. "I said: 'What happened?' She said she went up to Rob and said, 'You're the best person I ever had sex with.' She said he told her, 'You shouldn't have said that.'

"That really hurt her," Alex said. "It offended her."

When LaGatta decided to go home between one-thirty and two, she informed Jennifer that she was taking along her boyfriend, Robbie Banker.

"She said she wasn't coming home yet. I told her I would leave the keys under the mat," Alex testified.

By 2:30 A.M. both Jennifer and Betsy had switched to drinking ice water exclusively. "Alcohol is empty calories," Shankin told the jury. "After a while I drink ice water . . . because of the conscious awareness of my mind to clean out my system."

Jack Dorrian said he noticed Jennifer looking forlorn just before three o'clock. When he asked what was wrong, she told him, "I'm in love." With who? "Robert Chambers."

Dorrian said he advised her: "Forget him. You can do better than that. Before you get married, you'll have twenty different guys."

She brightened up and said: "I wish that was true, Mr. Dorrian."

After that, Levin managed to make contact with Chambers again. "She was talking to Robert, they were leaning against the bar," recalled Edwina, who was about to go home.

"She wasn't as happy. Rob had the same kind of look on his face," said Edwina, who decided not to bother saying good-bye to Jennifer. "It looked like she was having a serious conversation, and I didn't want to interrupt them."

Dorrian's was emptying now. The two bartenders were still there, along with three members of the Dorrian family and a few customers. Among them were Shankin and her boyfriend, Paul Delaney, who had moved to a table in the back. Jennifer joined them briefly, Betsy remembered.

"Then I saw her sitting at the bar with Rob. It was late, between four and four-thirty A.M. Rob and Jennifer were the only ones at the bar. They were sitting six or seven feet away. I couldn't hear what they were saying, but I could see their faces. They were facing each other."

Neither one was smiling, Shankin testified. Jennifer was noticeably less animated than before.

"About four-thirty I saw the two of them get up from the bar and proceed to walk toward the door," Betsy said, her voice trembling. "I said, 'Where are you going?' She said not to worry about it—'it'll be all right.'

"I said good-bye. She said, 'Good-bye. I love you. I'll call you tomorrow.'

"I called out: 'I know what you're going to do.' And she just winked at me and smiled.

"Rob opened the door, and they left together."

3

THE CRIME SCENE

It took only a glance for Sergeant Anthony E. Michalek to know that the battered young woman under the elm tree in Central Park was dead. Still, he went through the motions.

"I was going to check the carotid artery for a pulse. But when I saw the damage, the injuries to her neck, I decided not to touch that area," Michalek testified seventeen months later. He looked for a pulse under the breast. Nothing.

"She hasn't been dead long, because she's still warm," cyclist Pat Reilly thought she heard Michalek say.

And at 6:30 A.M. on August 26, 1986, in the shadow of the Metropolitan Museum of Art, one of the city's most turbulent homicide investigations in many years got under way.

A four-wheel-drive Jeep-type car with two cops from the sergeant's Central Park precinct came up on the grass south of Lamppost E8201 and rolled toward the body. Michalek told them to bring some yellow tape from the precinct to rope off the crime scene.

Pat Reilly waited with McCreary, just north of E8201. It was only twenty minutes since her grisly discovery. While McCreary covered the body with a sheet of brown wrapping paper, Michalek asked the biker if she had seen anything unusual.

Reilly mentioned the brown car with tinted windows going the wrong way, at high speed, near the boat-house. The sergeant radioed in the car's description. He also summoned Nightwatch detectives, the Crime Scene Unit, an ambulance, and more uniforms.

By now there were about fifteen joggers gawking from the East Drive and the low stone wall beyond it. Later in the day, McCreary would remember one of the faces at the wall.

Michalek started looking around the elm tree. He saw tire tracks "thirty to forty feet" from the body and ordered traffic cones to mark them.

"I attached the tire tracks to the brown car," Michalek testified.

It seemed logical—unless the Jeep had made the tire tracks. But Michalek wasn't alone. In a few hours there would be many cops milling around E8201, some with gold braid. Even the biggies figured the corpse had been dumped under the elm tree from a brown car with tinted windows.

Linda Fairstein, the assistant district attorney who became the trial prosecutor, labeled the wrong-way car a "red herring" that diverted attention from the actual killer.

Defense counsel Jack T. Litman had his own novel theory about the tinted windows and the tire tracks, but he kept it to himself until the trial was over. In the courtroom, Litman used the confusion to create a mosaic of police ineptitude.

Nightwatch is the newfangled dawn patrol unit that investigates any crime reported to the NYPD between midnight and eight A.M., from muggings on up. On that summer Tuesday the call came in at 6:45 A.M., a "possible homicide" in Central Park.

Detective Sergeant Wallace Zeins took off with four other Nightwatch plainclothesmen. They joined Michalek at the elm tree within twenty minutes, Zeins testified.

The first thing he noticed was a thong bracelet on the dead woman's right ankle, "a leather shoestring," Zeins said. Despite the disheveled clothing, her white shoes were still on. "On the right wrist were green-and-yellow rubber-type bracelets and a chain of white beads. She had two yellow metal rings, one on each index finger."

While the jury looked at two-by-two-foot blow-ups of the body, Zeins described the wounds. Some jurors winced visibly, biting their lips, covering their mouths. "The left eye looked to me as if it was bruising," concluded Zeins, still boyish-looking with a salt-and-pepper beard.

An older Nightwatch hand, white-haired George Gillner, questioned Reilly again about the brown car with tinted windows. Then McCreary drove her to the precinct for more questions.

Another plainclothesman was sent to talk to museum construction workmen watching the cops from the low stone wall across the East Drive. "I thought it possible some of the crew saw something," Zeins testified. "I also saw a video camera mounted on the wall, and thought it might have caught something on tape."

The workmen had little to say. And the camera on the museum wall was not only pointed in the wrong direction, it had been out of order for six months. The killer's videotape debut would be delayed a few hours longer.

His victim, now under a white plastic sheet, was uncovered again when the Crime Scene Unit arrived at 7:20 A.M., trailed by a TV news van and a big EMS truck, orange and white. CSU specialists took more than a dozen pictures, looking for obvious gunshot or stab wounds. They found none but didn't turn the body to look closer. Not then.

CSU Detective Paul Chu removed all the victim's rings and bracelets for safekeeping and took off her shoes to check them. "Some people keep currency in their shoes," Chu explained. There was only a torn half of a dollar bill in her pockets, found when Richard Ferro of Nighwatch examined her clothing for some hint of her identity. First he picked up the faded jean jacket.

"The jacket was laying across the left arm. It was stonewashed denim, size forty-six, Levi jacket with red stains on it," testified Detective Ferro. "From the inside left pocket I extracted a black Pierre Cardin leather wallet." It contained a few photographs, several pieces of paper, the torn dollar, and a plastic Citibank card "in the name of Jennifer Levin, but not signed."

That was it for Ferro, a veteran of 750 homicides. Another investigator said the "pieces of paper" included "two birth certificates, some entrance stubs from Manhattan nightclubs, a check stub from Fluties, and a miniature copy of a high school diploma in the name of Jennifer Dawn Levin."

But birth certificates and diplomas were easily forged. The plastic card, giving access to Citibank's computerized cash machines, was Nightwatch's first solid clue.

"That's how we learned her name," Zeins said.

It was their last moment of triumph.

Zeins walked about fifty yards south, near Cleopatra's Needle, to check out a pair of dark blue woman's underpants crumpled in the grass. There were no panties on Levin's body, but these were a long way away. Still, they were photographed and tucked into an evidence envelope. It was a routine move that would cause trouble later on.

At 8:20 A.M. the park precinct sent its own detective to take charge of all the physical evidence—this being their turf. Their sleuth was Detective Michael McEntee. He had a bushy mustache, but this was his first homicide investigation.

And soon McEntee made his first big find, near a small crabapple tree, under some branches on the ground. At first, McEntee said later in court, he thought it was "a hankie."

Everyone gathered around. Someone picked it up. It was a second pair of panties. "They were white, with embroidery on the side. And they were dirty," Zeins told the jury.

"They appeared rolled," Gillner testified. "They looked like someone had rolled them down, taking them off."

And most significant, whereas the blue panties were fifty yards distant, these dirty white ones were only about forty-five feet north of the body.

But somehow nobody bothered to write down their exact location before McEntee carried off the embroidered panties on the end of a pencil.

Of course they were photographed first—weren't they? That was the nasty question Litman put to Zeins at the trial.

"Not to my knowledge," Zeins admitted.

Litman paced back and forth. Zeins sat unsmiling, watching him pace.

Q. Are you telling me that the blue panties were photographed, but not the white ones?

A. Yes, that's what I'm telling you.

Q. Is there a shortage of film in the police department?

The rout was on.

About six feet from the panties, near the crabapple tree, there was a ground disturbance. In court, Ferro called it a ten-foot "drag mark" and said "it appeared as if something had been moved." Michalek put it slightly farther northwest, stretching eight to ten feet in his testimony. Zeins made it five to ten feet, Gillner ten to fifteen feet.

Was the body dragged? How far? The cops couldn't agree on the size or location of the ground disturbance, Litman pointed out to the jury. Ten feet was a sort of common denominator, but nobody actually measured the "drag marks." Nor were they photographed.

"This is a homicide investigation?" Litman asked disdainfully in the courtroom.

He spent a long time on it. Later he dug out a TV news clip showing an unmarked car parked ten feet north of the crabapple. It was Paul Chu's car. Chu testified that he moved it there to pack his equipment just before leaving. Litman suggested for the jury's benefit that Chu and his men trampled the nearby ground for an hour first—actually creating the "drag marks" with their feet. Chu was stung. He maintained the ground disturbance was there beforehand.

In the park, Ferro found a gold-trimmed black lipstick case near the crabapple, along with a black cloth hairbow. Chu's men dusted them for fingerprints but took no notes, no photos. McEntee just collected all physical evidence and carted it to the Central Park precinct.

The hairbow eventually was lost there.

Everything found near that little crabapple tree, forty-five feet north of the body, seemed to be discounted by all the homicide investigators. Why?

Chu testified that the white panties in particular were "not connected with the victim because of the state they were in, the dirty condition. They appeared to have been there for a long time."

And, inevitably: "We had information of a car leaving the scene. It seemed like the victim had been assaulted elsewhere and dumped in the park."

And there were undisturbed dried leaves surrounding the body under the elm tree—also a sign it was dropped there, Chu testified.

"You're telling this jury," said Litman, "that a person stopped, got out, carried a 135-pound body eighty feet, and then dropped it under a tree?" He walked toward the witness with his arms outstretched, as if carrying a body.

"Yes," Chu said.

At 9:15 A.M. in the park, a half hour before the city medical examiner's arrival, Zeins ordered Polaroid snapshots of the victim. A canvass might be needed to verify her identity.

Crime Scene decided to cover her exposed breasts. They could have left the sheet on up to her shoulders, but instead they draped it over her legs and hips.

Chu helped another detective hold the body and turn it while the sleeveless white blouse bunched at her throat was tugged down to cover her bare chest.

"I did the actual turning," testified the bespectacled Chu, one of the rare NYPD detectives of Chinese descent. "Holding the left arm, I turned the body on the right side." Chu then took ten identification shots.

"We covered the body from the neck down so she wouldn't be exposed. For privacy. There were already a lot of media and onlookers around," Zeins explained to the jury.

"Aren't you instructed in the Crime Scene manual

not to touch the body before the ME arrives?'' Litman asked Chu.

"Unless the body is in a public place," Chu replied.

That burst of chivalry might have served to destroy evidence of how the victim was killed. A prosecution medical witness would later insist that the "pushed-up" blouse had in fact been twisted around Jennifer Levin's neck—and demonstrated it.

The bid for privacy was revealing, however. With the blouse pushed up, the full damage to the neck was hidden. Now it could be seen clearly—a band of raw red streaks that ran from her chin to the base of her neck, from ear to ear.

Zeins assured the jury it was a "gruesome" sight.

Litman quickly objected. From the bench, State Supreme Court Justice Howard E. Bell ordered the loaded word stricken from the record. While instructing the jury to disregard the word "gruesome," the judge repeated it several times.

Zeins edited his recollection and said: "I observed multiple horizontal red wounds across her neck."

Some wounds had the shape of a rectangle, he recalled in court, and there were yellow flecks of metal on the neck. He thought the rectangle might have been imprinted by the face of a wristwatch. That was another police theory to bedevil the prosecution.

But in the park, where the neck wounds were perceived as the sign of a violent struggle, Zeins had Levin's hands "bagged"—placed in simple brown paper bags taped at the wrist. That was to preserve any evidence of a fight, maybe chipped fingernails. Zeins wanted to convey that to the jury. He never got the chance.

"Sometimes during a struggle—"

Litman cut him off—and the judge did his thing again. Telling the jury to ignore Zeins' comment, Bell managed to emphasize the words "sometimes during a struggle."

In the park since nine A.M., some heavy artillery had been moving in—"a lot of bosses," said McEntee, from his own precinct captain up to division commanders, straightening their ties—even the borough commander. Several TV crews were buzzing around.

One homicide bigshot was there on assignment, though. And he would be working for at least thirteen hours more.

Detective Michael Sheehan of the Manhattan North squad was a beefy Irish cop with an educated eye after fourteen years of viewing battered corpses.

This one was now beneath a yellow plastic sheet and—it turned out—the blouse had been raised up again. By then it was almost nine-thirty.

"I took the sheet off," Sheehan testified. He knew one thing right away: speculation about the victim as a prostitute who'd been dumped in the park would probably prove untrue. She had a deep tan, and most working prostitutes avoided the sun, hoping to look palely innocent.

Sheehan did not mention that to the jury, of course.

"The body was lying face up, covered with dirt," he began his testimony. "Her hair was dirty, with leaves and twigs entwined in it."

He would regret that opening remark, along with his many other references to dirt. The victim's nostrils and one ear were filled with dirt, Sheehan said. "Both knees were dirty. There were four inches of dirt on her thighs, particularly the right one."

His rundown of Levin's injuries was clear and concise. "On the right side of her forehead there was a dark mark just above the eye, and what appeared to be a bruise just above that. The left eye was swollen, discolored, just about closed. It was a tiny slit. The right eye was slightly open, and fixed. On the bridge of the nose, there was a dark mark. Her mouth was caked with dirt and what appeared to be dried blood. I was wearing plastic gloves. I placed my hand around her lips to see where the blood was coming from.''

Sheehan said he found a front tooth loose, a detail not verified by the autopsy. He also cited what every cop had mentioned: the dark red wounds across Levin's neck and chin.

But a body "covered" with dirt? While some Crime Scene Unit blow-ups showed more dirt than others, this hyperbole opened a new door for the defense. Litman hinted that "someone" dropped Levin's body facedown in the dirt before Sheehan saw it. He also suggested that with all the lowering and raising of the blouse, Levin's body was "manipulated" by the cops for hours.

At 9:45 A.M., a new face arrived at the crime scene—the first woman there with authority. She was Dr. Maria Luz Alandy, thirty-nine, assistant medical examiner for the city of New York.

Alandy testified about her Central Park assignment eighteen months later—a short, chunky Filipino woman with fat cheeks and short curly hair, sort of a plump Corazon Aquino. She had a Spanish accent but was very fluent in English, especially with medical terminology. Alandy trained as a pathologist at Manila's University of Santo Tomas, then practiced at Metropolitan Hospital in Manhattan before becoming a resident in the Medical Examiner's office a month earlier. While she had performed some 750 autopsies, this would be her first experience with death by nonligature (usually manual) strangulation.

In the park, as Alandy approached the body, twenty cops formed a blue wall between the elm tree and East Drive to shield the pathologist and the body from onlookers. She wanted the blouse raised to the neck again.

"The buttons were intact. . . . There were a few blood drops on the front of the blouse," Alandy said in court, but an important piece of evidence had been altered—the body.

"One of the detectives positioned the body the way it was when first found," said Alandy. What had to be moved? "The legs and the head. He flexed the legs slightly, so they were in a slightly bent position. He turned the head slightly to the left. Nothing else was done."

Before touching the body, Alandy photographed it twice, one overall shot and a close-up. She used a camera with a built-in flash, but in court one picture seemed darker than the other. "The close-up has more resolution," she explained to the jury, "and is taken from a different point of view." It magnified the dirt Sheehan had seen.

When Alandy first touched the body at about ten A.M., she said, "it was cool." The pathologist also noticed what Jennifer Levin's admirers had noticed. "The deceased had a nice tan."

But Alandy was the first in the park to make two observations that would play a major role at Robert Chambers' trial.

One was that the victim's brassiere, pushed up to the neck, "was twisted at the center," Alandy testified, "so that the middle of the bra rested on the sternal notch, the top of the breastbone. The brassiere was hooked at the back, but twisted in front."

Alandy's second observation regarded the victim's eyelids. "The lids had hemorrhages, small, pinpoint hemorrhages," she said in court, identifying them as "petechial" hemorrhages. These could have various causes, including heart disease, and were found in many regions of the body. They occurred "any time there's a compromise in the blood flow to the brain."

But in the eyelid, petechial hemorrhages have a

more specific meaning, she explained to the jury. "They occur in cases of asphyxial death, caused by constriction of the blood vessels in the neck." And in this case, the extensive neck wounds were even more persuasive.

While still at the elm tree, Alandy had drawn her conclusion about what had killed Jennifer Levin. "I thought the deceased was strangled," she said in court.

Time of death? "Rigor mortis had already begun to set in. [It] is evident from four to five hours after death. I noticed some lividity [the settling of blood] was present but not fixed. It is manifested after four hours. I estimated she had been dead at least four hours."

Sometime, that is, before 5:45 A.M. It could not be fixed more closely except by Jennifer Levin's killer.

Alandy said she twice made written notes of her observations—once during her examination of the body and then "immediately after leaving," at 10:45 A.M., "on my way to another DOA."

Sergeant Michalek was still at the scene with his DOA when the morgue ambulance arrived at 11:00 A.M. It backed along a footpath as close as it could get to the elm tree. Two EMS technicians slid a scoop stretcher beneath the body, then lifted it onto a wheeled gurney, strapping it in.

Michalek, on the witness stand, described putting the body into an ambulance. In the spectator section, Ellen Levin bit her lip, one hand gripping the other.

The body was taken about fifty blocks downtown to the Bellevue morgue, where Alandy would conduct an autopsy the next day, Wednesday. Among other things, she would try to determine just how long it took the young woman to die.

Someone else would have to solve the two pairs of panties. Then there was that torn dollar—was Jennifer

Levin a robbery victim? Was her body dumped at the elm tree, carried from a car, or half dragged from the crabapple tree? By whom?

A half hour before noon that Tuesday, the center of the homicide investigation shifted from Lamppost E8201 to the Central Park precinct on the 86th Street transverse.

The NYPD's all-points alarm was still out then for a brown car, the one with tinted windows.

It never would turn up.

4

THE INTERROGATION

Robert Chambers emerged from his wake-up shower a few minutes after eleven o'clock that Tuesday morning, just as stretcher bearers lifted the stiffening body in the park.

His mother told Robert that Alex LaGatta had just called . . . something about Jennifer being missing. Then Phyllis Chambers saw her son's handsome face. Why was it so badly scratched?

Robert blamed the scratches on their Siamese cat, Rasta.

It was his first lie of the day. And for the next ten hours he would blame Rasta, over and over.

An hour earlier, Detectives Frank Connelly and Al Genova had walked into Steven Levin's SoHo realty firm with some Polaroid prints. They had Levin sit down in his private conference room. His painful memory of that moment was recorded in a letter dated April 4, 1988, later published in the New York papers.

"In a slow, deliberate manner," recalled Steve

Levin, "they asked me if I had a daughter named Jennifer. I replied, 'What's wrong, what's going on?' One of the detectives said Jennifer may be hurt. I said, 'Where is she?' The other detective drew a breath and said Jennifer may not be with us any longer. They asked me if they could show me pictures of a young girl found strangled in Central Park. I nodded yes and with that became aware of the gruesome fact that my youngest daughter, Jennifer, was dead.''

Connelly and Genova had located the father on a tip from Nightwatch's Wally Zeins at the scene. A driving learner's permit reportedly had been found, showing Jennifer Levin's address and a birth date of May 21— either 1964 or 1968. A maid at the Mercer Street loft had directed them to Arlene Levin's lingerie shop on lower Broadway. Arlene had sent them to Steve.

Now they escorted the shaken father home to the nearby loft to see if they could trace Jennifer's path after her weekend in Southampton with LaGatta. Steve Levin may have thought she was still at the beach—the two girls had returned to town impulsively on Monday—or maybe he knew she was staying at the LaGattas' East Side apartment. In Jennifer's frenetic world, parents were not always kept fully informed.

In any case, he needed both LaGatta phone numbers now. There were no messages on the answering machine in Jen's bedroom to provide any clue, and her Filofax phone book wasn't there. But as Steve Levin showed the two cops around, the phone rang.

It was Alex LaGatta.

Steve answered, talked to her briefly, then handed the phone to Genova. The detective told LaGatta only that he was trying to find Jennifer.

It had already been a nerve-racking day for the seventeen-year-old Alex. When her alarm clock went off at 6:30 A.M., she realized her boyfriend, Robbie

Banker, was still asleep beside her—with her parents just down the hall.

"I was so frazzled that he was still there. I rushed him out and rushed myself out"—to apply for a driver's license, LaGatta testified seventeen months later. "I didn't realize that Jen wasn't there until I returned and found the keys were still under the mat."

It was after ten then. Soon LaGatta found herself talking to Detective Genova, then to Betsy Shankin, who said Jennifer had left Dorrian's with Robert Chambers.

LaGatta dug the Filofax out of Jennifer's bag and located Chambers' number. Then she waited for him to finish his shower.

Now, in a packed courtroom, LaGatta re-created their conversation about her friend who was missing.

"I said, 'Robert, is Jen there?'

"He said, 'No.'

"I said, 'Do you know where she is?'

"He said, 'No.' "

She told Chambers that Jennifer's father was very worried and that detectives were at Jennifer's home. "I said, 'You've got to tell me where she is. Weren't you with her at Dorrian's?'

"Then he said, 'Yes. I was with her last night at Dorrian's, but she left me to go see Brock.' "

Chambers would tell that one over and over, too—Jennifer was with Brock Pernice. "He repeated that several times without my asking," Alex testified. "I was so happy."

In her relief that Jennifer seemed all right, LaGatta forgot one detail. She remembered it moments later: Jen had seen Brock Saturday night out on Long Island, at Stony Brook. And he had stayed there.

Before noon, two plainclothes cops came to La-Gatta's apartment. Nobody had yet told Alex that

Jennifer was dead, and neither did the two detectives. But she told them what Chambers had said to her.

And one cop picked up the phone.

The Central Park precinct is housed in a string of ancient two-story buildings with soot-blackened stone walls and barred windows. Inside, several generations of detectives had heard almost everything. But the story of Jennifer Levin's fatal rendezvous would be different in a lot of ways, with small twists and turns normally reserved for fiction.

Michael McEntee coordinated the homicide investigation from the precinct's Anti-Crime Unit office, making phone calls and conducting interviews.

Pat Reilly sat wearily through one of McEntee's earlier interviews—her third on the brown car sighting. Reilly's seven hours in the precinct were notable mainly for a phone call she made to a Wall Street friend, alerting him to her involuntary role in a homicide case. By sheer chance, apparently, the friend was Joe Dorrian, a younger brother of the proprietor of Dorrian's Red Hand.

A later McEntee interview was with William Thrush III, who knew both Chambers and Levin very well. It was Thrush's oversize denim jacket that Jennifer had carried into Dorrian's and beyond. And it was Thrush who told McEntee: "It was common knowledge around Dorrian's that Robert Chambers was heavily into cocaine."

That may have been the first tip to the cops that Chambers had a coke habit.

McEntee had Manhattan North's crack homicide squad at his disposal. When the phone call came in reporting Alex LaGatta's conversation with Robert Chambers, several plainclothesmen were sent to interview Dorrian's patrons on who had left with whom.

Chambers' address was unknown but obtainable

through a driver's license or car registration—or perhaps an arrest record. Only the license turned up when Connelly, just back from SoHo, ran a computer check at 1:30 P.M. "We did a group search under the name Chambers, first initial R, and found his address," McEntee testified.

Connelly and Genova headed for 11 East 90th Street. It was a five-story townhouse next to the old Andrew Carnegie mansion that now houses the Cooper-Hewitt Museum. The detectives circled the block, looking for a brown car with tinted windows. "We saw one that was remotely similar," Connelly testified, almost triumphant.

Inside the window-paneled front door, after identifying themselves as cops on the intercom, a woman buzzed them up to the top-floor apartment. When Robert Chambers' mother opened the door, they told her they were on a missing-persons case and hoped he could help.

Within minutes a tall young man appeared, wearing a white polo shirt, dark sweatpants, and white sneakers and introduced himself. Connelly: "He had quite a few scratches on his face, and the back of his fingers had several cuts."

Al Genova said Jennifer Levin was reported missing and asked him to go back to the precinct with them, bringing any names or phone numbers that might help.

"Chambers left the room for a minute and came back carrying a small black book," recalled Connelly, describing him as "responsive, attentive, and in complete control of himself. He didn't show any nervousness. When asked questions, he seemed to be looking directly at Detective Genova."

Phyllis Chambers, an experienced nurse, had seen the scratches on her son's face. She had to wonder what was up now. Only three months earlier, after returning from Hazleden, Robert had been questioned by the police about a series of East Side apartment burglaries. His mother had retained a lawyer, Henry (Pete) Putzel III.

Months later she would recall advising Robert to "call Pete Putzel" before he left with Genova and Connelly. If so, it went unheard by both cops.

As Connelly remembered it, while they waited for the down elevator Genova informed Mrs. Chambers that Robert would be at the park precinct "to help us find a missing girl." And her only advice to Robert was to take his keys.

News of the dead girl in Central Park was all over the radio by then—but without a name. Only the Levin family knew her name. Her uncle Dan Levin and grandfather Arnold Domenitz knew—they went to the morgue at 2:00 P.M. to identify Jennifer. Her distraught mother, Ellen, had now joined Steve and Arlene at the SoHo loft in secluded grief for the slain teenager.

Chambers was not yet a suspect in her death. He wore no handcuffs on the ride to the precinct with the two veteran detectives. But when they got there at 2:30 P.M., as Genova described it later, he asked young McEntee:

"Did you notice the scratches on Robert's face?"

McEntee looked, and Connelly said:

"Maybe you better read him his rights."

What did the cops know of Chambers at that stage? Only whatever Robert chose to tell them. A few discreet phone calls by any handy Irish cop might have fleshed him out, but if any phone calls were made, they stayed private.

From accounts that would eventually emerge, Robert Chambers began life in conventional obscurity on September 25, 1966, and spent his first eight years in the Jackson Heights section of Queens. His Irish-born mother, Phyllis, had come to America dirt poor, worked as a nurse, and married a younger New Yorker of middle-class origins with colonial British antecedents. While his name was Robert Fowley Chambers, the son born to Phyllis was never an ordinary "Junior." He was named for Robert Emmet, a famous patriot who led the Irish rebellion of 1798 and was dead at twenty-five.

At age six Robert was enrolled at St. David's School in Manhattan with the offspring of the Catholic elite. By 1975 the family lived on Park Avenue. Where the money came from for this upward spiral is not clear, but it's easy to believe that Phyllis Chambers worked like a horse and saved nearly every penny for the sake of her son.

Robert joined the Children of the American Revolution and the Knickerbocker Greys, a toy-soldier drill group that straightened spines for generations of Vanderbilts, Roosevelts, and Rockefellers. An altar boy at the parish church, St. Thomas More's, young Robert was all that a mother could ask.

Phyllis Chambers' fierce ambition would be widely examined, but simple bad luck might be blamed for what happened in 1980. First her hard-drinking husband, a middle-level record promoter for years at MCA, lost his job. After moving to East 90th Street, they separated briefly. And thirteen-year-old Robert, who had made Central Park a city boy's backyard, couldn't enjoy it for long.

That fall he was sent to Choate, a high-priced Connecticut boarding school with an incipient drug reputation. Chambers reportedly tried cocaine as a freshman. He wasn't invited back. At the exclusive Browning School in Manhattan he was a habitually stoned truant, soon expelled for allegedly stealing a teacher's wallet.

When Bob and Phyllis Chambers separated for good
in 1984, Robert was at low-rated York Prep, near his
home. He managed to graduate—barely, in what was
now a cocaine haze—but academically the die was
cast. Even when high scores on the Scholastic Aptitude Test eased him into a basic studies program at
Boston University in the fall of 1984, Chambers lasted
just one semester before flunking out. He didn't seem
to realize that one needed initiative in college. Chambers used his educational ticket mostly to party and
hang out, friends said. A faculty adviser recalled: "He
wasn't handing in assignments. He never caught on
from the start."

In 1985 he attended a few classes at Hunter College,
did occasional odd jobs, and gradually slid down the
tubes. He was a cokehead. On a spring day in 1986,
his mother found drug paraphernalia in Robert's room.
Whether rolling papers or a free-base pipe or whatever
was not disclosed, but Phyllis shipped him off to
Hazleden on March 25. She knew all about the Minnesota rehab clinic. In the mid-1970s, Robert's father
had sought treatment there for alcoholism. Now it was
Robert's turn. He stayed until May 1, and when he got
back to Dorrian's he told his pals he had kicked
cocaine.

But by June, when he eyed Jennifer Levin for the
first time, he was already implicated in a $70,000 East
Side burglary spree.

And now Robert Emmet Chambers was being questioned about a homicide.

While lawyer Pete Putzel had told him never to talk
to the cops about anything unless he was present,
Putzel's warning was not heeded. Four times that
Tuesday in the park precinct, Chambers was told of
his constitutional right to call a lawyer. Each time, he
declined.

Michael McEntee told the jury that he took Connelly's advice. Before asking Chambers anything about Jennifer Levin, he took him into the precinct's Anti-Crime Unit office and read him the Miranda warning. "I told him he had a right to remain silent and refuse to answer any questions. I told him he had a right to a lawyer and could call one at any time. I asked if he understood. Mr. Chambers nodded that he understood."

Then the first tentative questions came. It was no grilling, and it was no dungeon, just "a room about ten feet square with two desks, a wastepaper basket, file cabinet, locker," as McEntee described it in court. There was a clock on the wall and a phone on one desk.

Robert seemed relaxed, said McEntee, and answered questions easily. Yes, he knew Jennifer Levin. Yes, he had talked to her at Dorrian's. Yes, he had been told she was missing now. No, he had no idea what had happened to her.

But he did have a lot of other ideas. Piece by piece, Chambers told what was perceived later—much later—as a highly inventive and involved story.

He said that when he left Dorrian's—Chambers put the time at about 2:30 A.M.—Jennifer was standing in the doorway. She asked him for a cigarette, but he didn't have any, and she said she was going to a Korean deli across the street to get some.

He said he didn't know where she went from there but suggested she had gone to visit Brock Pernice on the West Side, across Central Park. He went to a doughnut shop on East 86th Street, said Chambers, bought a doughnut, and walked home.

"About the scratches," McEntee testified, "he said he was watching TV and playing with his cat. The cat scratched his face, kicking with his hind legs, and as he lowered the cat, it scratched his chest and stomach.

Then he pulled his shirt up to show the other scratches.''

Chambers carefully explained that only the cat's front paws were declawed. He repeated that the hind legs had scratched him. As for the bloody marks on both hands, he said he had cut them when a sanding machine jumped while he was working on a neighbor's floors.

He said he had watched a game show on TV, *The Price Is Right*, then saw part of a movie. Chambers couldn't remember its name but said "it was about a man and a woman who had a messed-up kid."

McEntee listened for about two hours.

At four-thirty Betsy Shankin called Dorrian's. Michael Dorrian put a cop on the phone, and the cop told Betsy that Jennifer was dead. By six o'clock Betsy had been picked up and brought to the Central Park precinct.

Edwina Early got the bad news on the phone from Betsy's mother. Edwina grabbed a cab at eight P.M. and went to the precinct alone.

Larissa Thomson heard it from a detective at nine o'clock. She gave him the undeveloped roll of film from her camera, full of farewell photos from the night before.

In the intervening hours, Robert Chambers continued helping the detectives working on the case—McEntee, Lafferty, Doyle, Sheehan, Gill, Mullally. Later, *New York Newsday* columnist Denis Hamill likened it to "an Irish wake."

Detective John Lafferty told Chambers about the legend of the Red Hand that had given Dorrian's its name, according to Cynthia Carr of the *Village Voice*. It was the fable of an Irish king "who had two sons, one good and one bad," wrote Carr. "To choose who would succeed him, the king asked his sons to race from a boat to the shore; whoever touched it first would win. The bad son swam faster and seemed certain to touch first. So the good son cut off his own hand and threw it ashore.''

Lafferty was also the first to level completely with Chambers. He told him that Jennifer Levin was dead. And at a pretrial hearing months later, Lafferty recalled Chambers' immediate reaction:

"He said, 'Oh, no! How did she die?' "

Until that moment Chambers had been "cool," Lafferty testified. But now "his eyes got misty."

He still was not a suspect. He was merely regarded as the last person known to have seen Jennifer alive in Dorrian's doorway.

As the evening began, Detective John Mullally made a food run, bringing hamburgers for all hands, including Chambers. At 7:45 P.M. the veteran Mike Sheehan took over the questioning.

And it was Sheehan, according to his pretrial testimony, who first injected a jocular hint of skepticism.

When Chambers assured him that the long wounds on his face were cat scratches, Sheehan said he responded: "I have a regular house cat at home. What do you have—a mountain lion?"

Sheehan went over the rest of Chambers' story with him for about an hour.

Betsy Shankin, in another room, was telling the cops that Jennifer and Robert had left the bar together at 4:30 A.M. Alex LaGatta had already told them that Brock Pernice was not in Manhattan—he was out on Long Island. And both of her close friends confirmed that Jennifer never smoked cigarettes.

Yet Chambers' story was still officially unchallenged at nine P.M. The ranking officer in the investigation, Lieutenant John Doyle, told a pretrial hearing that he was still impressed at that point by the nineteen-year-old youth's coolness after six hours of questions.

No cop was sent to determine whether Chambers

even had a cat at home. But Doyle said he never doubted his story of the cat scratches until Chambers himself recanted.

The break came between nine and ten o'clock. When Chambers was confronted with the contradictions of Shankin and LaGatta, he got a little nervous. "He was fidgeting—fingering a wound on his hand," Detective Martin Gill said at a pretrial hearing. As the tabloids put it later, Robert Chambers was ready to crack.

Describing how he got his cat scratches for the umpteenth time, Chambers finally drew a serious challenge from Gill, who was nearing retirement.

"You know, there's a difference between animal and human wounds," Gill said he told Chambers. It was a fairly explicit nudge. After a brief hesitation, Gill said, Chambers responded:

"I got them from Jennifer."

Gill and Sheehan, who was now back in the room, wanted the whole truth. Gill said he asked Chambers, "Why don't you get it off your chest?" Gill recalled that his pale blue eyes got damp—"sort of glassy, like they were filling with water." And what Robert said was:

"What will my mother think?"

Now Chambers no longer claimed he had parted from Jennifer in Dorrian's doorway. There was no "Korean deli," no cigarettes, no doughnut, no game show, no TV movie and—the real breakthrough—no cat scratches.

Instead there was Chambers' second version of what had happened:

He and Jennifer had walked north from Dorrian's for two blocks to 86th Street, then two blocks west to Lexington Avenue. They quarreled there, said Chambers—and Jennifer scratched his face.

Gill told him he knew a doughnut shop on that

corner. He said maybe someone there noticed the quarrel, saw the scratching. Now Chambers revised the location. He shifted it a block west to 86th and Park Avenue.

That was where a male friend of Jennifer's approached them, and Levin introduced them, said Chambers. He couldn't remember the man's name, but he was blond and in his twenties, and Jennifer had walked off with him, said Chambers. And that was the last he saw of her.

"It was the first time anyone had heard him deviate from his story," said Sheehan.

By now Chambers was "visibly nervous . . . rubbing his hands," said Sheehan, who decided to read him his Miranda rights again.

"He took a few deep breaths, sighed a few times, and his eyes filled up with tears," Sheehan recalled. And he asked Sheehan:

"What will my mother say?"

Doyle said he tried to comfort him. "I told him how he had completely fooled me, and I prided myself as a judge of human nature," the lieutenant testified. "And I told him I liked him."

But while Chambers admitted that Jennifer had scratched him, he was saying nothing more. Doyle said he patted him on the shoulder and told him, "I'm sure you'll feel better if you get the whole matter off your chest."

When Chambers remained silent, Doyle asked him what he had used to strangle Levin, where he got it . . . but Chambers only shook his head.

"I told him I didn't understand," the lieutenant testified. "With that, he raised his left arm."

When Doyle saw the watch on Chambers' wrist, he thought he knew what had left the distinctive imprint on the victim's neck.

An assistant district attorney was needed to take

Chambers' statement on videotape. Bypassing the ADA on call, they decided to bring in Sheehan's friend Stephen Saracco, an ADA all the cops there knew well. Sheehan and his partner, Detective Joseph Brady, went to fetch Saracco.

While waiting, McEntee repeated the Miranda warning to Chambers a third time. Then he took notes of the new version of Chambers' story. McEntee's raw notes, never before published, read this way:

"I got to Dorrian's at 2300 hours to meet Alex, one hour late. Hanging with David, Sandy. Jen came to table where I was with Peter. She talked on and on about tan. Went to bathroom and then to bar away from Jen. Two shots tequila, Rolling Rock. One pint Bass. Friends says go to back of bar to talk. I did. I went to leave. She followed. Wanted cigar(ette). Go to store. I said I don't give a fuck. She follows. Asks me to go park to talk. I say yes.

"We get to park. Start talk. Don't want anything to do with her. She gets mad, curses, scratches, spit on me. Don't sit near me. I don't want to commit. Nice, but one time. She says go to bathroom. Rub shoulders. Ties arms with panties. Sits on my face. Pulls pants down. [*Margin at that point says* Cute/cuter tied up.]

"Hit me with stick. Slap dick. Lick dick. Masturbate hard [*Margin on the left says* Playing with me.]

"Sat on chest. Scratches. It hurt. She's strong. Sat on face. Jogger passes. Sitting on chest. Jerk off hard. Hitting balls. Got hand free. Grabbed around neck. Left arm watch. I was pissed. Pulled hard. She fell over. She didn't move. I said, Get up. Thought she was kidding me. She didn't move. I knew she was dead.

"I went across street, sat on cement wall. And then it was bright. I saw ambulance. Biker, girl. Cop car.

"Wandered home. Fell asleep. Thought it was a dream. Mom woke me up. I went to Columbia. [*Aster-*

isk says I liked her. She was nice person. Easy to get along with. Nice to talk to. She was too pushy, friends bothering me.]''

When Chambers finished, McEntee took his notes to Lieutenant Doyle just as Sheehan and Brady returned with ADA Saracco. Now all that was needed was a videotape technician.

While waiting, Sheehan and Brady joined Detective Gill in the Anti-Crime Unit room with the suspect, to formalize McEntee's notes.

"I explained I was about to take a written statement and that he could write it or I would," Sheehan recalled in court. "He chose to have me do it, saying his right hand was sore. . . . He had the opportunity anytime to change it. He could read it, and if he was not satisfied with it, he didn't have to sign it."

On the witness stand, the detective identified the four pages—each signed at the bottom by Robert Chambers—taken just before midnight on August 26. Sheehan then read the full statement aloud:

"I, Robert Chambers was present at Dorrian's Restaurant on 84th Street and Second Avenue. I met Jennifer Levin there about twelve midnight. I had known her about two months. During that time, I had sex with Jennifer three times, twice at a friend's house and once on the roof on the West Side.

"I didn't plan to meet her that night. We just ran into each other. A girl I didn't know but recognized was a friend of Jennifer's said she said I was better in bed than her boyfriend Brock.

"Alex Kapp was angry at me, and Jennifer laughed as I was being yelled at. I was pissed off. Jennifer stated that she wanted to speak with me about something important. She waited for me in the vestibule while I finished a shot of tequila.

"We walked down 86th Street. Jennifer suggested Central Park where we could talk. At Fifth Avenue,

Jennifer suggested a particular path, and inside Jennifer suggested we go behind the museum, so we crossed the road and went under a tree. It was darker than near the museum, and no one could see us.

"We started talking about why I wasn't interested in her. She freaked out and began screeching and scratched my face with her hands. I stood up and started to leave. She apologized and still wanted to talk. I agreed if she didn't sit next to me. I was sitting on the ground, facing the museum.

"Jennifer excused herself and then came up behind me. She massaged my shoulder and said I looked cute, but I would look cuter tied up. Jennifer began cackling and tied me with her panties.

"She pushed me down and took off my pants. She grabbed my dick and jerked me off. I said it hurt. She picked up a stick and hit my dick with it. I yelled out, and a jogger passed and asked if everything was all-right. She sat on my face and dug her nails into my chest. I screamed, and she squeezed my balls.

"I couldn't take any more. I got a hand free and around her neck. She flipped over and landed on her side, twisted next to a tree. I stood up, pulled on my pants, and said, 'Let's go.'

"I shook the body, but it didn't move. I knew then something was wrong. I walked to the museum and sat on the wall. I saw the woman with a bike, saw a police car come and an ambulance. I went home and went to sleep.

"All this time, all this jerking off, and I didn't come."

On the last page of Robert Chambers' formal statement was the time, 12:03 A.M. Sheehan said he then walked the suspect to the men's room.

Under cross-examination by Litman, Detective Sheehan acknowledged that the final sentence of the statement was not volunteered by Chambers. It had been in response to a question.

The suspect asked for one clarification. Sheehan recalled that after looking at his written statement, Chambers said:

"There's nothing here about what she did to my hands. She bit my hands."

Sheehan agreed to an addendum. He also read that to the jury:

"P.S. I told Jennifer after she scratched my face I would talk to her, and she began kissing my hands. I tried to pull away, and then she bit my hands. It didn't hurt then, but it does now. I also hurt my right pinky knuckle when I leaned on it as she flipped over."

In the detective squad room at the Central Park precinct, a small group of participants gathered for a memorable videotape session.

Robert Chambers was brought in front of a camera for what would be his final version—and his only public explanation—of how Jennifer Levin died.

Only Saracco, Sheehan, McEntee, and a videotape technician were present, but in the course of time millions of TV viewers would see brief film clips.

At ten minutes past midnight on August 27, the videotape began to roll.

5

THE VIDEOTAPE

What follows is a word-for-word transcript of the full videotaped statement made by Robert Emmet Chambers shortly after midnight on August 27, 1986, about nineteen hours after Jennifer Levin was killed.

The sixty-five-minute videotape was played in the courtroom twice during Chambers' trial for murder—and at least six more times in the jury room during deliberations on the verdict.

No transcript was made available in the jury room, however. And since Chambers did not take the witness stand to testify in his own defense, sitting silent and slumped at the defense table throughout the trial, the jury could know his voice and facial expressions and persona from only one source: the videotape.

In a sense, Chambers did not exist except on the videotape. He is more animated throughout the one-hour tape than he was at any single moment of his eleven-week trial, and infinitely more vocal.

I compiled this transcript myself, working from the videotape provided by the New York County district attorney's office as well as an incomplete CBS transcription.

While there are at least a dozen other copies extant, this is the first time to my knowledge that the Chambers videotape transcript has been published in full.

A few minutes of audio were deleted by court technicians because sarcasm toward the defendant by Assistant District Attorney Stephen Saracco was ruled inadmissible—for its potential effect on the jury—by presiding Justice Howard E. Bell. There are no other gaps in the transcript.

I have interpolated italicized depictions of Chambers' near constant gestures and physical movements.

Saracco asked all the questions here except for a few from Detective Michael Sheehan, as noted. Detective Michael McEntee remained silent. So did the videotape technician.

Chambers, wearing a short-sleeved white polo shirt, sat behind a desk facing the camera and his interrogators. Saracco and Sheehan sat to the right of the camera, rarely visible from a three-quarter rear angle.

As the questioning began, Chambers brushed his long hair back with his right hand—a characteristic gesture throughout—then put both hands on the desktop blotter. His fingers, especially on the right hand, were curled upward, held gingerly. They looked swollen and sore.

SARACCO: My name is Stephen Saracco. I'm the assistant district attorney in New York County. I want to ask you some questions about the death of Jennifer Levin. Before asking any questions, I want to warn you of your rights. Okay? You have to speak up so that we can get this down here. *(Camera quickly pans right to show Saracco sitting next to desk.)*

CHAMBERS: Okay.

SARACCO: You have the right to remain silent and

refuse to answer any questions. Do you understand that?

CHAMBERS: Yes.

SARACCO: Anything you say may be used against you in court. Do you understand that?

CHAMBERS: Yes.

SARACCO: You have the right to consult an attorney before speaking to the police or to me and to have an attorney present during any questioning now or in the future. Do you understand that?

CHAMBERS: Yes.

SARACCO: If you cannot afford an attorney, one will be provided for you without cost. Do you understand that?

CHAMBERS: Yes.

SARACCO: If you do not have an attorney available, you have the right to remain silent until you have an opportunity to consult with one. Do you understand that?

CHAMBERS: Yes.

SARACCO: Now that I have advised you of your rights, are you willing to answer my questions and tell me the truth about what happened that night?

CHAMBERS: Yes.

SARACCO: Tell me in your own words. I know you—you've talked to detectives, and they've given you your rights and—and you've spoken to them. Is that correct?

CHAMBERS: Right.

SARACCO: I'm from the district attorney's office. That's another *(inaudible)*. Just tell me in your own words as best you can how she, you know, came to be dead.

CHAMBERS: Last night I was supposed to meet a girl named Alex Kapp at Dorrian's at ten-thirty. And I got to Dorrian's late. I got there about eleven-thirty. I was hanging out with my friends, a guy named—I can't remember their names now. A girl named Sandy and her boyfriend named David Smith, and we were just talking.

I hadn't seen Jennifer yet. And then I guess about, sometime around midnight, she came over and started talking to me. Started talking about herself and her trip to California and her tan. *(Right hand touches mouth.)* And you know Betta, my friend Betta, [he] knew I wasn't really all that interested.

SARACCO: In her?

CHAMBERS: Yeah. And I kept making faces about it and stuff. And then she walked away. And I talked to Betta. Then about ten minutes later, she came back and sat down. And at this point I said, "I'm going to get a beer." So I got up and I walked to the bar and I just stood there with some of my friends and she walked to the back of Dorrian's.

Then, I don't know, about twenty-five, thirty minutes later, somewhere around there *(right hand drops out of sight below desktop)*, one of her friends came up to me and told me that Jennifer really wanted to talk to me about something important.

SARACCO: Did you know this friend from before?

CHAMBERS: I knew her face. I don't know her name. *(Right hand moves back to desktop.)* And I didn't want to go. And she knew that. But she told me that it would make Jennifer happy and that I should go. So I walked to the back of the bar *(gestures with right hand)* or to—down near the bathrooms at Dorrian's and—I was there for about a minute. We got like two words out each, then Alex Kapp, the girl that I was supposed to meet—that I hadn't talked to all night—came over and started yelling at me in front of everybody. While this was going on—

SARACCO: What was she yelling about?

CHAMBERS: That I stood her up. That I didn't meet

her on time. That I didn't come over and talk to her. And—

SARACCO: Did she know Jennifer?

CHAMBERS: I don't know. I'm not sure if they'd known each other. And—while this was going on Jennifer was laughing at me and talking to another guy at the same time.

SARACCO: Did this get you annoyed?

CHAMBERS: Yeah, because she came—she asked me to come over and talk to her and—then I'm getting in trouble and she's laughing at me and also the fact that the girl I was supposed to meet, Alex, the girl I like, was yelling at me in front of everybody, so it was embarrassing. So Alex left, and then I walked back to the bar to talk to my friends because I was all pissed off now.

SARACCO: Who were you pissed off at?

CHAMBERS: Well, A, at myself, because I ended up standing Alex up, and B, Jennifer, because she's just laughing at me and she's supposed to be talking to me and that she's talking to another guy. She's flirting with this guy.

SARACCO: Jennifer?

CHAMBERS: Right. And—I was standing at that bar and then she came over. Some of her friends had already left. And she came over and said that she wanted to go outside and talk. So I said, "Well, let me finish"—I had a shot of tequila and I said let me finish this and I'll be outside. She went outside.

And I did my shot and I said good-bye to my friends and I went outside and I met Jennifer. And then we started walking up towards Eighty-sixth Street.

SARACCO: About what time of day is this?

CHAMBERS: This is—I thought it was about two-thirty, quarter of three. It might be later.

SARACCO: How were you feeling at this point? You're not—?

CHAMBERS: I was fine. I wasn't feeling drunk or high or anything like that. And we started walking and talking. I was trying to explain to Jennifer that I wasn't interested and I wanted to go home. *(Leans back, both hands in lap, out of sight.)* And I told her that.

And she said, "No, well, let's talk, you know. Come on, let's walk and talk." So I said fine. And we got to Eighty-sixth Street and we walked up Eighty-sixth Street towards Central Park and—she said, "Let's go in the park." And I was saying, "No, no," you know. "I want to go home."

And she was like, "No, let's just go sit in the park and talk." So I said fine. *(Hands brought back on top of desk.)* And she said, "Let's go, you know, behind the museum."

So we walked to Eighty-fourth and Fifth, and we took this path that goes right along the museum and into the park. *(Right hand gesture traces path.)* And then she pointed and said, "Let's go over here, across the road and sit under this tree." *(Right hand props side of head.)* So while we were there we started talking, and I was explaining to her that I was interested in other people, not interested—

SARACCO: *(Overlap)* Are you sitting there with her under the tree?

CHAMBERS: Yeah. And I started—

SARACCO: *(Overlap)* Have you made any moves towards her or her towards you?

CHAMBERS: No, I wasn't interested at all. I didn't even want to be with her.

SARACCO: Well, she obviously was interested in some excitement—

CHAMBERS: Well, yeah, she was.

SARACCO: Did she do anything towards you as you were walking towards the park?

CHAMBERS: No, we were just walking and talking. And while we were sitting there and I was explaining this to her, you know, saying I'm interested in other people. And that you're going away and I don't want to be bothered.

And she freaked out. I mean, I—I wasn't rude about it. I was just like telling her straightforward how I felt.

SARACCO: While you're sitting there—?

CHAMBERS: Yeah, and she freaked out—and she just—she like got up and—knelt in front of me, and she just scratched my face. *(Both hands make single clawing gesture across front of face.)* And I have these marks here. *(Right hand rubs cheek.)* I didn't even notice them till this morning.

And—I got all upset and I stood up and I was saying, "I'm going to go. I'm going to go. This is crazy."

SARACCO: She's still remaining sitting?

CHAMBERS: She was kneeling.

SARACCO: Mm-hm.

CHAMBERS: And—she said, "Oh, I'm sorry. I'm really sorry. Sit down. Sit down." And I said, you know, "I'll sit and talk with you, but I don't want you to sit next to me. You know, you can say whatever you want to say and then I'm going to go." Because I was really pissed off at this time. I mean—she laughed at me and she scratches me.

SARACCO: She had laughed at you in the bar that night?

CHAMBERS: Yeah. And—she'd also spit on me— after scratching me. Didn't really say anything. Didn't call me any names. She just had this look on her that she—I don't know. She was insane. I don't know what was wrong with her.

And—so I said, "Okay, you know. I'll talk to you. Just don't sit next to me."

And she said, "Well, let me go to the bathroom." And I said, "All right, you know. I'll wait here." So she went to the bathroom and—I suppose—she went *(right hand points away)* behind these bushes. I guess she went to the bathroom.

And during this time I was facing the museum. I was leaning back on my hands like this. *(Leans back in chair, arms thrust straight behind hips.)* Sitting on the ground. And I didn't see her. And she came up behind me, and she started to give me a massage *(hands back atop desk)*, saying how cute I looked and that I would look cuter if I were tied up.

SARACCO: Your face is scratched at this point, right?

CHAMBERS: Right. And this was before she went to the bathroom she had scratched me. And she seemed calmed down and she came over and she seemed really nice, giving me the massage.

SARACCO: How long had she been gone?

CHAMBERS: Hmmm. Two minutes? And—she said I looked really cute and that I would look cuter tied up. And I thought, you know, that she was just horsing around.

SARACCO: Why did you think she was horsing around?

CHAMBERS: Because it just didn't seem like Jennifer. At least the way I knew her. And—all, you know, I started to say that this is crazy, whatever. I mean, she scooped my hands with both her arms and like held them together. *(Arms thrust forward, wrists crossed.)* And took her underwear that was—

SARACCO: From behind or—?

CHAMBERS: Yeah, this is from behind because I'm facing away. And she wrapped up her underwear around my wrists *(wrapping motion, right hand over left wrist)* so they were locked and they were behind my back. *(Hands together behind back.)* Because I was leaning on my hands. And she just pushed me back. Like this. *(Leans way back in chair, hands still behind him.)* And then got on top of my chest and she was facing my feet.

SARACCO: *(Inaudible)*

CHAMBERS: And—she began taking off my pants. *(Sits up again, hands on desk.)*

SARACCO: You're still by that same tree you were sitting under?

CHAMBERS: We never moved from the tree. And she started to take off my pants, and she started to play with me. She started jerking me off. And—

SARACCO: Did she take your pants down?

CHAMBERS: Yes. Not all the way off. Just, she just pushed them down. *(Makes pushing gesture with both hands.)* And she was doing it really hard *(makes masturbation movement with right hand)*, and it really hurt me and I—you know, I started to say, "Stop it. Stop it. It hurts."

And she kind of laughed in a weird way—like more like a cackle or something. *(Right hand touches mouth.)* And she, then she sat up *(both hands on desk)* and she like sat on my face and then she dug her nails into my chest and I have scratches right here *(lifts shirt to neck with both hands, looks down at scratches)* from where she scratched.

SARACCO: Can you show me?

CHAMBERS: Along here *(both hands holding shirt up)*.

SARACCO: Where?

CHAMBERS: See? And—

SARACCO: You're wearing the same shirt you were wearing when you were with her?

CHAMBERS: *(Lets go of shirt, hands return to desktop.)* No, this—I was wearing a different shirt. *(Plucks at shirtfront with right hand.)* And—she—she seemed to be having a great time. And I was—you know, at this point, I was beginning to scream—

SARACCO: *(Overlap)* What do you mean she was having a great time?

CHAMBERS: She was laughing and giggling and making weird kind of laughing-type sounds while digging her nails into me. And I was—you know, and she's sitting on my face. And I'm trying to get away *(jerks head to side)* by wiggling all over and I'm screaming. And at this point, a jogger came by. And—he yelled out—

SARACCO: At three o'clock in the morning?

CHAMBERS: Yeah. It was a jogger, and he yelled out—you know, "Is everything all right?" And she was like, "Shh-shh-shh"—like that.

SARACCO: You're the one that's yelling, right?

CHAMBERS: I'm—I'm screaming. I'm, like, you know—get off!

SARACCO: What—?

CHAMBERS: And then she's like, "Shh-shh." And the jogger was like, you know, "Is everything all right?" And I was like, "Yeah, don't worry about it."

And then the jogger left and then she began to jerk me off again. And then she squeezed me—she squeezed my balls. And this really hurt. And I just—I couldn't take it anymore and I was screaming in pain.

SARACCO What kind of a—what type of time are we talking about from when she comes back from going to the bathroom and—

CHAMBERS: This is—it was in like a ten-, fifteen-minute time—

SARACCO: *(Overlap)* This is going on about ten, fifteen minutes?

CHAMBERS: Yeah, And—it was nonstop. She was just having her way. And then she squeezed my balls and I just could not take it. So I was wiggling around *(leans back, hands behind him, hips moving in chair)*, wiggling around, and she was, you know, leaning forward, jerking me off and squeezing my balls and laughing. And I managed to get my left hand free. *(Pulls left hand from behind him.)*

So I kind of sat up a little and just grabbed at her

(left hand and arm arcs in front of him and to right), and I—she—she's sitting in the—she's still facing— she's facing in towards the Great Lawn into the park.

SARACCO: Away from you.

CHAMBERS: Yes. Facing my feet.

SARACCO: Okay.

CHAMBERS: All right.

SARACCO: And where is she sitting like that?

CHAMBERS: She's sitting on my chest, leaning forward. And I just leaned up and grabbed her like this from up around the neck *(arching motion, crook of left elbow rests briefly under chin)*, and I just yanked her, and she could have—

SARACCO: You're indicating with your—?

CHAMBERS: It was my left hand.

SARACCO: *(Inaudible)*

CHAMBERS: Because my right hand was—I was still lying down, kind of. And I sat up and grabbed her and pulled her *(yanking motion with left arm)*, and when I came down I landed on my knuckle. *(Brings right arm forward, holds hand up.)* I don't know if I hit a rock or—something. *(Looks down, rotates right hand)*. And I hurt my knuckle doing that.

SARACCO: You grab—did you have the watch on when you—when you grabbed her?

CHAMBERS: Yeah. I did. I was wearing a watch.

SARACCO: The same watch you're wearing now.

CHAMBERS: Yeah, the exact same watch. And I just pulled her *(yanks with left arm)*, and she kind of flipped over on the side near the tree.

SARACCO: Right. I just don't understand how you hurt your—your right hand.

CHAMBERS: Well, when I grabbed her I leaned *(leans back, right hand behind him, brings up left hand in arc)*—I leaned up like this and grabbed her. When I came back down this hand was still behind me. Because I was still lying on it a little bit. *(Brings right hand forward, rolls edge of palm on desk.)* When I came down I twisted it and landed. I don't know if it was on a rock or whatever. And I don't know if I jammed it or broke it.

SARACCO: You came down how? If you can, then say—

(JUDICIAL AUDIO DELETION)

(Chambers looks around, leans back in chair, then stands up. Video widens. He walks to left side of desk, leans body backward across desktop, hands behind him.)

CHAMBERS: I was lying like this.

SARACCO: Right.

CHAMBERS: Okay? On my back. And I couldn't move and I managed to get this hand free and my legs are out. And she's facing this way, kneeling on my chest. So I reached up like this *(left hand comes up as torso rises off desk, left arm swinging forward)* and grabbed, and I came down like that on my hand. *(Sprawls twisted to right side on desk, his weight on edge of right hand, left arm arching across chest).*

SARACCO: All right. She's—she's flipping backwards.

CHAMBERS: She came over this way *(left hand traverses chest to right shoulder)* and landed right there. Right next to the tree. And she was kind of twisted along next to the tree.

SARACCO: Did she groan—or say anything—or—?

CHAMBERS: *(Rises off desk, sits in chair.)* Nothing. It—it was just really quick. *(Left hand yanks sharply.)* She just flipped over and then—landed, and she was kind of twisted on the tree. On her side. *(Pantomimes her—face down, elbows out, hands up, fingertips nearly touching.)* So I stood up and I—

SARACCO: *(Inaudible)*

CHAMBERS: No. I don't. So I stood up and *(cough)*

I pulled on my pants and I said, "Jennifer, let's go. Let's get out of here. Now!"

And she didn't move. And—I still thought she was just kidding around. So I came over and I shook the body. *(Shaking motion with right hand.)*

SARACCO: You thought she was kidding around about what? I mean, she—?

CHAMBERS: She was just lying there not moving. *(Pantomimes face down, right hand to forehead.)* I thought she was trying to scare me. So I went over and I shook the body *(repeats shaking gesture)*, and there was—nothing happened. You know—?

SARACCO: Did you know it was a body at that point or—?

CHAMBERS: At that—

SARACCO: A dead body?

CHAMBERS: No, I had no idea. I thought she was kidding around. So I shook her *(shaking motion)*, and there was nothing. And I got really scared. And I just—I stood there for like ten minutes waiting—about I don't know how long. About ten minutes. Five minutes. Trying to see if she'd move. If she's just trying to, you know, scare me.

SARACCO: That's a lot of time—you mean like five or ten minutes you're standing there?

CHAMBERS: Yeah, I was just standing there looking at her, waiting for her to move. And if she moved, I was just going to—I don't know what I was going to do. I was going to get really pissed off and yell at her and this and that.

But she didn't move. So I got really scared and I just kind of like went into my own little daze. And I walked back across the road *(points right forefinger)* and sat on this stone wall *(hand moves back and forth)*—that was—

SARACCO: Across—across what—what road?

CHAMBERS: From—there's like a little road *(right*

hand traces road) that goes through Central Park between where we were and the museum, the back of the museum. And there's a stone wall there.

So I sat on the stone wall *(leans back, left hand now in lap, right hand held up)* just looking at the tree. I couldn't see Jennifer. She—because the tree was like ballooned out around *(both hands sketch large circle in air)*—she was behind it, and I couldn't see. *(Puts hands in lap.)* But I just kept staring at the tree.

And then a lady came by with a bike, and she was walking the bike and—she looked at me and then I guess she saw Jennifer and then she—I found out later that she went and got an ambulance. *(Leans forward, puts hands on desk.)*

And the next thing I knew it was light. At this time, it was still kind of dark. And then—the next thing I knew is that I—I looked across and I noticed that this lady—the lady with the bike is sitting in a police car staring at me, and the police are walking around with these people from the ambulance. I don't know if they were taking pictures or what. I just noticed the police walking around. *(Leans back, puts hands in lap.)* And I was in shock. I didn't know what was going on. I didn't—

SARACCO: What—what were you in shock about?

CHAMBERS: That this girl that I knew and I left the bar with and just wanted to talk to—you know, was—what—did what she did to me. And that now she's not moving.

And that there were police there and there was an ambulance there and there's a lady looking at me and I was all nervous.

SARACCO: I assume like you walked up and said—?

CHAMBERS: I didn't say anything. I stood. I—I stood—I got off the wall and I just walked in the park slowly just looking around and then I got home. Then I—

SARACCO: *(Overlap)* Were you trying to avoid people or—?

CHAMBERS: No. If I was trying to avoid—I was sitting there in plain sight.

SARACCO *(Overlap)* I'm just asking—

CHAMBERS: No. I was sitting there in plain sight. *(Leans forward, puts hands on desk.)* And—just looking at this lady who was looking back at me. And I—she's looking at me like she knew that it was me.

SARACCO: She knew that it was you that what?

CHAMBERS: That I had hurt Alex. *(Pause.)* Not Alex, Jennifer. Sorry.

SARACCO: Alex was the other girl?

CHAMBERS: Yeah. And so I'm—

SARACCO: Did you check her pulse or anything to see if—

CHAMBERS: No. I was scared. I didn't want to touch her. Because I—when I shook her *(shaking motion)* and she didn't move and I stood there. I got scared and I—I didn't want to touch her. I didn't know what to do.

SARACCO: You told me that you thought she might be faking or—

CHAMBERS: *(Overlap)* Yeah, at first I shook her really hard. *(Shaking motion.)* And nothing. And she just didn't move. Then—she didn't move a muscle, not a finger, anything.

Then I got really scared. So I just sat across the street.

SARACCO: You told me you stayed there for about five to ten minutes.

CHAMBERS: Yeah. I was standing there watching her at first.

SARACCO: Right by her?

CHAMBERS: Yeah. And I just—I just stood there and I stared. And I didn't know what was going on—

SARACCO: *(Overlap)* Scared of what?

CHAMBERS: No. I stared at her. And I was scared because I didn't know really what was going on. Just that—then I went across and I sat on the wall and the lady with the bike came and then the police came and an ambulance came.

And then I just walked through the park all the way up to Ninetieth Street at the engineers gate, which is an entrance that goes right off on my block *(right hand gestures)* because I live on Ninetieth between Madison and Fifth.

And I just—I went upstairs and got undressed and went to sleep. And I don't know how long I was home for or what time it was. Then my mom just woke me up and she said, you know, it's eleven o'clock. Get up. You've got to do things. And when I woke up I thought it was a dream. Because nothing really hurt. And I didn't look at my hands *(looks down at them)* and I didn't think about—

SARACCO: *(Overlap)* But you're saying that you were all scratched?

CHAMBERS: But it—nothing hurt me. I woke up and I was just—I was tired and I didn't know what was going on. I didn't know if it was a dream or what. So I went and I got in the shower. And at this point a girl named Alex, one of—

SARACCO: Did your mother see you?

CHAMBERS: No. She just yelled into my room, like, get up, you know, it's eleven o'clock. And I went in the shower.

SARACCO: Because I imagine she would have asked you some questions about your face.

CHAMBERS: Well, when I got out of the shower she told me that this girl Alex called, a friend of Jennifer's. And asked where Jennifer was.

SARACCO: Did she see you at this point?

CHAMBERS: My mom? Yeah, at this point she did and she said that Alex wants you to call her. And then she looked at my face. And I told her, you know, I was nervous because I knew as soon as I heard the name Alex and where's Jennifer, I knew exactly that everything that I'd thought I'd dreamt was real.

SARACCO: You thought this was all a dream?

CHAMBERS: When I woke up at first I was, like, you know, that had to be a dream.

SARACCO: You weren't drunk or anything?

CHAMBERS: No. But I just woke up.

SARACCO: *(Overlap)* Drugs or anything?

CHAMBERS: No. I just—I woke up and I was in a daze and I was, like, wow, that must have been a dream. So then my mom looked at me and I was, like, oh, it's from the cat. We have a cat. And I told her how the cat scratched me. Because I didn't know what to say at first. I was—you know, I was really nervous. Then I had to go up to school. And I—

SARACCO: Where's school?

CHAMBERS: Well, Columbia. I—you know, I want to take some courses there in September. And I talked to a few people about placement tests and things like that for certain courses. And—when I came back, I—I'd talked to Alex before I left for Columbia. And she asked—

SARACCO: The girl that you were supposed to meet?

CHAMBERS: No, this is Jennifer's friend, Alex.

SARACCO: Right.

CHAMBERS: And she said, "Do you know where Jennifer is?" And I said, "I have no idea. Why don't you try Brock, her boyfriend"—who isn't around the city, I guess, at this moment. And she said, "Okay."

And then I went off to Columbia and I came back and I was lying down and I started to fall asleep again because I was exhausted because I really wasn't sure what I did. And—at this point, the cleaning lady came, a lady named Mary Ray.

And about ten minutes after that the police rang up.

And came upstairs to ask me some questions and then I've been here since one-thirty. So I've been here for about twelve hours.

SARACCO: You've been treated pretty well?

CHAMBERS: Yeah. I feel good—

SARACCO: *(Overlap)* Treated you like gentle—like a gentleman?

CHAMBERS: Yeah. I got something to eat. I felt better. So I mean, I never meant to—to hurt her or anything. I just wanted to go home. That was the whole point. And then now I'm just completely drained. I cried—I cried during the day or night. I don't know. *(Right hand smooths top of desk.)* I was just worn out. I didn't know what to do. I was nervous. I felt nauseous.

SARACCO: When the police started to talk to you, you lied to them, though?

CHAMBERS: Because I was scared. I didn't know what was going on.

SARACCO: You did lie to them, then?

CHAMBERS: Yeah, I did. I told them that—

SARACCO: I think in fact you told them you weren't even at Dorrian's when they first started questioning you. Is that right?

CHAMBERS: No. I never told them that. I told them I was at Dorrian's. I was not there—I had no intention of meeting Jennifer. I never talked to Jennifer—

SARACCO: What did you lie to them about when they first questioned you?

CHAMBERS: About when I left with her. Whether she was with me or not. And where I left her. And I said that she wasn't with me and that I had lost her somewhere off—off Eighty-sixth Street and Second Avenue. But actually she was with me. Because she was arguing and, you know, we were arguing together.

SARACCO: So those were lies.

CHAMBERS: Yeah, it was at the time, yeah. Because

I was scared. I didn't know what was going to happen to me.

SARACCO: I think you even lied to them about, you know, the scratches on your face.

CHAMBERS: I told them it was the cat, also.

SARACCO: Which was a lie, also?

CHAMBERS: And people have been—I've been shaking hands with the detectives and I have a hurt knuckle and I didn't say anything. (*Raises right hand, looks at it, rotates it slightly.*) So—I was just scared.

You know, I—I'm not—I'm not somebody that hurts other people. That's just a reaction. She was hurting me. I told her to stop and she wouldn't.

SARACCO: But you said—that—?

CHAMBERS: She spit on me. She hit me with a stick.

SARACCO: I wasn't there. You weren't—the detectives weren't there. But there were certain things that just don't lie. The condition of the body. The condition of your face and your chest and—How tall are you? Six four?

CHAMBERS: Three. Six three.

SARACCO: How much do you weigh?

CHAMBERS: One ninety.

SARACCO: What is she, about five eight, maybe five ten?

CHAMBERS: Five nine. Probably weighs like one twenty something. But she was strong. I mean, she—she would just burst into these like fits and freak out, and she was strong.

SARACCO: What was your relationship like with her prior to that night?

CHAMBERS: I had—we didn't really have—she felt it was more special than I did. I saw her—

SARACCO: When did you first meet?

CHAMBERS: I met her probably about two months ago.

SARACCO: (*Overlap*) Where was that?

CHAMBERS: At Dorrian's bar on Eighty-fourth Street. And—we liked each other. I mean, we got along. We were nice to each other. And . . . *(Right hand combs through hair, then props face.)*

SARACCO: Had you taken her out or—?

CHAMBERS: No, I—I'd only seen her in Dorrian's. I'd never gone anywhere else with her. And—

SARACCO: Had you had sex with her?

CHAMBERS: I had sex with her three times. Twice at two different friends' house and once on a roof where she took some pictures.

SARACCO: Of—?

CHAMBERS: Of me while I was asleep. I fell asleep on the roof. And she had a—

SARACCO: Where did she have the camera?

CHAMBERS: She had it with her. We were at a friend's house. And she had keys to her friend's house on the West Side. Just like another time she had keys to her friend Laura's house on the East Side. And—because she lives way downtown. And she didn't want to go all the way downtown.

SARACCO: *(Inaudible)*

CHAMBERS: Yeah. I didn't know that. I found that out while I was talking to everybody.

SARACCO: When you had sex with her the three times, did you use any protection or did she use any prophylactics or—?

CHAMBERS: It—

SARACCO: *(Overlap)* Concern of either party?

CHAMBERS: It never even entered our minds at all.

SARACCO: Was she pregnant, do you think?

CHAMBERS: I don't know.

SARACCO: You don't know?

CHAMBERS: I don't know specifically, no. But—I—

SARACCO: You had sex with her those three times, was—was there anything *(Chambers lowers right hand to desk, raises left hand to chin)* out of the ordinary with the tying up or anything, like, or just regular, you know, regular sex?

CHAMBERS: Just regular sex. Except for the third time on the roof where she took pictures, and I don't know what happened—

SARACCO: *(Overlap)* How did you know she took pictures of you?

CHAMBERS: Because she woke me up and showed them to me saying, "I thought you looked cute like this."

SARACCO: These are Polaroids?

CHAMBERS: Yeah.

SARACCO: So, you fell asleep on the roof naked?

CHAMBERS: Yeah, I was exhausted.

SARACCO: And you didn't realize that she had taken the pictures of you?

CHAMBERS: Not until she woke me up, no.

SARACCO: And what was your reaction to that?

CHAMBERS: I was shocked because I had no idea. I—I just thought it was odd. It was out of the ordinary. I'd never, like, come across somebody that did that.

SARACCO: I—I reckon so. Did you take them and try to rip them up or—?

CHAMBERS: She kept—I didn't think she was going to do anything with them. I didn't think she was going to—

SARACCO: Did she do anything with them? Did she—?

CHAMBERS: I've never seen them again. I hardly ever see her. And she—she's been away for two, maybe three weeks.

SARACCO: Where was she?

CHAMBERS: She went to California. But I think she also went to Montauk. She was talking about Montauk.

SARACCO: Was the extent of your relationship to her, prior to last night, was it about a month? With—?

CHAMBERS: I—I had slept with her the night before

she left for California at her friend's house. And her friend drove her to the train station and dropped me off on Seventy-seventh and Lexington.

SARACCO: Did you ever give her any—for want of a better term, any sincere lines? I mean, that she may have felt that the relationship was different than you would?

CHAMBERS: No, I—

SARACCO: You know—you know what I mean by that. *(Inaudible)* phony lies?

CHAMBERS: No. Not at all. I was—I was always nice to her. I was just always nice to her. Because we got along. She was very easy to talk to. She's a really nice girl.

SARACCO: What did you talk about?

CHAMBERS: Talked about—what, last night? Or any time? Any time we just talked about whatever. *(Leans back, left hand in lap, right hand on desk.)* What we're doing, where we're going to school, what we want to do in the future. Just—talking. Talking about where we've traveled. Who we saw, what movies we saw. Just usual kind of stuff. Nothing out of the ordinary. *(Right hand brushes hair off forehead; leans forward, both hands on desk.)*

I mean, her friends knew that—I mean, she would come on to me. And her—my friends knew I didn't really want her around all that much. And then when she used to walk into a—some—when she used to walk into Dorrian's, I would say, "Oh, God, here she is." And I was interested in other people, and my friends knew that.

SARACCO: I want to be perfectly frank with you. Let's—we assume that you're telling the truth *(Chambers rests chin on right hand)* and a lot of people investing a lot of time and *(JUDICIAL AUDIO DELETION)*—it just strikes me as a little odd that—that she would be able to—be able to tie you in some fashion without your consent to it.

CHAMBERS: Well, at first, I thought she was just joking around. That's what I said. I mean—

SARACCO: I mean, it seems like you'd be able to get out of it—?

CHAMBERS: Well, I was lying on my hands like this *(puts both hands behind him)* with her kneeling on top, and it's kind of hard.

SARACCO: *(Overlap)* I mean, it seems like when she comes up behind you you can—?

CHAMBERS: Mmm-hmm. *(Sits forward, hands on desk.)*

SARACCO: Then all of a sudden you find yourself— and you're tied up.

CHAMBERS: She just *(inaudible overlap)* she took the underwear and just put my hands together *(wrists crossed in front of him)* and wrapped it up.

SARACCO: What kind of underwear?

CHAMBERS: I don't know what kind of underwear they are.

SARACCO: How did you know it was underwear?

CHAMBERS: Because that's the only thing that it could have possibly been. Plus I felt it. And when I ripped my hands off *(flings left hand in air, then right hand)* I saw it. I don't know where they went. I just threw it.

SARACCO: Was it panty hose, panties, a bra?

CHAMBERS: Just panties.

SARACCO: Just a pair of panties?

CHAMBERS: Yeah. And she—she had them twisted *(makes twisting motion, then crosses wrists, palms up)* and she put my hands in—you know, in a joking manner. Because she said, "You'd look cuter tied up." And I was, like, you know *(both hands on desk).*

SARACCO: I mean, your face was scratched at this point. You're mad at her for two reasons.

CHAMBERS: Mmm-hmm.

SARACCO: You're mad at her from—

CHAMBERS: But each time—

SARACCO: For laughing at you in the bar.

CHAMBERS: Right. And then for scratching me.

SARACCO: And spitting at you.

CHAMBERS: Right.

SARACCO: You're *(inaudible overlap)* accessible at this point for—?

CHAMBERS: But each time we've talked.

SARACCO: Some sort of adventure with her at this point about being tied up. I mean, you're mad at her.

CHAMBERS: I was mad, but each time that she came over and talked, we just—we'd start to get into a serious conversation, and I liked that.

SARACCO: Your face was scratched at this point.

CHAMBERS: I know it is.

SARACCO: And you must—you know that your face was scratched at this point.

CHAMBERS: I know it is.

SARACCO: I mean, you know that you're bleeding?

CHAMBERS: No, see I had no idea how bad it was, where I was scratched. It was just like, oh—

SARACCO: *(Overlap)* But you felt her when she scratched you? *(First close-up of Chambers's face shows scratches along right cheek and jaw.)*

CHAMBERS: Yeah, yeah.

SARACCO: That certainly would have—upset you?

CHAMBERS: I was. I told her not to come and sit next to me again. I said, "I will listen to what you have to say and I'm leaving." I told her the whole way up Eighty-Sixth Street, "I just want to go home. That's all." I wasn't even going to go out that night.

SARACCO: I mean, you're not drunk.

CHAMBERS: No.

SARACCO: You're sitting under a tree with your face scratched, you've been spit at, you've been laughed at in a bar. By some girl you're not really—not too much of a romantic attachment with.

CHAMBERS: At this point, no, I didn't.

SARACCO: And now comes up with all—she has you tied up and she's sitting—

CHAMBERS: It's not like—it's not like she's not—

SARACCO: *(Overlap)* Where it really doesn't—it—?

CHAMBERS: It's not like if she knocked me out and tied me up

SARACCO: I know this. I—

CHAMBERS: She just came up and was like kidding—

SARACCO: It would be different if she did, like *(Chambers sits back, arms drop to sides)*, come up and hit you over the head with something and you found yourself tied up. You—you were perfectly conscious, right?

CHAMBERS: Right. But I figured that she was just joking around at this point. And she's like talking—when she pulled my hands together *(puts hands behind him)*, and she said, like, "You'd look cute tied up," I thought she was just joking around. I never—

SARACCO: *(Overlap)* At this point. You've been scratched, you've been spit at, you've been laughed at. There's—

CHAMBERS: *(Overlap)* She wasn't in a normal way. She wasn't in a normal state of mind. She was just laughing. I was, like, well, this is a weird kind of humor. And the whole time, I'm still talking to her at this point, saying, "Jennifer—"

SARACCO: *(Overlap)* But that—but that doesn't make any sense. *(Chambers sits forward, hands on desk.)* You're not talking—you're not talking to her. *(Inaudible)* When she's come—if she comes back and she's going to start tying you up, after she'd scratched you, spit at you, and laughed at you at the bar—?

CHAMBERS: Right—

SARACCO: You're six foot three, a hundred and ninety pounds. When you've had enough—?

CHAMBERS: But I'm not going to do anything to harm her at all.

SARACCO: You're going to stop her.

CHAMBERS: I'm going to stop her, but I'm talking to her. And she's just joking around. I didn't take it seriously like she had any intent—

SARACCO: *(Overlap)* You just told me that she's gone—she's gone nuts on you.

CHAMBERS: She did go nuts and she came back and then she started to *(sits up, makes kneading motion)* massage my—massage my back.

SARACCO: After you're tied up or before?

CHAMBERS: No, before. That's what I said. She came over and she started to give me a massage. And she said, you know, "you look really cute," and she started to try and sweet-talk me. And the whole time I'm saying, "Jennifer, you know, this isn't going to work. Jennifer, I'm interested in other people." And she said, "But you look—"

SARACCO: *(Overlap)* Aren't you saying anything about, "I've got scratches all over my face. You just spit at me—"

CHAMBERS: *(Overlap)* Yeah, we got into a—we got into a long argument—

SARACCO: *(Overlap)* I mean, aren't you talking to her about that?

CHAMBERS: We got in—yes, of course. We got into a long discussion about it and why she's so weird and why she freaks out and why I can't hang out with her.

SARACCO: I would imagine you were a little bit upset?

CHAMBERS: I was very upset. I was very upset. But I'm not paying attention to her. I'm like explaining to her that I don't want to, you know, continue any kind of relationship. We don't have any kind of relationship. I saw her three times and I see her in Dorrian's every once in a while. She flirts with a lot of guys. I don't know who she's gone home with. I know nothing about her.

SARACCO: That's not the point—was it at the point where you were under the tree?

CHAMBERS: Right. *(Right hand combs forelock.)*

SARACCO: *(Inaudible)*

CHAMBERS: I wasn't taking her seriously when she was doing it. I thought she was just playing a little game.

SARACCO: Now you had to be taking her seriously.

CHAMBERS: I took her seriously when she's scratched me. When she was tying me up, I didn't take her seriously.

SARACCO: What happened to the—to the underwear?

CHAMBERS: I don't—I think they found it or something. They said *(inaudible overlap)*.

DETECTIVE SHEEHAN: No, not by us.

CHAMBERS: Then I don't know. Then it's still there.

DETECTIVE SHEEHAN: No underwear at the scene.

CHAMBERS: I didn't take it.

DETECTIVE SHEEHAN: No panty hose at the scene.

SARACCO: Now, according to you, all you did was, like, just grab her around the neck once.

CHAMBERS: Well, I just grabbed her *(left arm swings up toward right shoulder)* and yanked her as hard as I could. And she just flipped over me and landed right next to the tree. And then she didn't move.

SARACCO: It's been described to me that you may have some *(JUDICIAL AUDIO DELETION)* on her breast area. Do you—?

CHAMBERS: No, see, that's—that's what I don't know. When I reached around *(leans back, left hand reaches out, yanks, then drops to lap)*, I might have grabbed one of her breasts. I don't know. Because I was in a frenzy. She was squeezing my balls. So I just reached and grabbed. (*Left arm swings repeatedly across body.*) So I might have like yanked, pulled, twisted. I don't know. (*Hands on desktop.*)

SARACCO: Do you have any marks on—on your genitals from—from the squeezing? Is there any scratches around—?

CHAMBERS: No, there's no scratches—there's no scratches. There's just—you know, squeezing hard. She wasn't scratching or biting or anything like that.

SARACCO: Did you ejaculate at any time?

CHAMBERS: No, I never did. Never did.

SARACCO: Were you erect at any time?

CHAMBERS: Yes, I was. Never had an orgasm. (*Right hand brushes hair off forehead.*) Never ejaculated or anything.

SARACCO: You became erect?

CHAMBERS: I was in too much pain. I wasn't even thinking about it.

SARACCO: So she did arouse you when she came back?

CHAMBERS: Well, she did because—

SARACCO: To a certain degree, I mean—?

CHAMBERS: To a degree until it started to hurt and I told her to stop. And she just kind of laughed and sat up on my face and dug her nails into my chest. (*Inaudible overlap.*)

SARACCO: I don't mean to upset you. I (*overlap*)—

CHAMBERS: (*Left hand shields face, head turns right, eyes down.*) Please, I really don't want to see—

SARACCO: You've seen these photos?

CHAMBERS: (*Looks away.*) I haven't seen the photos, but I'd really rather not see the photos.

SARACCO: Well, let me just describe them to you. (*Chambers turns toward him. Wide-angle glimpse of Saracco holding Polaroids.*) Her neck area—depicts

markings of a degree a lot more severe than could have
been inflicted by the way you describe it, just by one—

CHAMBERS: That's all I did. *(Swings left arm in arc.)*
I just—

SARACCO: Bringing her back—

CHAMBERS: I reached up—

SARACCO: There was nobody there except you and
her.

CHAMBERS: Yeah, I know. And some joggers.

SARACCO: And some jog—but nobody else laid their
hands on her as far as you know.

CHAMBERS: As far as I know. I didn't even move
from the scene. I sat on the wall. I didn't run. I didn't
do anything. I was in shock.

SARACCO: These are not—these are not tough, really. *(Chambers turns head away.)* Take a look at these.
(He glances down at Polaroids, again turns away.)
Take a look at her neck, Robert. *(He glances at them,
then leans forward, studies them intently for five seconds.) (Inaudible overlap)* Do you see how discolored
and even bleeding her neck is? *(Chambers turns
away.)*

CHAMBERS: *(Very quietly, after long pause.)* Yes, I
can see that.

SARACCO: All right. I mean, is there any way you
can account for this?

CHAMBERS: Yeah, because when I pulled her back
she—landed against the tree and just laid there like
this *(pantomimes right arm across her face)* against
the tree.

SARACCO: But not her neck, though. I mean—?

CHAMBERS: I don't know what she hit. I don't know
if she hit a root on the tree or something like that.

SARACCO: Was she wearing what she's wearing in
these photographs?

CHAMBERS: Yeah.

SARACCO: Detective, if you'd like to ask him a couple questions?

DETECTIVE SHEEHAN: Robert . . . *(Chambers brushes hair back with right hand.)* The photographs we have here, okay—what do you recall her wearing?

CHAMBERS: Well *(elbow on desk, right hand up)*, as I said—

SHEEHAN: Would you describe what she was wearing?

CHAMBERS: Well, as I said—before like I said in there—in the other room, I said that she was wearing some kind of light colored clothing. A skirt and, like *(right hand plucks front of shirt)*, a skimpy little top.

SHEEHAN: A skirt as opposed to slacks?

CHAMBERS: Right.

SHEEHAN: And a what?

CHAMBERS: Sort of like *(plucks shirtfront)* a small top.

SHEEHAN: A scanty top?

CHAMBERS: Yeah.

SHEEHAN: It was kind of *(Chambers brushes hair back)* cool last night. Did she have a sweater with her or anything?

CHAMBERS: *(Sits back, arms at sides.)* That I don't—I don't remember. I have no idea. I didn't notice.

SHEEHAN: Did she have a jacket?

CHAMBERS: I don't know. *(Right hand on desk makes impatient gesture.)* I don't know if she had a bag. I didn't notice. I had a jacket, but I ended up leaving that at Dorrian's.

SHEEHAN: In other words, you didn't have a jacket when you went to the park?

CHAMBERS: No.

SHEEHAN: But you don't recall whether or not she had a jacket?

CHAMBERS: I don't remember. (*Shrugs right shoulder.*)

SHEEHAN: Okay.

CHAMBERS: The whole (*shrugs again, waves right hand*), the most important thing was just explaining to her that I wanted nothing to do with her and that she was bothering me. Even her friends knew that she was bothering me. Her friends saw—everybody in the place saw her, like, coming up to me, rubbing up against me, doing these things, telling me things, telling me I'm better in bed than her boyfriend. She told her friends that she was definitely going to have sex with me.

SARACCO: I believe you to that point. I believe pretty much what happened in there. It's just when you get out it just—it doesn't make any sense to me. I think that—that you were upset, that she was pestering you. You want no part of her. Maybe you do walk her out. And maybe she does get upset when you're—you— tell her you don't want any part of her, maybe she does scratch you. And that certainly upset you.

CHAMBERS: Mmm-hmm.

SARACCO: And—you're not drunk. But you're mad at her. And you are—you are mad at her?

CHAMBERS: (*Nods.*) Yeah.

SARACCO: And you're real mad at her. Spit at you. Marked up your face. She'd laughed at you in a bar. In front of your friends. And—whatever overtakes you at that point, I mean—?

CHAMBERS: Nothing overtook me because I had no intention to hurt her. I was not in the frame of mind to hurt her. If I was—

SARACCO: I'm not saying it's something that—it's premeditated on your part, something that you're thinking about doing as you walk out like—I'm sure it's not that way. I'm not saying that you're walking out of that bar and saying to yourself, I'm going to kill this girl in Central Park. I'm sure it didn't happen that way. But something triggered you.

CHAMBERS: *(Waves right hand.)* She *(overlap)* she molested me in the park. She hit me with—

SARACCO: How did she molest you? You're—we're talking about—?

CHAMBERS: What, girls *(puts hands on desk)* girls cannot—girls cannot do it to a guy?

SARACCO: *(Overlap)* But you can't—tell me, she's *(inaudible)* she's raping you in the park? Robert, come on.

CHAMBERS: She's having her way with me without my consent. With my hands behind my back. Hurting me. The jogger heard me scream.

SARACCO: Are we from Iowa or someplace? What—?

CHAMBERS: *(Sharply.)* I don't know where you're from. That really doesn't concern me. But you see, the jogger heard me scream. The jogger even asked, "What's wrong?" *(Turns palms up on desk.)*

SARACCO: *(Inaudible)*

CHAMBERS: I'm hurt. *(Holds hands in air.)*

SARACCO: You're hurt from what? I know that you're hurt from your language from her scratching you. *(Chambers leans back, turns away, looks up at ceiling.)* *(Inaudible background words)* I mean *(Chambers shakes head, brushes forelock with right hand)*, if I was sitting here telling you this story—

CHAMBERS: Yeah?

SARACCO: You'd be laughing.

CHAMBERS: No. I doubt I would be laughing.

SARACCO: And not laughing because it's funny. But laughing that—it just doesn't make any sense.

CHAMBERS: It makes no sense—that somebody could do that? It makes no sense that somebody could put your hands behind your back and push you down and then get on top of your chest?

SARACCO: Exactly. You're exactly right. Exactly.

CHAMBERS: So you can't move. You have no arms to push anybody off—

SARACCO: There's no *(JUDICIAL AUDIO DELETION)* you're not unconscious.

CHAMBERS: But I'm also not taking her seriously when she's doing it because she's talking and trying to be sweet and this and that and at the same time—

SARACCO: But you've already been scratched up. You've been—

CHAMBERS: I know—I'm explaining to her—

SARACCO: *(Overlap)* And you've been laughed at.

CHAMBERS: I'm explaining to her why she should stay away. Why I'm not interested and why I'm interested in other people. She's just laughing and having the time of her life.

SARACCO: I understand. *(Chambers brushes hair back.)* But what I'm trying to suggest to you *(JUDICIAL AUDIO DELETION)* mad enough and something goes *(Chambers shakes head)* and—whatever happened between the two of you was apparently— did you do anything to her besides—besides grab her around the neck? Did you punch her or slap her?

CHAMBERS: No. I grabbed her. I just reached around and grabbed her and threw her over. *(Yanks left arm.)*

SARACCO: So there should be no—no other marks on her?

CHAMBERS: Not of mine. No.

SARACCO: Okay, Detective, you want to—?

DETECTIVE SHEEHAN: *(Chambers brushes hair back.)* Why is that—you grab her, the actual grabbing, okay? You say you grabbed her around the neck?

CHAMBERS: Yeah.

SHEEHAN: *(Chambers brushes hair back, right hand props forehead).* It sounds like an ongoing argument, right? Did there come a time where after she spit at you and everything else, did you slap her in the face

(Chambers shakes head) or shove her away from you or punch her in the eye or something?

CHAMBERS: I never slapped her or punched her or anything.

SHEEHAN: After she scratched your face there's no way that you would have even raised your hands to her or—?

CHAMBERS: I wasn't going to hurt her at all. I just wanted out of there. I wanted to leave.

SHEEHAN: But you didn't even push her away or anything?

CHAMBERS: I pushed her—I had to stand up because she was kneeling in front of me when she scratched me.

SHEEHAN: Well—well, in the process of standing up, did you—?

CHAMBERS: Yeah, I went like this *(he stands suddenly, shoving with both hands against edge of desktop)*, to the left. And I stood up. That's it. *(He sits down.)* I didn't strike her. I didn't do anything to her. I had no intentions to do anything.

SHEEHAN: You just let her scratch you?

CHAMBERS: What am I going to do? Hit her with a stick or something?

SARACCO: I don't know. *(Chambers puts hands on desk.)* I mean, she's dead. You're not. Something happened. *(Chambers shifts sideways, rests left arm on back of chair.)* I mean, that's—that's a fact. Isn't it, Rob?

CHAMBERS: Yeah. *(Long pause.)* That's all I did. And that's what she did. It's not impossible for somebody to do that.

SARACCO: Well, it is impossible. There are certain things, I told you, that don't lie. The condition of the body and condition of your face, condition of your chest. Your size. Her size.

CHAMBERS: She's a big girl. She's strong. She was

strong last night. She was drinking. They said she was on pills.

SARACCO: The detectives didn't even find any underwear. Nothing that'd tie you up.

CHAMBERS: She had to be—was she wearing them? There had to be some. They're still there. There have to be something—

SARACCO: *(Overlap)* Anything you want to ask, Detective?

DETECTIVE SHEEHAN: Yeah, I have one question for you. When you put your arm around her neck, okay, you indicated before it was your left arm.

CHAMBERS: Yeah.

SHEEHAN: Are you sure about that?

CHAMBERS: Yeah *(raises right hand from desk)*, because I landed on my right arm because my knuckle is hurt.

SHEEHAN: Let me ask you this, were you wearing the watch?

CHAMBERS: Yeah. *(Raises left wrist from chair back.)* I never take this watch off.

SHEEHAN: Now would you—would you demonstrate for us how that watch opens?

CHAMBERS: Yeah.

SHEEHAN: Because it's a bracelet, right?

CHAMBERS: Basically it just pops open. *(Right hand opens watchband bracelet.)*

SHEEHAN: *(Overlap)* Now, in other words, after opening that—that lock—?

CHAMBERS: Yeah?

SHEEHAN: That watch could still bang along your arm?

CHAMBERS: Right.

SHEEHAN: Am I correct?

CHAMBERS: Yeah.

SHEEHAN: All right. Now in the force—you grabbed her with some force?

CHAMBERS: Yeah. *(Refastening watch, returns left arm to chair back).* Grabbed her as hard as I could. I wanted her off.

SHEEHAN: Okay. Around the neck?

CHAMBERS: Yeah.

SHEEHAN: Over the back, towards you?

CHAMBERS: Yeah.

SHEEHAN: Do you remember if that watch popped open?

CHAMBERS: I don't remember. It's possible.

SHEEHAN: Let me ask you this, in your experience, does that watch—?

CHAMBERS: Yeah?

SHEEHAN: Like if you slammed it against a—?

CHAMBERS: Oh, it—it pops open a lot. *(Raises and turns left wrist.)*

SHEEHAN: It pops open without much—without much force?

CHAMBERS: Yeah, it's weak. It's not that strong.

SHEEHAN: So in other words, there's a strong possibility that it could have opened up?

CHAMBERS: Yeah.

SHEEHAN: All right? Am I correct?

CHAMBERS: Right.

SHEEHAN: And is that the portion of your arm that was around her neck?

CHAMBERS: My arm was like this. *(Puts left palm to neck with base of thumb under right ear.)*

SHEEHAN: Okay.

CHAMBERS: And I just pulled her back. *(Jerks head back.)*

SHEEHAN: Let me ask you this, in relation to that. How hard did you squeeze her neck?

CHAMBERS: I don't know. I know I pulled her back hard. I pulled her. *(Yanks with left arm, returns it to chair back.)*

SHEEHAN: Just what you've been saying, as hard as you could.

CHAMBERS: Right. I don't—I guess I squeezed very hard.

SHEEHAN: And—and how long did you—in relation to time, how long did you maintain this—this hold on her?

CHAMBERS: I don't know. It seemed like an instant.

SHEEHAN: But you don't—?

CHAMBERS: I don't know. I have no idea.

SHEEHAN: Could it have been seconds or—?

CHAMBERS: It might—it was only seconds. I mean, I wasn't holding it or anything like that. I just threw—I yanked her back as hard as I could. Threw her over my shoulder *(glances over right shoulder)*, and she just didn't move.

ADA SARACCO: When did you first find out she was dead?

CHAMBERS: When I first found out she was dead? When I saw the ambulance come. And I was sitting on the wall. And the lady on the bike was looking at me.

SARACCO: You knew she was dead when you went home?

CHAMBERS: Basically, yeah. And then I woke up and I had—I didn't know.

SARACCO: You did nothing about it?

CHAMBERS: I was—I was in a daze. I was scared. I didn't know what was going on. I didn't know what had happened. I didn't—I couldn't believe that she'd just lie there. I couldn't believe what had happened that night.

SARACCO: Let's just take it a little bit slow. *(Chambers leans back, elbow on chair back, props head with left hand.)* All right. You know she's dead. Maybe five or ten minutes after she probably is dead. While you're in the park. Or at least assume she's dead. Before you go to sleep that night you know she's dead.

CHAMBERS: *(Nods.)* The police are already there by then.

SARACCO: You don't bother to talk to anyone or try to account to anyone—for what happened to her at that point? Is that correct?

CHAMBERS: I stood there and I just looked at her for—for I don't know how long.

SARACCO: You've explained that to us—

CHAMBERS: I was scared. And I didn't know what to do. So I just walked across the street and sat down. And I don't know if it was two minutes, ten minutes, an hour, five hours. I don't know how much longer. But then the lady with the bike was there, then the ambulance was there, then the police were there. I don't know how long it was.

SARACCO: Did you try to assist her medically in any way or try to get any aid for her? Did you try to—mouth-to-mouth resuscitation or—?

CHAMBERS: No, I didn't want to—I was scared. I didn't want to touch her. I was really freaked out. I did not want to touch her.

SARACCO: What are you—according to you, all you did was grab her around the neck and pull her back. I'm—

CHAMBERS: I don't know if I broke her neck. I don't know what happened.

SARACCO: Why would—why would you think that you might have broken her neck?

CHAMBERS: Because she didn't move and all I did was yank her back.

SARACCO: Weren't you concerned about it?

CHAMBERS: Yeah.

SARACCO: But you didn't do anything?

CHAMBERS: At first I thought that she was just kidding around. And then I stood there and I waited and I waited and then nothing happened.

SARACCO: Then you know she's dead.

CHAMBERS: Then *(inaudible overlap)* scared.

SARACCO: Or she's injured or at least—?

CHAMBERS: That's when I got scared. She didn't move at all. Didn't budge at all.

SARACCO: What did you do?

CHAMBERS: Her eyes were open just looking down at the ground. *(Pantomimes glazed staring look.)*

SARACCO: You didn't do anything? Did you try to assist her in any way?

CHAMBERS: All I did was cross the street and sit down. And sit there and stare.

SARACCO: So your answer is no?

CHAMBERS: No, I just stared. That's all I did. That's all I could do.

SARACCO: And when you see the people arrive, the ambulances and the other people, you—just disappear and—?

CHAMBERS: No, I stayed there and I watched.

SARACCO: You don't bother to go up to them and volunteer as to your account as to what happened?

CHAMBERS: No, I just stood there and I watched. And I stared at this lady.

SARACCO: If the police hadn't found you or discovered that you were the last person with her or left Dorrian's, you wouldn't even—?

CHAMBERS: If Alex, her friend, hadn't called me this morning out from where I was, I don't even know if I'd have known it had happened.

SARACCO: You told Alex, her friend, that she should check her boyfriend when you knew she was dead, is that correct?

CHAMBERS: Yeah. Because I was scared. I didn't know what to do. Because then I—it all came and I was, like—it wasn't a dream. *(Puts fingers through hair with left hand, then holds head.)*

(There is a delay while technician changes cassettes.)

SARACCO: I think we've gone over enough. These answers just don't make any sense—the fact that she—your account on how she tied you up, your account as to what you did to her doesn't correspond to her injuries. If, as you say, it was just some freak accident as to why you don't remain there and try to render some sort of medical assistance. You don't say to people: I'm here, this is what happened—telling them like you're telling us now. It seems to me that you were—you were angry at her for what she did to you—it's understandable that it wasn't her that freaked out, that it was you that lost your temper to some degree. *(JUDICIAL AUDIO DELETION) (Chambers sits forward slightly, left forearm still on chair back.)* You went home. You went to sleep. And through good police investigation they found you. The account you give is just an accommodation because there's no way you can deny that you left the bar with her. You can't deny the scratches on your face because they're there.

CHAMBERS: I know. I'm not denying them. They are there.

SARACCO: Is there anything you want to change? Do you want to maintain this?

CHAMBERS: I'm telling you exactly what happened. I'm sorry if you can't see—I'm sure that I've heard of other men being—being raped, men being tied up.

SARACCO: Well, I'll tell you one thing, I haven't.

CHAMBERS: Well, good. You're lucky. You're very lucky. It's not a matter *(overlap)*—

SARACCO: I've been in this business for a while and you're the first one I've seen raped in Central Park.

CHAMBERS: Good. That really makes a difference to me. It happens. It can happen. It did happen. Her friends knew she was all over me. She told her friends she was definitely going to fuck me tonight. My friends know I didn't want to go with her. I didn't even want to talk to her. They knew I wanted to go home. They knew I was there to see other people.

SARACCO: You didn't wind up raped and she wound up dead, that's all I know, all right?

CHAMBERS: I didn't mean to hurt her. I liked her very much. She was a very nice person, easy to get along to—easy to talk to. She was just too pushy, and she liked me more than I thought. More than anybody actually thought. Her friends were in here telling the other detectives that she was crazy about me. I don't know. It made no difference. I didn't pay attention.

The girl was hyper all night. Everyone was talking about how she was bouncing around. My friend Betta made a remark about it. I laughed. He laughed. She was on cloud nine all night. Then she said she had something very important to talk to me about. She wants to go to the park. She picked the place. I could have talked to her in Dorrian's. Her friends asked me to talk to her in the back. That's when my friend came up and yelled at me and she laughed.

Her laughing at me isn't going to hurt me because at that point I wasn't interested in her. I was interested in the girl that yelled at me. I couldn't care less—I didn't even want to go to talk to Jennifer so she can laugh.

SARACCO: Yeah, but you're sitting in the park and your face is scratched, you're being yelled at, and still getting an erection when you're tied up—this is what you're telling me, right?

CHAMBERS: If somebody takes your dick and starts to jerk you *(masturbation motion, right hand)*—

SARACCO: After my face is scratched and I'm mad?

CHAMBERS: The point being that when you're being jerked off *(masturbation gesture)*, after a while you're going to get erect.

SARACCO: How long did this take?

CHAMBERS: This was going on for a while. *(Leans sideways against chair back.)*

SARACCO: Detective, is there anything you want to ask?

DETECTIVE SHEEHAN: No.

SARACCO: Okay, this concludes the statement. Thank you.

6

TAKING SIDES

When he was done acting out Jennifer Levin's sexual performance and his pain, Robert Chambers dropped his pants one more time.

He had said Jennifer hurt him but left no wounds. Now Mike Sheehan checked him out and found that portion of his statement truthful. Sheehan testified that Chambers' genitals showed no sign of damage twenty hours after the pain he said he "couldn't stand."

His scratched torso and face and his finger bites were documented by a Crime Scene Unit photographer on the graveyard shift that Wednesday. It was about two o'clock in the morning.

The suspect wondered if he could go home now.

"Chambers asked me, 'What happens to me next?'" Sheehan testified. "He thought he gave a logical explanation for his acts and he was going home."

Surprised or not that he was under police arrest, Chambers was certainly upset when he saw his father, who had waited for him for seven hours in another room. Detective Mullally was the only other person there to hear their words, and Mullally would testify to it under oath:

"Don't worry, I'm here now," the father said. But Robert Chambers didn't sound worried. When it came to blaming the victim, the suspect was first in line.

"That fucking bitch—why couldn't she leave me alone?!"

He just spat it out.

Sheehan testified that he chatted with the father, who was an old acquaintance, very briefly in an ante-room.

He said Chambers' father asked, "What do you think I should do now?"

And Sheehan said he replied, "If I were you, I'd get a very good lawyer."

When they brought Robert Chambers outside in handcuffs at three A.M., the Central Park precinct parking lot was crowded with reporters and photographers. In the glare of TV lights the suspect turned his head away so the cameras caught his left profile.

The long scratches on his cheek were visible. It seemed clear in the early newspaper photos that Levin had struggled desperately for her life.

In *The New York Times* lead paragraph that morning of August 27, the police said Levin was "sexually abused" and strangled—found with her bra wrapped around her neck.

As vivid as it was, that image would not survive the next eighteen hours.

Tidbits from the videotape statement began to leak. Chambers' scenario—that Levin had died by accident during a sexual tryst initiated by her—caught the public's attention. In retrospect the first whisper was immediate: she asked for it.

Most of the media willingly trashes any pretty teen-ager. Some New York editors with a sense of restraint—and there are some with children in Manhattan prep schools—gradually got swamped as Chambers' erotic quotes about Levin got pumped out. Most of them reached print more than a year before videotape excerpts reached TV. Defense counsel Jack Litman was repeating Chambers' statements for two weeks before Litman himself got to see the videotape.

The product was plugged indirectly—and most effectively—by Chambers himself.

He had a gift for suggestive phraseology, if indeed it was his, that played into the sexual prejudices and fears of many men—and some women.

Chambers found code words worthy of a lyricist to make Levin's sexuality sound more menacing. She was "pushy" and "insane," he said, and finally she was cruel to him.

He claimed she masturbated him "really hard," and he told her it hurt. "And she kind of laughed in a weird way—like more like a cackle or something," Chambers said. Levin was eighteen, but "cackle" summoned up the cruel old witch of "Hansel and Gretel."

"She molested me in the park," he said. "Molested" was linked to perverts and other males on police blotters. That even stumped his interrogator.

"How did she molest you?" asked Saracco. "You're—we're talking about—?"

CHAMBERS: "What, girls—girls cannot—girls cannot do it to a guy?"

He was yelling rape but could not yet say the word. Saracco could. "She's raping you in the park? Robert, come on."

CHAMBERS: "She's having her way with me without my consent. With my hands behind my back."

Having her way? The lawmen in the squad room just stared at him. Isn't role switching in bondage a porn-flick fantasy? Then the soigné man-child told these slow adults pityingly:

"I'm sorry if you can't see—I'm sure that I've heard of other men being—being raped, men being tied up."

He was an authority. "It happens. It can happen. It did happen."

In light of the tawdry post-trial revelations about Chambers, it seems likely now that he had "heard" of Manhattan dolls who violated six-foot-four guys in bondage. But that happened with ropes, not dinky underpants.

For me Chambers' whole story was undercut by his glib exaggeration of what he "knew." I thought it began twelve hours before the videotape—as soon as he got out of the shower—with the systematic and excessive facticity of his lies.

He had Levin, a known nonsmoker, leaving Dorrian's not only to buy cigarettes, but at a specific location, the "Korean deli." He described in detail the TV movie he hadn't watched. He repeatedly blamed his Siamese cat, Rasta, for his scratches.

And Chambers' lie about Levin having gone to former boyfriend Brock Pernice was a pathologically ornate gem of nastiness. "It is not easy to warm to someone who can think of no way to dispose of his mess except by fingering someone else," wrote Murray Kempton, the Pulitzer Prize-winning columnist at *Newsday*.

Yet a legal pundit evaluated the suspect's defiant demeanor on the videotape as "compelling." And Chambers sold his fantasy of helpless panty bondage to some New Yorkers. They seemed to be in the minority—but they included at least one juror.

Some Americans still believe Chambers' story, and many more did then. Especially vocal in their belief were certain doting mothers and grandmothers. Maybe it was Chambers' altar-boy look mixed with indolence, a hint of brutality in the pale blue eyes, a mouth molded by tantrums and a thousand secrets.

Everyone has the right to an opinion. This time, however, opinion was shaped by Chambers' artful words. He stirred primitive sexist passions that had remained under the surface in public for twenty-five years.

A drumbeat against Jennifer Levin began at Chambers' postmidnight arraignment early on Thursday, August 29.

Bare-bones police reports Wednesday hinted at casual sex and underage drinking among good-looking rich white preppies. It was irresistible for the media. Reporters from every news organization in New York were in night court.

Bob and Phyllis Chambers showed up together, everyone noticed. She stood tall and gazed straight ahead. He wore a safari jacket and scarf, a heavy tan, and made notes in a leather-bound notebook. They had taken Sheehan's advice and hired the best criminal lawyer in town.

Jack T. Litman was on the case.

He never would divulge who first contacted him. Litman told me he first spoke to Chambers' father about eight hours after the videotaping. That placed it about nine A.M. It left Litman fifteen hours to plot his strategy for *Night Court*. But it may have taken him only fifteen minutes.

"I'm good, but I'm expensive," the $300-an-hour counselor was rumored to have told Bob Chambers. It's doubtful he charged the defendant's hard-up family that much over nearly twenty months.

But if worldwide attention paid off, this case could be a million-dollar bonanza for Jack Litman. Especially if he won.

Chambers pleaded not guilty to a charge of second-degree murder when arraigned before Criminal Court Judge Richard Lowe III.

Litman wasted no time making his central point. He established that Levin had approached his reluctant nineteen-year-old client in the bar.

They had a past relationship, Litman said. "But that night, she was the one who was the aggressor."

Cynics in the press row who knew him may have glanced at each other and grinned. Jack was at it again.

His celebrated defense of Yale student Richard Herrin in the 1978 bludgeon murder of Bonnie Garland had adapted the old "blame the victim" technique in an up-to-date cause: to tarnish a sexually liberated twenty-year-old woman.

Herrin confessed he had deliberately clubbed his sleeping sweetheart with a sledgehammer in her Scarsdale bedroom. He was distraught that Garland was ditching him, fornicating with other men. Many other men, emphasized Litman. He had to "taint her a little" to win the case, he conceded later. His concessions often came later.

He was widely criticized, but Herrin got off with a manslaughter conviction. And Herrin's brilliantly ruthless defense lawyer, then only thirty-three, was on his way to stardom.

Litman primarily represents wealthy white-collar criminals now. He still sways juries his way. "I come across terribly sincere," he once confided, but now he mentions a more cerebral talent—careful preparation. He told me after the Chambers trial:

"It's important to know what you're doing, to control the courtroom, so people focus on what you're doing. If you come across as intelligent and reasonable and sincere, they will accept what you're saying."

He indulges a lifelong appetite for theater. "That's

one of the things you must love if you want to be a criminal defense lawyer,'' Litman said solemnly.

Mostly he plays a pit bull in ferocious combat on the courtroom stage, using the whole floor, pacing to and fro, then veering abruptly for effect. Eyebrows arching, arms flailing, he mutters theatrical asides to the jury. His sonorous voice rises in tone as he salts questions with sarcasm and incredulity to taint a witness.

His thick glasses—a boyhood accident left Litman blind in one eye—sit atop his head as he peers at a photograph, bringing it close to his nose, sincerely tainting the photo with doubt. Reasonable doubt is Litman's holy grail.

His incessant objections and a maddening penchant for bench conferences are legendary. "Jack will sidetrack you if he can with sidebars that take the flow of your case away," said Herrin prosecutor William Fredreck.

Litman did all of that at the Chambers trial. It started at the midnight arraignment.

He assured Judge Lowe that the young woman had been sitting on top of his client, hurting him, when tragedy struck.

"She was straddling his body, sitting on top of him with her back to his face," Litman explained. "He said, 'Let's stop,' and she said, 'No.' And when she refused, he leaned up and pulled her back, causing the fatal trauma."

The judge asked: "Are you saying this was an accident?" Litman couldn't have imagined a better word.

"Yes, Your Honor," he said.

"At the hands of the defendant?"

"Yes, Your Honor, a tragic accident," Litman said. As Chambers was jailed without bail at pusher-packed Riker's Island, that afternoon's tabloid *New York Post* unveiled the first tainting headline: WILD SEX KILLED JENNY.

On inside pages it hardened into "rough sex"—a Litman quote. "Jack's the one at arraignment who coined the term 'rough sex,' " a prosecutor remembered bitterly.

Soon Chambers' hardest words, "masturbated" and "testicles," were in print on a daily basis. The *Times* resisted that for a while but moved its second-day coverage to the front page, a "darkness beneath the glitter" look at the Levin and Chambers life-style— "private schools, fancy apartments, foreign vacations, and underage drinking at a preppy hangout called Dorrian's Red Hand." The rough sex stuff was inside in section B, page 7, but the *Times* story set a golden example for the tabloids.

Steven Levin tried to stem the tide. He said his daughter liked to go out nights but was "always the straight kid of her crowd," and "maybe she was too trusting." Her stepmother, Arlene, said Jennifer could have been considered "a prude."

As other New York parents realized that these tragic children were as spoiled and aimless as some of their own, Litman quickly put the thought into words: "The sad part of this story is that this could happen to anybody's kids."

Perhaps to remind us that not all nineteen-year-olds use cocaine, Jack Dorrian told the *Post* he had warned Phyllis Chambers that her son was a habitual druggie. But no police reporter seized Dorrian's tip and followed up on it that day. Journalists were busy with Jennifer's "sexual aggressiveness."

Several of Dorrian's teenage barflies voiced their disbelief that Chambers was "the violent type." They said he had wimped out of fights with shorter guys. None seemed to notice Jennifer Levin's vulnerability as a woman—seven inches shorter and fifty-five pounds lighter than Chambers even by his shrunken numbers. He told the cops he was six-three and 190. The papers made him six-four and 220—and made Levin one hundred pounds lighter—but even that disparity got little space.

Chambers' nonmacho style made better copy. One close friend, however, said he had seen Robert lose his temper once in a wrestling match, caught in a painful crotch hold. "He picked me up and threw me against the wall," the friend said. "I had to calm him down before he let me go."

But drinkers unacquainted with his temper insisted someone else must have killed Levin. One young woman at Dorrian's declared herself a friend of both. "We have to fight for Robert's rights," said the friend, Norah Bray. "There's nothing we can do now for Jennifer."

It was about a year before that same line would be heard in the film *River's Edge*.

When Chambers' success with teenage girls bored editors, one tabloid headline gave it a twist: FRIENDS CALL ROBERT A RELUCTANT ROMEO, SHY WITH GIRLS. For proof there was a familiar quote from York Prep classmate Larry Greer: "He didn't have a way with women. Women had a way with him."

So in or out of bondage, Robert Chambers was a victim.

To counter Litman's "tragic accident" headlines, Manhattan District Attorney Robert Morgenthau chose that Thursday, thirty hours after Chambers' arrest, to release the first official excerpts from his videotape statement.

A wave of lurid new headlines hit New York streets on Friday—just in time for Jennifer Levin's funeral.

Her uncle Dan Levin, once a *Sports Illustrated* writer, invited some newspaper people into the mortuary chapel. Mourners sickened by "rough sex" stories tried to throw them out. A rabbi marveled at how the Levin family, cleft by divorce, was bonding again in its hour of grief.

Dan Levin delivered the eulogy for Jennifer. "Anyone who has ever been eighteen years old knows that nothing bad can happen to you," he said. "That's the way it's supposed to be. Well, I guess we know now that isn't true."

He closed by reciting a nineteenth-century poem with a lasting theme: "They are not long, the days of wine and roses . . ."

The New York Times story that day emphasized that Chambers had exhibited no remorse on the videotape. It also noted both his wounds and hers as evidence that Jennifer had fought her killer, not dying from one quick blow. It was one of her few portrayals in print as a victim.

Litman hired former city pathologist Dominick DiMaio to discount Levin's bruises and to say her strangulation could have been caused by "one blow."

While the public feasted on fantasies of Jennifer's panties around Robert's wrists as she squeezed his testicles painfully, it became clear that his and hers factions were taking sides.

Geoffrey Stokes, the *Village Voice* media critic, was the first to notice that Jennifer's side was losing.

In an irony-laced column with the head BUBBLE-HEAD SLUT DIES, DESERVES IT, Stokes wrote:

"For a while, when there was a chance a stranger did her in, the press was kinder to young Jennifer Levin than her murderer had been. But as soon as it appeared that she'd willingly accompanied her killer to the park, the dailies turned vicious."

The *Times* had "stiffly observed," he noted, that Levin's Baldwin School prepared "mediocre or troubled students for middle-level colleges," and that no

Scholastic Aptitude Test was required at the junior college that admitted her, Chamberlayne in Boston, her father's hometown.

Stokes advised parents to warn children to "do well on your SATs, dear. If someone strangles you, you don't want the *Times* to call you 'troubled and mediocre.' "

He concluded the New York media had "savaged Levin because she was a lively young woman who willingly left a bar and headed for the bushes with a young man in the early morning hours. And since sex, especially female sexuality, is filthy and disgusting, she deserved whatever she got—even after she died."

Beth Fallon of the *Post* asked Litman if he and Chambers were not in fact defaming Levin. "No," Litman said. "The truth is never defamation." Fallon roasted him in her column, expressing hope that Chambers' prosecutors would get even.

But it was both too early and too late for that.

The crowning irony of those first two weeks came September 10, when Chambers was cast as a winner at the press conference announcing his indictment.

Since the suspect's "compelling" videotape statement was the only eyewitness testimony available, the prosecution case seemed burdened under its rock of circumstantial evidence.

A grand jury indicted Chambers on two counts of second-degree murder—of equal weight but "mutually exclusive." He could not be convicted on both counts. One charged him with intentionally killing Levin. The other charged "depraved indifference to human life."

While the depravity count relieved prosecutors of proving intent, it served no other apparent purpose. Nobody seemed able to clearly define depravity, not then and not later.

Conviction on either count meant a minimum prison term of twenty-five years, and Chambers was facing a possible maximum life sentence. But since judges tend to leniency on depravity, Litman exulted over his "victory."

He called the depravity count a clear sign that not even the DA was sure Chambers had intended Levin's death—or as Litman now referred to it, "this unfortunate incident." And when asked how Chambers would plead, Litman replied quickly:

"Are you kidding? Not guilty."

Morgenthau said the autopsy showed "substantial pressure" was applied to Levin's neck for at least twenty seconds and summed up the basis of his intentional murder charge in one sentence: "He cut off her air supply for a substantial period of time."

The DA then departed. He wanted no part of Jack Litman, who laughed off the twenty-second estimate. When it came to timing fatal neck pressure, Litman announced, "No one can say with any certainty." He would eventually reduce the time to two seconds.

What nearly went unnoticed was the DA's other announcement. A grand jury was hearing evidence in a number of burglaries and would bring in indictments soon.

Chambers' fingerprints had turned up in two East Side apartments.

The Dorrian's crowd wasn't rich, *The New York Times* decided. It was just "affluent" and deeply troubled by an epidemic of divorced parents. A Manhattan mother was quoted:

"It's very frightening. We are raising children who have to circulate. Where do you let them go? How much 'no' can you say?"

East Siders didn't know how to be a family anymore, the paper reported, searching for an intact family. It found the Dorrian family together one noontime in the homey saloon—from patriarch Red down to granddaughter Laura, nineteen.

Jack Dorrian and his wife had eight children. Maybe not your ideal family, said the *Times*, but "at least intact."

A community activist up the block on East 84th Steet, however, said she warned Jack Dorrian of trouble a week before the Levin tragedy.

"I said one of the girls you serve will drink too much and pass out on the street and some of the low-lifes around here will rape her or worse," Nancy Hunt recalled.

She said it wasn't just routine drinking—the young barflies threw up and urinated in public, smashed windshields, and wrecked shrubbery.

Not at noontime, but at four A.M.

People magazine dropped into Dorrian's to research casual sex in nearby Central Park and published this insightful report: "The bar is the meat market," explained one young cynic, "and the park is the grill."

Her principal at the Baldwin School called Levin a "magnet" because "everyone seemed to gravitate toward her." But the story otherwise made it clear that at Dorrian's, her killer was the reigning sex object.

"Girls throw themselves at his feet," marveled one friend.

And Jack Dorrian said: "He was a lollipop."

Litman said he received about one hundred offers from a variety of agents in those early weeks. One promised that Chambers could play himself in the movie. "Oh, to be young and attractive and under arrest in New York" an agent burbled in the *Times*.

On September 11, the day after his client's indictment, Litman got something more palpable: his first look at the now notorious Chambers videotape.

That viewing cost Stephen Saracco any chance to

prosecute the case of a lifetime. While a skeptical Saracco seemed to have questioned Chambers rather gently, Litman objected to his irreverent sarcasm. It could have triggered an appeal if Chambers was convicted. So Saracco was out of the picture.

Enter Linda Fairstein.

If anyone had a chance to counteract the videotape's defamation of the victim, Fairstein could. She understood sexism in its most ruthless forms.

Tall, blond, just turning forty, Fairstein had spent fourteen years in the DA's office. She pioneered reforms in rape prosecution as the chief of the DA's Sex Crimes Unit, largely by investigating rape victims' stories carefully enough to find the truth. Her novel approach raised the existing 10 percent conviction rate in Manhattan rape cases to 75 percent. Now she was deputy chief of the DA's trial division as well.

She had yet to try a murder case. But she wanted this one. "I was interested from the first moment I knew about it," Fairstein told me. She had been, vacationing on Martha's Vineyard when the case broke.

"I immediately called the office because my assumption was that it was, as the headlines were saying, a sexual assault case. The routine is for me to call up and see if it's someone I prosecuted previously based on M.O. and if I can be of any help." She learned there had been an overnight arrest. "It was not someone from my files, it was someone else. But when I came back, Mr. Morgenthau wanted me to be a part of the team. . . ."

Morgenthau evidently saw that in a homicide case with a sexual dimension, Fairstein would have more empathy than a male prosecutor working with Ellen Levin and the rest of Jennifer's grieving family and friends. She lets victims and witnesses phone her at home in the middle of the night.

And Fairstein wanted to salvage Levin's tattered reputation. Just before Chambers went to trial, she told *New York* magazine's Linda Wolfe: "Every girl who calls my office says she was Jennifer's best friend. She must have been a wonderful friend."

When Fairstein graduated Vassar and the University of Virginia Law School, her first job was as a lowly assistant to a young Harvard-trained Manhattan prosecutor—the cerebral, mercurial Jack T. Litman.

Soon Litman became a criminal defense lawyer, dropping in occasionally to say hello, Fairstein told me. "It was on that level. He's a brilliant lawyer. Our passions are very different, and I'm glad that I don't do what he does, but I certainly respect his right to do it."

They crossed swords for the first time at the Chambers trial. Fairstein shepherded Levin's best friends through searing testimony about Jennifer's open sexuality that seemed damning to many, but not to her. While she also worked to protect her detectives and medical witnesses from Litman's lash, Fairstein fought hardest to restore a teenager's honor.

She tried to give Jennifer a clear voice in the courtroom, the last time anyone would hear Jennifer's voice.

It said: "Don't blame me."

State Supreme Court Justice Howard E. Bell was chosen in mid-September to preside at the high-profile Chambers trial. It was a random selection, they said—but not as random as most judicial assignments, reported the *Post*'s perceptive courthouse regular Mike Pearl.

A two-wheel lottery system had been installed nine months earlier to discourage clever lawyers from "shopping" for a judge. One wheel contained the names of all available judges among the fifty serving

Manhattan's Supreme Court. The smaller P-wheel held the names of those available among fifteen judges deemed "best qualified" for protracted and complex trials. Hence the "P" for protracted—though some claimed it denoted a flair for coping with heavy publicity.

Pearl wrote that Litman had a good idea who was available on the small P-wheel—mostly tough judges impervious to his "razzle dazzle." Litman had the option, so he opted for the big wheel.

When the name Howard E. Bell popped out, courthouse insiders grinned. Bell's name was said to be on the P-wheel, too, so someone upstairs must have liked him.

While regarded as plodding but fair, Bell's reluctance to crack the whip would make him a target of media scorn late in the eleven-week Chambers trial. One columnist called him Ding Dong in print for two days, putting court administrators in a tizzy.

But his fairness was needed with the volatile Litman, who described himself as "zealous" but might also answer to "abusive." A more volatile judge might have jailed Jack once or twice a day for contempt of court.

With it all, the vital element brought to the courtroom by Bell as a black jurist was ethnic balance.

Most of the Manhattan judges were either Jewish or Catholic and had many political obligations. Bell was from the now defunct Harlem democratic machine, among the last relics of Tammany Hall.

In the trial of an Irish Catholic youth charged with killing a Jewish girl, Bell was clearly "best qualified" to preside.

Litman had to be content. A Jewish judge might have been under pressure from supporters of the victim. A Catholic judge might have bent over backward not to favor Chambers.

And those were not minor considerations. There was an ethnic storm on the horizon.

On Robert Chambers' twentieth birthday, September 25, Litman made an application for bail. Most second-degree murder suspects await trial in jail. But Litman offered forty-five character references in support of bailing Chambers. Most came from prominent Catholic friends of his parents.

One was from Newark Archbishop Theodore McCarrick, who had known the Chambers family since 1972, when he was Father Ted. And he had been secretary to the late Terence Cardinal Cooke in 1983—when Phyllis Chambers was a special-duty nurse for Cooke during his final illness.

While McCarrick had not seen Phyllis's son in "four or five years," he lauded his virtues. Young Robert had a "gentleness and a very special respect" for people, McCarrick wrote, reflecting "his unwillingness to cause pain."

Steven Levin begged Judge Bell to consider the circumstances of his daughter's "horrible death" before considering bail.

Litman personally attended to the seating of his key supporters at the bail hearing, including Monsignor Thomas Leonard, who had once taught religion to Chambers in grammar school.

"Put the monsignor in there. You guys go next to him," Litman was heard instructing two youths, one white, one black.

Fairstein protested the intervention of both McCarrick and Leonard. "Their faith is misplaced," said the prosecutor, arguing that the bishop's positive memory of Chambers had "no relevance to his current life." He was no longer an altar boy.

Bell listened. He weighed her protest against McCarrick's letter. The judge then set bail at $150,000, on condition that Chambers report regularly to Monsignor Leonard at his Church of the Incarnation in Washington Heights. Should he fail to report—or be charged with another felony—bail would be revoked.

Most second-degree murder suspects get either no bail or prohibitively expensive bail, so $150,000 was very low. Bell justified it in terms he may have later regretted.

"There is a letter here from the archbishop of the diocese of Newark, indicating that he knows the mother of the defendant," said the judge. "When I receive letters from a person of that stature, I do give it consideration."

A month later Archbishop McCarrick told *Post* gossip columnist Cindy Adams he was having second thoughts. He said:

"Had I known about those things like the boy being on drugs, I'd probably still have helped . . . but I'd probably have written a slightly different letter."

Eleanor Chambers, his grandmother, put up her $125,000 house as partial collateral for the bail bond. Monsignor James Wilder offered $21,000 from his meager savings. He had known Robert as an altar boy at St. Thomas More's, but Wilders said his donation was "out of empathy" for Phyllis Chambers.

It still wasn't enough, so Jack Dorrian came to the rescue, borrowing against his $600,000 Manhattan townhouse. And skeptics wondered why.

Dorrian explained that he had visited Phyllis Chambers. "She was sitting by herself, with her cat. She was crying. She was wondering what she was going to do, because there wasn't enough money." What could he do?

"It's no big deal," said Dorrian, who couldn't put up the bar—his wife and daughter were its legal owners. "All that bail means is that he's going to show up. At least his mother has the comfort of having him out of jail for now. I'm sure the mother of the victim would understand that."

But the father didn't. Steven Levin hung up when the saloonkeeper phoned. "I called him up as one father to another," Dorrian told *New York's* Linda Wolfe. "I was going to say I felt sorry for him, but that, you know, death is really a continuation of life. . . ."

Monsignor Leonard invited Chambers to live at his rectory. That rankled Jewish critics who remembered that priests and nuns had sheltered another Litman murder client—Richard Herrin—and that Yale Catholics had raised $30,000 for his defense.

Although Jennifer's stepmother, Arlene, was Catholic, Arlene's brother told me that even their devout relatives were somewhat "disillusioned" by the mounting Church support for Chambers.

John Cardinal O'Connor, successor to Cooke in the New York archdiocese, sent a "letter of condolence" to the Levin family. Archbishop McCarrick and Monsignor Leonard were said to have gotten some death threats that worried O'Connor. His letter was not released, but courthouse talk later was that the cardinal had urged the Levins to turn the other cheek.

A Levin family spokesman disclosed only that O'Connor had tried to explain Archbishop McCarrick's intervention. "It was a lame excuse," the spokesman said. "The family thinks the Church is taking sides."

O'Connor now responded to the rising tension with statesmanlike alacrity, in an article in the weekly *Catholic New York*.

"I am worried," wrote the cardinal, "that mercy toward a Catholic boy could be perceived as callousness toward a Jewish girl.

"I am worried that the Catholic Establishment will be seen as rallying around its 'own' . . . while a Jewish girl lies dead and her family is shattered with grief. I worry that some Catholics will fail to recognize the potential for resentment on the part of some Jews.

"If I were a member of the girl's family, I would be terribly frustrated and prone to anger. If I were Jewish, and the media were saturated with what Catholics are purportedly doing for a Catholic, I might well feel troubled."

He said he hoped his comments would head off potential trouble amid the certainty of "enormous publicity" when the Chambers case went to trial.

The message from on high was heard and obeyed. No Catholic collars were visible at the trial.

Afterward, Litman shrugged off the issue of Church intervention.

"When I represent a Jewish client, I get rabbis to the extent that they know them and they write letters," he said. "It's just the inevitable way of properly promoting your client's best chances of a bail application."

Two weeks after the explosive bail hearing, Chambers was back in court. The grand jury had his burglary indictment ready. Morgenthau said it crystallized because witnesses saw Chambers' picture in the newspapers and came forward.

Chambers pleaded not guilty to three separate counts. Bell had warned him that another felony charge would put him back at Riker's. But now the judge reasoned that the burglaries were a year old. Bell just added $7,500 to Chambers' bail costs, raising the total to $157,500.

With Litman's huge fee looming, Chambers was in dire straits financially. But then he always had empty pockets to fill.

He had stolen more than $70,000 in jewelry, silver, and furs from three luxury East Side apartments during one week of September 1985, the grand jury said.

Chambers' twenty-year-old black co-defendant, David Fillyaw, maintained that he had stood lookout while Robert rifled the apartments. That explained the fingerprints police had found, but Chambers claimed at a later hearing that Fillyaw had coerced him into the thefts with "threats of physical violence."

He said he feared Fillyaw.

Allan Freiss, Fillyaw's lawyer, reminded the court that his client was slightly built, five nine and 140—quite a bit smaller than Chambers. It had a familiar ring.

Freiss laughed and said:

"My quick read of the papers seems to indicate to me that Mr. Chambers is always the victim."

7

THE DIARY BATTLE

November 12, 1986: Jack Litman escalated his war against Jennifer Levin. He did it by turning her into a physiological wonder.

It developed that one impact word from Robert Chambers' videotape statement had not yet seen print. Now it reached the media in a sheaf of court papers filed by Litman.

The tabloids did the rest of it. The first headline screamed:

SHE RAPED ME

Not even seasoned rewritemen could explain how Jennifer had "raped" Chambers. They didn't try. It mattered not to the Chambers defense strategy.

The "R" word was now imprinted in the public mind.

November 13: Now Litman had another ace up his sleeve. For anyone who didn't accept Chambers' words, Litman would have Levin herself say some of the same words.

He went after her little black book.

Teenagers for generations have kept intimate personal journals. This one came under legal attack from a taint master.

Litman asserted in court papers—his favorite medium—that Linda Fairstein had first told him about a Levin diary.

He claimed she "indicated" that the police had it—a diary "which among other things chronicles the sexual activities of Jennifer Levin."

Litman wanted her diary handed over to him for his private perusal—on behalf of Robert Chambers.

He said all he wanted were the names of Levin's other lovers. What he got were huge headlines. One read:

"SEX DIARY" KEPT BY JEN?

Like rough sex, the "sex diary" catch phrase was now firmly linked to Jennifer Levin's name. Litman's blame-the-victim strategy was in high gear.

Fairstein fiercely denied that she had told Litman the diary was hot stuff.

"I never told him anything like that," she said to reporters. "I refuse to participate in Mr. Litman's campaign to vilify the victim. There is not a sex diary. There is a school datebook, but nothing chronicling her sex life."

Litman wanted something more than a school datebook.

He had told psychiatrist/author Willard Gaylin after the Herrin trial that his tainting of Bonnie Garland had an "important" purpose: "so the jury would not believe as the parents wanted that she was this ingenue who fell in love for the first time with this wily man."

Now Litman demanded not only Levin's diary, but also the copies made by detectives, who reportedly photocopied twenty-three pages.

He wanted "any material suggesting sexual activity or violent behavior by Jennifer Levin during which she caused pain to a man prior to August 26, 1986."

In her lifetime, that was.

Litman also sought the nude rooftop photos Chambers claimed Levin had taken of him—Polaroid shots. They never did turn up.

But the "sex diary" had a long run.

November 19: A Justice for Jennifer task force would combat defamation of her character. The organizers said Levin is "maligned by innuendo, misinformation, and outright distortion," while Chambers is depicted as "at worst a Huck Finn who gets into mischief from time to time."

Steven Levin originally gave his daughter's black book to detectives on August 26, said Fairstein, because he hoped it would help them find her killer. When the search ended with Chambers' arrest that night, the diary remained in prosecution hands.

Litman insisted he needed it. Fairstein made her move to deprive him of it.

She returned the diary to the Levin family.

"It was their property," she said. And since it contained nothing that would "exculpate" Chambers from guilt, it never had been considered evidence.

Fairstein's decision had one important side effect. Returning the diary in the middle of a court battle for it, according to legal scholars consulted by *The New York Times,* "made it a three-corner game, directly involving the Levin family."

Litman had the option of backing down or subpoe-

naing the diary from a family in mourning. Character-
istically he attacked—on Thanksgiving Eve.

November 26: A subpeona for the diary was served
by Litman on Jeffrey Newman, the Levin family's
lawyer. Newman said he would challenge it in court.

The Levins were steaming.

The legal scholars debated Litman's audacity. It
was one thing to subpoena defamatory documents
from the public prosecutor. To force a private family
to cooperate in a slain daughter's defamation was
another thing.

November 28: The Levins struck back. They demanded an investigation into whether Chambers had
robbed their daughter.

When last seen alive, Jennifer had been wearing a
$400 gold ring with a diamond stud, they said—an
eighteenth birthday present. It was missing. So was
about $70 in cash they said she was carrying. Only the
torn dollar found in her denim jacket was returned to
the family.

"We are looking into whether jewelry and money
were taken by Chambers," a police source told the
UPI wire service.

December 3: Fairstein divulged publicly for the first
time that Chambers cursed Levin while talking to his
father after the videotaping—when he blurted out,
"That fucking bitch—why couldn't she leave me
alone?!"

The nature of Chambers' angry outburst was inconsistent, Fairstein said, with his story that Jennifer had
died by "accident."

Most people expressed remorse about accidents.
Chambers blamed this one on the victim—and made
himself her victim.

December 5: Steven Levin begged the judge not to
surrender Jennifer's diary to Jack Litman. He didn't
quibble that it was a "school datebook."

Some wondered: what was in the diary, and why was Jennifer's father trying to suppress it?

Steve Levin tried to explain it to the judge.

"The diary contains, as one would expect, the most private and innermost thoughts of my teenaged daughter," he wrote. "The thought of disclosing the diary to the attorney for the man who killed my daughter is so horrifying as to border on the obscene."

How do you explain your stomach turning? The Levins had a visceral revulsion to the idea of cooperating with Chambers or Litman, however indirectly.

They also had a well-founded fear that Litman might try to distort anything possible to twist—sexual or not—in Jennifer's diary. He and Chambers both had demonstrated a cruel way with words.

The last entry in the diary was July 12, Fairstein said. Chambers' name appeared on only two pages, months earlier.

Litman argued that it still might contain material proving that Chambers had no motive—"no intent to do anything to this woman in Central Park."

"This woman." Jennifer Levin had no identity now—and no rights.

Newman said that because the diary was "never vouchered as evidence" by the police, Litman had no right to see it.

"Some things are sacred," Newman said. And to let Litman "paw through Jennifer's most confidential thoughts and musings" would be "gratuitous cruelty" to her family.

Litman argued that Levin had no right to privacy anymore.

"Her constitutional rights—and there are none here—terminated at the time of her death," he said.

Even if that sounded like gratuitous cruelty, the scholars agreed that Litman was on firm legal ground.

What was paramount, he insisted, were the rights of

the defendant. The issue was whether Levin was "utilizing . . . unusual sexual activities against Mr. Chambers," he said.

"It goes right to whether he had the right to use reasonable force in response to that act and if reasonable force caused her death accidentally."

With twenty-three diary pages floating around, rumors were rife.

By one cop's account, Jennifer had recorded several penis sizes—something never before imagined in the history of teenage girls.

Judge Bell ordered another hearing.

Elizabeth M. Schneider, associate professor of law at Brooklyn College, commented on Litman's constant inference that Jennifer Levin's sexuality made her partly responsible for her own death.

"Somehow we'd be more at ease if Chambers had dragged her unwillingly into the park," Schneider said. "What Jack Litman's done is a common defense ploy. And the most troubling part is that it's not individual, but systemic.

"If she was involved in unusual sex, that's not a defense for murder."

Stephen Gillers of New York University Law School wasn't troubled. The diary was a regular topic of his evidence course.

It is, maintained Professor Gillers, "not unethical to try to cast aspersions on the character of the victim. It's ethically the lawyer's duty to do that if it will succeed in a not guilty verdict or conviction on a lesser charge."

Rose Jordan, a freelance photographer and organizer of the first Justice for Jennifer group, ridiculed any legal necessity for Litman's tactics.

"He doesn't have to defend Chambers by killing her again," Jordan said.

In the growing victims' rights movement, Jennifer was becoming a symbol.

"Other women who die violently remain virtually nameless and faceless," Jordan said, "but are victims of the same distortions to justify the violence against them."

December 12: Another diary hearing. Litman was still escalating his attacks on the slain teenager.

First it was Levin's "chronicle of sexual activity." Then she was "utilizing . . . unusual sexual activities." Now it was that the bruises on her body could have been put there by "other men, other lovers on other occasions." Jack Dorrian said Jennifer had sat on a barstool that night between two young men who gave her hickeys. Did those nips translate into the deep red scrapes across her throat?

Her "other lovers" were the real reason he wanted the diary—for the names in it, Litman argued today. He said an "investigation of those individuals may produce critical witnesses."

Again insisting that Fairstein had first tipped him off to the diary's contents, Litman now typified it as "kinky and aggressive sexual activity by Jennifer Levin with many lovers."

Fairstein waited until she was outside the courtroom to explode. She said:

"That's an outrage and a lie! He said to me that he had heard that the diary contained such things, but he refused to say where he had heard it."

Judge Bell scheduled another hearing—but warned: "There comes a time when I will put a stop to all motion papers coming in and get on with the trial."

The trial was still more than a year away.

December 15: Today Robert Chambers paid a $20 fine for disorderly conduct in the street last July.

Police said Chambers got a summons when he and a chum, acting loud and boisterous, were ordered to be quiet by a Hispanic cop. Chambers allegedly shouted in response:

"Why don't you go up to Harlem and arrest some spics and niggers?"

Litman wasn't an eyewitness, but he had no difficulty denying the charge, declaring flatly: "He never said any such thing."

Fairstein said Chambers had ripped up the summons and affixed it to a patrol car windshield. He failed to show up for an August 20 court date.

Seven days later he was under arrest for murder.

December 16: Disclosing that Chambers was under the care of a psychiatrist for drug and alcohol abuse at the time of the murder, Fairstein said she had subpoenaed the shrink's records.

Diane McGrath of the state Crime Victims Board complained bitterly last week that Chambers was freed on bail without "an extensive and exhaustive psychiatric examination."

McGrath said: "Here is a guy who has a record of drugs and is walking free. If he was black, he would have been treated differently, I am sure of that."

In today's diary hearing, Fairstein said she didn't read it until October—a month after Litman claimed she told him how "kinky" it was.

"I learned that Mr. Litman's sensational charges were a figment of his imagination," said Fairstein. "There is no mention of kinky or aggressive sexual activity."

December 18: Judge Bell lost his patience with the Levin family today, and with their lawyer.

"I direct Mr. Newman to produce the diary for the court's eyes only," said Judge Bell. He said he would then decide whether to let Litman see it.

Newman refused to surrender the diary.

"This diary is so sacred to the family," he said, "they feel even the court should not see it.

"I mean this as no sign of disrespect, but Your Honor has granted the defense request [by demanding to read the diary]."

Bell retorted angrily: "I have no personal interest in the diary, but I feel I must see [it] before ruling."

Litman tried a diversion. He accused the prosecution of orchestrating a publicity campaign against Chambers and called for a gag order on all parties. Bell turned him down.

"No one in this town has done more to besmirch the reputation of Jennifer Levin," Newman said of Litman's gag motion. "This man has milked the case for all it's worth."

Even so, her family's impassioned and costly battle to defend Jennifer's privacy seemed to be boomeranging. Many observers, even sympathetic ones, thought it only provided support for Litman's "kinky" claims.

Why not turn the diary over to the judge?

The Levin family finally consented to give the diary to Judge Bell.

December 30: Litman was not quite finished. He brought a four-page letter to court urging, in his peremptory way, that Judge Bell not "play the role of defense counsel."

Don't read the diary, Litman said. Let me do it. It's my role.

But Bell was clearly in the mood to read. He had some theatrics of his own ready for the diary drama's final act.

When Newman unlocked his briefcase in court, a detective hovered nearby. It looked as if someone thought Litman might grab the precious diary and memorize it instantly.

But no one had more than a glimpse of what appeared to be a standard appointment book, a five-by-eight spiral with a black cover, as Newman handed it up to the judge.

There was a white heart hand drawn on the back cover of Jennifer's diary. There was writing scrawled inside the heart.

"I don't expect to be interrupted by anyone," Bell said as he withdrew to an empty jury room. It was 11:45 A.M.

The judge emerged at 3:30 P.M.

"I read it cover to cover continuously from eleven-forty-five to now, stopping only for some soup," Bell said. "It was handwritten, and some parts took me longer than others."

Cute, Judge.

He returned the diary to Newman and promised to offer a ruling on Litman's subpoena motion within "two weeks."

That was as optimistic as most New Year's resolutions.

January 28, 1987: Four weeks later the cliff hanger came to an end. Bell ruled in a six-page decision that Jack Litman could not have access to the diary.

He found "nothing in the document which was relevant and material to the defendant's case," said the judge.

Chambers' due process right to a fair trial would not be violated, Bell said, by depriving Litman of an "unrestrained tour" of the diary merely for "generally useful information."

That meant Litman had just been fishing—not seeking a particular fact. Fishing expeditions were not allowed.

As for Litman's "don't play defense counsel" thrust, Bell observed that the defense counsel was not best suited to determine the diary's relevancy. That was the judge's role. Litman's protest was "unfounded."

The diary, Bell said, could now go back to the bank vault for safekeeping.

The *New York Daily News* sang: DIARY HELD DEAR.

Jeffrey Newman put it another way: "If what happened today enables the Levins to bear their grief with an added measure of dignity," their lawyer said, "then something valuable happened in court today."

Bell's ruling, of course, did not diminish Litman's passion for the black book's irrelevant and immaterial contents. In a way it was his diary, after all—his invention, Fairstein said weeks after the trial.

"Jack's the one who called it a sex diary, who said things about what was in it. 'Kinky and aggressive sex' was his description," Fairstein said.

"It just isn't there. I put myself on the line swearing to that."

Litman made two more futile bids for the diary during the trial a year later.

"I think he backed off from it outwardly because he got killed in the press for doing it," Fairstein said. "The public perception was that he was doing exactly what he was doing. Jack's just smart enough that he outwardly backed off, but that was never not part of what he wanted to do."

Litman, too, remained stung by his lost battle.

"What is ironic about it is I was not seeking the diary to introduce [it] into evidence. I was seeking the diary as any defense lawyer would . . . because [of] the names of the young people in that diary. I wanted to speak to those people."

Even without the diary, Litman was able to learn a lot about Jennifer Levin.

"Myself or people from my office, we must have interviewed forty, fifty [people]," he said. "The group that hung around at Dorrian's in large measure. People that knew Robert and people that knew Jennifer. . . ."

Still, Litman thinks he would have loved that diary.

"I got an anonymous tip that such a thing might exist. But the first time that I found out that the diary had sexual references was from Linda Fairstein. She's the one who told me about it," he insisted.

"She told me, 'Boy you wouldn't believe what there is in here!' "

"That's an absolute lie, an absolute lie," said Fairstein. She believed Bell's ruling had backed her up. If the diary was dirty, the judge seemingly would have granted Litman the right to appropriate its contents. And if it wasn't dirty, why should Fairstein have tipped off Litman that it was?

One answer may be that someone else alerted Litman. He had mentioned "an anonymous tip" and alluded to "members of your staff" as well as Fairstein.

The judge had now issued two major rulings in the Chambers case, and the score was tied 1–1.

Bell had granted controversial bail to an unrepentant Chambers. But he had deprived Litman of what he badly wanted—a "sex diary" that he could wield as a weapon against Jennifer Levin.

Bell's diary ruling, predicted Jeffrey Newman, would now put the focus "where it belongs—on the conduct of the killer and not the character of the victim."

With Chambers about to take center stage, Litman had to turn a page in his strategy book.

Instead of digging up dirt, he needed to suppress it.

8

THE SUPPRESSION
HEARINGS

Out on bail, twenty years old, Robert Chambers was roughing it far from his East 90th Street home. For six or seven months he stayed nearly one hundred blocks uptown, in the Washington Heights rectory of the Church of the Incarnation, with his court-appointed overseer, Monsignor Thomas Leonard.

Social life for the celebrated murder suspect seemed tightly circumscribed. "He couldn't go out unless he had my permission," the monsignor recalled thirteen months later. "He couldn't receive a phone call without my permission."

But on occasion Chambers would venture into the night.

Informers tailed him. They reported that Leonard let him go to a midtown New Year's Eve party to ring in 1987. Six weeks later, law enforcement sources told *New York Newsday,* "Chambers reportedly deceived the monsignor about his whereabouts and went to another party." In April another source said, "That's just two of thirty rumors I've heard."

A story went around the courthouse pressroom that one night Chambers showed up at Nell's, a crowded disco. He couldn't get past the bouncer. "Don't you know who I am? I'm Robert Chambers," he said.

"I don't care if you're Charles Manson—you're not getting in," the bouncer said.

But the paparazzi were glad to see him. Photo editors paid well for Robert Chambers shots. Freelancers caught him bopping around town several times, once wearing a Walkman headset and a devilish grin.

Washington Heights was crowded with Puerto Ricans and Dominicans. Chambers briefly took a course in basic Spanish at NYU until the university asked him to withdraw.

Linda Fairstein spotted the suspect at Tiffany's one day and wondered what he was up to—"shoplifting?"

Ellen Levin wondered where justice had gone while Chambers roamed free.

"That was a sore point," Jennifer's mother recalled in May 1988 on Larry King's CNN talk show. "I go to visit Jennifer's grave and, you know—and see in a paper that he's walking around with a Walkman on and he's smiling and he's going to parties.

"I mean, that's not fair," Ellen said. "It's not right."

Litman did not comment in those days on the rumors he must have heard. He might have liked to see Chambers in church more, but Monsignor Leonard indicated that would not happen.

"He represents the whole crowd of that age who don't find the church very interesting," Leonard told *Newsday*'s Tim Clifford. "He comes to church when he wants to. He's not born again."

Phyllis Chambers reached her son that spring. He had resumed living at home in May, and one Sunday he was seen in church. But it was not at St. Thomas

More's on the next block where he had been an altar boy.

Chambers went to far-off Flatbush Avenue to attend services May 24 at the nondenominational Brooklyn Tabernacle Church, according to a brief story in the *Post*. It was his second visit, said the pastor's son, Sam Iampaglia. "His mother got saved here, and a few weeks ago she brought her son."

If his Irish-Catholic mother was straying, that was a surprise. But Chambers already had searched elsewhere.

Twice he had tried to join Scientology, an organization not noted for strictly limiting membership. But Chambers was turned down in October 1985 and again in May 1986 after returning from Hazelden's drug tank. "He didn't meet the standard of character and ethical behavior that our church sets," said a spokesman for Scientology, which had glady enrolled actor John Travolta.

Three months later Jennifer Levin's death in Central Park made Chambers an instant celebrity. But by May 7, 1987, he needed all the help he could find.

A series of pivotal pretrial hearings got under way that day. Chambers would be tied up—in court—for three months.

For Litman the pretrial hearings were an exercise in damage control.

The "sex diary" publicity had triggered a backlash against his taint tactics. "The press quickly cast Litman as an unscrupulous purveyor of a blame-the-victim defense strategy," wrote John Riley of the *National Law Journal*.

Litman told me later that he welcomed the criticism because it "deflected attention" from his client. But he didn't mention liking the word "unscrupulous."

As the case of the *People* v. *Robert Chambers*

began, however, Litman had to shift gears. After trying to expose twenty-three pages of Jennifer's diary, he now needed to suppress eleven hours of Chambers' statements to the police.

His full videotape statement was about to be played in court for the first time. The media, although Litman had tried to block it, would be there in force.

The videotape was Chambers' diary, in a way. While Litman had beaten it like a drum for the past seven months, it contained one passage he feared: Chambers had admitted killing Levin. An "accident," to be sure, but still the taking of a life. And with more than enough of Chambers' rough sex scenario in the public domain, Litman no longer valued the tape.

For Judge Bell to suppress it, though, he first had to watch it. Litman had demanded a closed hearing. The press would just "sensationalize" it, said the master of media hype. He argued that full public exposure of Chambers' videotape statements might well jeopardize his constitutional right to an impartial trial.

And Bell agreed, P-wheel or no P-wheel. It looked like Litman now had a 2–1 edge in Bell decisions.

But Linda Fairstein appealed the ruling and won a reversal of Bell's decision. Fairstein's victory came during the week before May 21, which would have been Jennifer Levin's nineteenth birthday.

A five-judge appellate panel unanimously ordered the videotape played in open court.

Bell got slapped down for "improperly" barring the press. And Litman, named the New York State Bar Association's outstanding criminal attorney of 1986, got a public spanking for trying to smash his toy drum.

"It appears that the defendant, through his counsel, has made detailed statements to the public and press, disclosing most, if not all, of the information he now seeks to keep secret. Defendant, by his own conduct, has undercut the position on which he now relies," the panel wrote.

"If our ruling in this matter discourages the bar from trying cases in the pressroom instead of the courtroom, it is a consequence which does not cause us dismay."

Bell, of course, still could suppress the videotape after he watched it. Some of its visuals were pretty raw—Chambers' masturbatory miming and whatnot—almost tantamount to soft-core porn. "Hated it," the judge could have said, and banned it from the jury trial.

Come what may, the videotape ran on schedule at a jammed suppression hearing on June 12, 1987.

All Litman could do then was embrace the video-tape, make it his own thing again. He did that boldly at the jury trial. He was still touting the tape he had tried to suppress when I asked him about it six weeks after the trial.

"Obviously, I can't walk away from the videotape," Litman said. "It's a very detailed account of what occurred. It doesn't dot all the *i*'s or cross all the *t*'s, but it lays out a very consistent and coherent story with reasons why things happened. And that obviously had to be the centerpiece of the defense in the case."

Litman got extra media mileage out of it at that, when Bell played the videotape in court on a Friday morning. While that afternoon's *Post* emblazoned it as CHAMBERS' CONFESSION—a word Litman abhorred—it also mentioned some of Chambers' code words for his victim, like "insane" and "cackle." The next day's *Times* led with "insane" and used "freaked out." It told how Levin had squeezed his testicles while holding him down. It ended with the six-four Chambers saying in awe, "She was strong."

All that weekend, the tale of Chambers' painful

struggle in panty bondage was must reading. Even normal people were riveted.

Litman still had something real to suppress—the two sets of inventive lies that Chambers palmed off on detectives in highly intricate detail for seven hours before he admitted killing Jennifer Levin by "accident."

The innocence of an apparently consummate liar might be hard to sell to a jury.

Of course if it got that far, Litman could challenge the credibility of any detective witness who took no notes of Chambers' intricate early lies. And none of them took any notes.

He was not a suspect then, remember—they were still looking for a brown car. And Chambers had an extensive alibi.

Rubbery, but an alibi. First he wasn't even with Levin at Dorrian's. Then he was with her, but she went to a Korean deli to buy cigarettes, then maybe went to Brock's house. Chambers went home to watch *The Price Is Right* and a TV movie. He knew the movie's plot. The cuts on his hands? An electric sander. The scratches? His cat did that.

And then, no, Jennifer had scratched him, in a quarrel on 86th Street. There she left him, disappearing with a blond guy.

Some cops were skeptical enough of the "cat scratches" to read Chambers his rights, but even they had no incentive to take notes. Why bother writing down lies? Eventually a liar cracks.

If Litman briefly considered swaying one more jury—his favorite pastime—he finally decided to take no chances.

He decided to depict Chambers as a suspect from the start of his all-day stint as a "cooperative witness." Actually his client was under steady interrogation for ten hours, Litman would argue.

Chambers was being detained incommunicado in a little room at the Central Park precinct—that was the scenario.

If Litman could demonstrate that the cops deprived Chambers of a phone call—to his lawyer, his parents, his priest—that would mean Chambers was deprived of his constitutional rights.

Litman could have all his client's statements suppressed and tossed out—including the videotape. Litman could erase the entire eleven hours of interrogation in the precinct.

To make it stick, Litman maintained that Stephen Saracco had not immediately told him all the varied details of Chambers' first two sets of lies—or in fact any details.

So those revealing details did not even exist legally, Litman argued. Notification of their intended use by the prosecution had to be given defense counsel within fifteen days by law. Saracco had not met that deadline.

There was a catch. Litman dealt with it.

The fifteen-day deadline was law, but the depth of detail required had long been left to individual judges empowered to waive the deadline. The waiver provision was currently being debated in a separate case. It would not be settled—or provide a precedent for the Chambers case—until November.

But Litman argued the point anyway at Chambers' summer hearings.

The rest of his suppression strategy was to taint the victim, discredit the cops, and show how the "incommunicado" defendant's constitutional rights were violated for want of a phone call.

Fairstein's mission was to prove that Chambers was "a pathological liar" who deliberately tried to fool the cops investigating Jennifer Levin's murder.

On June 15, Litman's cross-examination of Detective Michael McEntee focused on Levin's pursuit of Chambers and his avowed disinterest.

McEntee told of Betsy Shankin's precinct recollections—of Levin telling Chambers he was the "best ever" in bed, that Levin "wanted to spend the night with Robert" that night, that Levin had "just winked" at Shankin when she left Dorrian's.

That made the top of the *Post* story. McEntee told Fairstein of Chambers pal William Thrush's tip that Chambers was "heavily into cocaine . . . it was common knowledge around Dorrian's"—and that became one paragraph at the bottom.

The *Daily News* didn't mention Thrush's cocaine tip. *Newsday* did—and cited Chambers' drug abuse treatment at Hazelden—but also mentioned McEntee's revelation that Levin was into diet pills, as Chambers had helpfully noted on videotape. They turned out to be over-the-counter diet pills, not amphetamines.

It provided quite a contrast—the splashy attention given to Levin's alleged sexuality compared with Chambers' admitted cocaine abuse. It was probably the single most glaring example of distorted media play at the suppression hearings.

But upcoming testimony from a string of cops inflicted some damage on Chambers.

John Lafferty testified that Chambers under questioning had brought up the East Side burglary investigation himself—possibly thinking the cops knew anyway. But Lafferty recalled Chambers saying his role in the investigation was as a "character witness."

Litman pounced. Here was a chance to hint that the cops had kept Chambers from phoning Putzel the lawyer.

"Isn't it a fact that the reason he mentioned the

ressa Thomson, Laura Robertson and Jennifer Levin at
orrian's six hours before Jennifer was killed. *(NY Post)*

A second picture of Jennifer at Dorrian's taken the nig
she died. Judge Howard Bell ordered the piece of whi
tape to cover the earring Jennifer was wearing, fearir
it might prejudice the jury. The earring was not found ⊄
Jennifer's body. (AP/Wide World Photos)

Police examine the body of Jennifer Levin in Central Park, August 26, 1986. *(NY Post)*

Police arrest Chambers on charges of second-degree murder. Scratches are visible on the left side of his face. Detective Mike Sheehan is at right. (AP/Wide World Photos)

`08-7?-8b 00:51:19`

ambers reluctantly looks at police photos of Jennifer
vin's body. *(from his videotaped confession)*

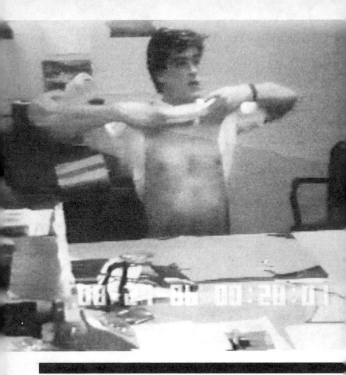

Chambers lifts his shirt to show scratches he claimed were inflicted by Jennifer Levin. *(from his videotaped confession)*

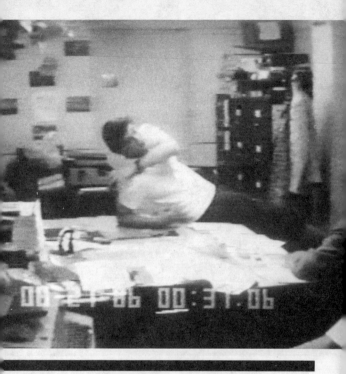

`00:2?:06 00:3?:06`

hambers demonstrating his version of how he
ccidentally choked Jennifer and fell backwards,
juring his hand. *(from his videotaped confession)*

Arlene and Steven Levin. *(NY Post)*

Robert Chambers and his parents leaving court. (Angel
Franco/*NY Times* Pictures)

Chambers briefly approaches the site where Jennifer Levin died. He quickly returned to the car while the jury examined the site. (AP/Wide World Photos)

obert Chambers faces his jury. (Drawing by Christine ornell)

Dr. Warner Spitz, Detroit Medical Examiner, demonstrates to the jury his theory of how Jennifer Levin was killed. (Drawing by Christine Cornell)

nnifer Levin's sister Danielle Roberts, her husband
ffrey Roberts and Ellen Levin. *(NY Post)*

Defense Attorney Jack Litman. *(NY Post)*

Assistant District Attorney Linda Fairstein. (Nancy Rica Schiff)

The Levin press conference after the plea bargain was announced. *(from l. to r.):* Linda Fairstein, D.A. Robert Morgenthau, Ellen Levin, Steven Levin and Arlene Levin. (AP/Wide World Photos)

other case is that he was a suspect in the other case?''
No. "That he had a lawyer?" No.

What gradually emerged was that Chambers had never mentioned Putzel—or any other lawyer—to any cop at the precinct.

Lafferty told of Chambers' misty-eyed reaction to the cops' first acknowledgment that they had a dead body: "Oh, no! How did she die?"

Litman cited Chambers' ingenuous question to Lafferty as a prime example of the details withheld from him by Saracco. He called it a "new statement" to him—a legalism that Fairstein quickly challenged. She said the remark "How did she die?" did not qualify as a "new statement." Saracco had implicitly included it in the whole bag of lies Litman had first learned of at Chambers' arraignment—confirmed by mail within fifteen days.

Implicitly, but not explicitly. The Saracco bag of Chambers' lies omitted crucial details. "How did she die?" Forget it.

Litman had his edge. But the charade of pretrial hearings dragged on.

Even after Chambers finally admitted killing Levin, the details of the deed itself kept changing.

Martin Gill heard first that Jennifer had "tackled" him in the park, then that she'd hugged him and pulled him to the ground. John Doyle said Chambers told how he had grabbed Levin by the neck and pulled her up as he stood, then dropped her. In that second set of lies there was no mention of "flipping" Levin over his shoulder, the accident Chambers described on videotape.

Lieutenant Doyle conceded that no other cooperating witnesses stayed at the precinct for more than two hours. Litman tried to establish Chambers' eleven-hour "incommunicado" status. "Did you ever tell him he could go home?" Litman asked.

Doyle said no, since Chambers had been "extremely cooperative" and was the investigation's "last hope." Until Chambers admitted that the scratches were made by Jennifer and not the cat, Doyle said, he believed the boy's whole story.

He never considered Chambers a suspect. Doyle, the boss investigator, said it never even occurred to him to check and see if Chambers had a cat.

Mike Sheehan testified that he knew Bob Chambers but had not seen him in five years. He said he did not connect the suspect to him. And he didn't know until he saw him in an anteroom that Bob Chambers had waited in the precinct virtually unattended during the last seven hours of Robert's interrogation.

All the other detectives swore the same thing.

It suited Litman's scenario: his client had been forcibly separated from his father while being detained incommunicado.

John Mullally recalled Chambers' "that fucking bitch!" outburst. His father told him to "calm down," said Mullally, but the suspect's outburst was all too memorable.

"It was in a loud voice—an excited voice," Mullally said. "It stuck in my mind. It was a violent statement. There was no remorse."

Litman floodlighted the fact that Mullally alone had heard the remorseless "bitch" outburst. Worse, Mullally didn't confide it to anyone, he said, except to his partner on that August night. Fairstein didn't get wind of it until that December. Mullally didn't file an official police report about it until January. Litman had a right to smile.

Yet it was the one instance where an unsupported allegation of Chambers' word usage worked against him.

Phyllis Chambers took the witness stand at the suppression hearing June 23 for two grueling days. She sat ramrod straight with short iron-gray hair neatly capping her head, but the overall effect was of fragility.

This would be her first and last testimony to her son's innocence. Before it was over she dramatically burst into tears several times.

Leading her through his "incommunicado" scenario, Litman helped her make three points:

• When the police picked up her son for questioning at 2:15 P.M. on August 26, she told him to phone Putzel the lawyer.

• The police did not let her talk to Robert by phone.

• She did not know his fate until his father called her at 2:30 A.M. and said Robert was under arrest for murder.

She had been home at 11 East 90th Street with her cleaning lady on that Tuesday afternoon when Detectives Frank Connelly and Al Genova dropped by.

"I asked them what the problem was," Phyllis Chambers testified. "I was told that a girl was missing and my son Robert was to help them. . . . [They] said it would not take long and that they would bring him home."

Connelly's recollection was that Phyllis Chambers had advised her son to take his house keys—nothing more—while they awaited the down elevator.

She swore that as Robert was leaving, "The last thing I said to him was, 'Call Pete Putzel.' That was the last I saw or heard of Robert on that day."

She phoned Dorrian's at 3:30 P.M. hoping to learn more. "The kids all went there," she explained in her Irish brogue. Jack Dorrian answered the phone.

"And he said, 'Phyllis, have you not heard? Did you not hear the news? A girl has been found dead in Central Park.'

"And I asked him, 'What has Robert to do with that?' " She said Dorrian didn't reply. His son Michael gave her the phone number of the Central Park precinct.

Chambers' mother testified that she called the precinct twice—at five o'clock and then at about seven.

Her first call was switched to a detective. She said she identified herself and asked to talk to her son.

"I was told, 'You cannot speak with him now, but we will be through shortly,' " Phyllis Chambers testified. She couldn't remember the detective's name.

Bob Chambers phoned her. She told her estranged husband where their son was and who had taken him there.

"He said he was on his way to the precinct," she recalled.

When she called the precinct again just before seven, Robert's father was there, and they spoke briefly.

While Mrs. Chambers testified that she tried to reach Putzel the lawyer all day, his office staff recorded no calls from her before six P.M. An answering machine was on after that. Fairstein said it recorded two late calls from Chambers' parents.

Putzel had testified the day before that he had given Robert two business cards in May of 1986 during the burglary investigation.

"I did not want Robert Chambers talking to law enforcement officials about anything without counsel," Putzel said. But Putzel was out of town on August 26, he said, and did not receive the two messages from Chambers' parents until August 27.

While his mother testified, Robert Chambers rubbed his teary eyes several times, noted in headlines: CHAMBERS WEEPS.

So even before Fairstein cross-examined the mother

the next day, journalists began researching Phyllis Chambers to find out what made her tick.

She was born Mary Phyllis Shanley near the end of the Great Depression on a County Leitrim farm in northwest Ireland, a region so poor its people still dig up their own peat for fuel. Educated by nuns and trained as a nurse, she came to America in the 1960s determined, by all accounts, to improve her station. But after she married Bob Chambers and bore their only child, she never was able to stop working. Her tall and dressy husband was a serious drinker.

For years Phyllis Chambers worked twelve-hour shifts, seven to seven, six nights a week, as a private-duty nurse for wealthy patients like Millicent Hearst and Dorothy Hammerstein. It helped pay for young Robert's private school tuition and a high-rent apartment on Park Avenue until 1980. With Bob Chambers unemployed and their apartment going co-op, Phyllis sold their insider rights for a chunk of cash. She found a two-bedroom apartment on the top floor at 11 East 90th, an eighty-year-old residence described as "elegant" by the New York City Landmarks Commission. She always was a doer.

Robert was her one blind spot, friends said. She gave up precious spare time to serve as president of the Knickerbocker Greys women's board and help make him a man. "The Greys teaches what society is about, the niceties of life," Phyllis said.

Her son's troubles are widely linked to her social climber image. She often said she wanted him to be a U.S. senator "like the Kennedys." She didn't specify which Kennedy.

As onetime girlfriend, Gail Cooley, put it two months after his trial ended: "His mother pushed him and pushed him and pushed him. It was very hard for Robert." And a source close to the Chambers prosecution called him an "emotionally lost kid whose mother tried to make him something that he wasn't."

His mother once caught Robert smoking marijuana in his bedroom with a friend, wrote *New York* magazine's Michael Stone. The friend described a sad vignette of parenting in the 1980s:

"She sat us down on the bed and put her arms around us and told us that if we had any problems, we should talk them out with her. Rob and I were doing all we could not to burst out laughing. I mean, she was very nice, but completely out of touch."

People who caught Robert stealing money or credit cards from their children reportedly told his mother, a law enforcement source told me. On her instructions Robert wrote them letters of apology on Tiffany stationery.

Phyllis Chambers repaid their losses. She said Robert was the victim of "bad companions."

Under cross-examination June 24, Phyllis Chambers did not hit it off with the prosecutor. Fairstein had spoken harshly of the son many times in print over the previous nine months. Now she was addressed variously as "Madame Fairstein" or "Madame Fearstein."

On the videotape Chambers had remembered his mother wondering out loud about the obvious scratches on his face when he got out of the shower at eleven A.M. August 26. She didn't remember it that way.

"He showed them to me," Phyllis Chambers told Fairstein as if her child had kept nothing from her. She recalled his scratches as barely noticeable.

Fairstein got rough. "Did he tell you at any time between eleven and two o'clock that there was a dead child in Central Park?" she asked.

"No," said Chambers' mother. She started weeping

ftly. Robert covered his face with both hands, wip-
g his eyes occasionally.

Fairstein asked when she first learned her son was
der arrest for the murder of Jennifer Levin. Mrs.
hambers said his father had phoned her regularly
om the precinct that night—the last time about 2:30
M.

"And what did he say?" asked Fairstein.

For twenty long seconds, Chambers' mother strug-
ed for control with her hand at her mouth, shudder-
g, pursing her lips. Then, dramatically, she broke
to racking sobs.

Judge Bell declared a recess. Court officers helped
e shaken mother leave the courtroom. Litman ob-
cted to the question. Two sets of lawyers approached
e judge's bench.

Robert Chambers covered his eyes for a minute,
oulders shaking. His mother took longer to regain
r composure and return to the witness stand briefly.
She never did answer Fairstein's question.

Members of the Levin family were in the courtroom.
even Levin said he "felt bad" for Chambers'
other.

"I think he's ruined a lot of lives, including hers,"
said.

But he didn't like her testimony. "I thought she was
vering for her son. She's doing the best she can as a
other."

And Jennifer's father expressed his contempt for
obert Chambers.

"He's shown not one second of remorse for killing
y daughter. He cries when his mother gets on the
itness stand, but not one tear for taking my daugh-
r's life.

"The kid has a history. He's a thief, a drug addict,
d he's a murderer," Levin raged to reporters in the

hall. "And everybody's been cleaning his dirty diaper for him his whole life."

In the Central Park precinct that August 26, across an alleyway from where Chambers was being questioned, Officer Nicholas Diomede came into his office about six P.M. and found the father waiting.

"He mentioned the fact that they wouldn't let him see his son," Diomede testified the following summer. "And he asked whether or not I thought his son needed a lawyer.

"I said to him, if he wanted, he could hold off to see how things developed. I didn't know what his son was actually involved in."

Diomede said he left at seven o'clock for an assignment, leaving the father behind for what would be a long wait.

Chambers' father, like his mother, adhered closely to Litman's "incommunicado" scenario.

He had a twofold reason for going to the precinct—not only to see his son, but also "to make sure he saw his lawyer," Bob Chambers testified at the June suppression hearing.

He said he asked to see Robert and was told to wait. "The man at the desk said the detective would come to see me in a few minutes. I asked if my son had seen his lawyer."

He was told to have a seat, recalled Chambers' tall, balding father. But instead he was escorted across the alleyway to Officer Diomede's office.

"I want to see my son," the father said he told Diomede. "He has a lawyer, and he should see his lawyer."

Bob Chambers testified that for several hours he either sat waiting or paced the precinct parking lot praying. It wouldn't be surprising if he wondered what

his was going to cost him. He had a job as a bill
ollector for a videocassette distributor, but he was a
ecovering alcoholic. He said the prayer he recited
was the Alcoholics Anonymous serenity prayer.

A couple of times he walked to the corner phone
ooth at Central Park West and 86th Street to phone
hyllis or Putzel the lawyer, he said, and intermit-
ently he asked to see his son. Each time he was told
hat a detective would speak to him shortly.

"Why didn't you go and slam your fist down and
emand to see your son?" asked Litman.

"I generally do what police officers tell me to do,"
Chambers' father replied.

About ten P.M. he thought he heard a cop—"a
oice," said Bob Chambers—telling him it wouldn't
e long now.

But it was an additional seventy-five minutes before
Doyle and "another man" showed up.

Doyle told him Robert was "busy" with Detective
heehan.

"Robert's made some statements, and he's been
rrested on murder charges," the father remembered
Doyle telling him.

"When I heard that, I sort of lost my breath."

Much as Doyle had comforted the son, now he
omforted the father. He testified that Doyle said:

"This is very tough. I am a father myself. It's like a
agic car accident where Robert is driving and there's
n accident and the passenger is killed. It's nobody's
ault."

A week earlier in the hearings, Doyle denied refer-
ng to Jennifer Levin's death as an accident.

Now, about 1:15 A.M., Bob Chambers was escorted
o another room. His son was there alone with Mul-
lly.

"I see Robert with his hands folded and his head
own on the desk, crying," the father testified. "I try

to console him. I put my arm around him. I mov
closer and hug him and I say, 'Don't worry. I'm here
I'm with you. Your mother is with you. We're behin
you.' "

And Robert's response? "Did you hear him curs
while you were there?" Litman asked.

"No," said the father.

It was Fairstein's turn.

Who were the police officers he spoke to that night
The father could name only John Doyle and Mik
Sheehan, his old acquaintance.

Had he mentioned Putzel the lawyer to either one?
Bob Chambers couldn't recall.

Fairstein returned to the same subject later.

"The only names of officers you remember wer
Sheehan and Doyle?" Yes. "Did you say to either c
them the name Putzel?"

The father now admitted he had not.

"Did you tell either of them that night that your so
had a lawyer?" No.

"The only ones you talked to about it were officer
you can't describe and whose names you don
know?"

Litman leaped up. How about Diomede? But Fai
stein's cross-examination of Chambers' father wa
over. And Litman's "incommunicado" scenario had
hole in it.

Watching Fairstein rattle both parents must hav
taught Litman a lesson, if any were needed, abou
putting any member of the defendant's family on th
witness stand. The question now was: should Rober
Chambers himself testify?

Litman pondered it over the Fourth of July week
end. A Sandoval hearing on the defendant's "prie
bad acts" was due July 7. That would determine ho
far Fairstein could dig into Chambers' cocaine an

urglary history on cross-examination in front of a
ury—if he took the stand.

There was no law requiring Chambers to testify at
ither the pretrial hearings or the jury trial. His past
istory had no direct bearing on the murder charge
gainst him. But Fairstein had submitted sealed
harges to Bell, disclosing "bad acts" of more recent
intage—subsequent to his 1985 burglaries and 1986
rug rehab—and Litman had no way of knowing what
he prosecutor could prove. Even if Bell ruled Cham-
ers' entire street history inadmissible, Fairstein's
ortrait of his "double life" as a cokehead thief would
nake hot headlines. It would wreck Chambers' altar-
oy preppy image. It would take the heat off Jennifer
evin.

Litman decided to withdraw from the Sandoval
earing. He told Bell that the "inflammatory" allega-
ions against Chambers would make it impossible to
nd an impartial jury.

Since Chambers would not take the witness stand,
nd Fairstein could not cross-examine him, only a
mall slice of his history could be revealed to his trial
rors. That slice covered the twenty-five hours from
hen Jennifer Levin walked into Dorrian's to when
hambers finished his videotape statement. The jury
ould know nothing about his "double life" of drugs
nd thievery.

"I can do without that," Litman told me later.
"Based on surveys we had done beforehand, people
eacted very negatively to that. And in order to bring
is individuality to the fore, I risked allowing the jury
o hear very pointedly and in great detail . . . every
ingle allegation they could have mustered. And I
idn't want that to happen."

Jennifer Levin's older sister, Danielle, thought at
he time that Litman showed his first sign of weakness
y keeping Chambers off the stand. "His history has

got to be really horrible," she said. "I think Litman is really scared. He's defeated."

But Litman soon struck back. In what legal scholars saw as a move to keep the prosecution on the defensive, he sought exhumation of Levin's body in order to explore "all possible causes of death." Specifically he asked for her spinal column. He wanted to dissect it.

Fairstein had no choice. While stating the obvious— that dissection could damage the spine and whatever medical evidence it held—she was forced to disclose that Jennifer's cervical spine section had been kept by the city medical examiner after the autopsy. That grisly detail not only made exhumation of the body unnecessary, it made everyone sick.

Litman, arguing that the prosecution feared discovery of a different cause of death, managed to deepen the enmity of the Levin family.

He was "tapdancing all over her heart, soul, and reputation," said Danielle's husband, Jeffrey Roberts. "This is the act of a desperate lawyer with a loser for a client. Chambers killed her, but what Litman is doing is almost worse. It's almost like he's backing up a truck to finish the job. Can't they leave Jennifer alone?"

Yes, said Judge Bell. When chief medical examiner Elliot Gross confirmed that dissection might destroy the spine, Bell ruled Litman's exploration "too speculative" to justify the risk.

With the suppression hearings winding down, Fairstein filed a brief calling both of Chambers' parents out-and-out liars. Her main target was their claim that they tried to get Putzel the lawyer on the case to help their son before he was arrested.

"The very last thing they wanted to do was to make

the police aware that their son had any earlier police involvement for fear that it would cause the police to view Robert in a different light,'' Fairstein said.

She argued that they had not hired a lawyer during his first ten hours of questioning by detectives at the precinct for another good reason.

''Mr. and Mrs. Chambers were very familiar with their son's ability to talk himself out of criminal liability, as he had done with their assistance so many times in the past.''

Fairstein also ridiculed Phyllis Chambers' ''incredible'' testimony about her son's badly scratched face.

''She didn't recall ever talking to Robert about the obvious scratches on his face, whereas he admits telling her the cat scratched him,'' said the prosecutor's brief.

''It is entirely incredible that Mrs. Chambers, a trained medical professional, would neither observe nor question such serious marks on her son's face when she first saw them.''

On the first anniversary of the August 26 tragedy, *The New York Times* reported that a citywide police crackdown on teenage drinking wasn't helping much. Fake ID cards were still prevalent. An eighteen-year-old, who said her friends knew Jennifer Levin, was interviewed at Dorrian's. The crowd there had thinned out and seemed older, she said, ''because the carding got heavier.'' Most of the teenagers had migrated to other bars. Police Inspector Ronald Johnson said the fake IDs he was seeing were ''very, very good.''

Robert Chambers turned legal on his twenty-first birthday, September 25. Although it qualified him for his first legal drink, it would be his last birthday drink on the outside for some years.

Bell had just set a new trial date for him: October 20.

Four days before the trial began, the judge granted Litman's request to electronically erase some of Saracco's videotape opinions "regarding the defendant's guilt." He did not specify which passages would be erased. That was the minor news.

The big story of that October 16 was Bell's ruling that Chambers' differing statements to police about Jennifer Levin's death could be used as prosecution evidence of his guilt.

That included his conflicting versions of when he last saw her alive—first in Dorrian's doorway, then at 86th and Park Avenue, and finally behind the Metropolitan Museum of Art in Central Park.

Chambers' first story to police was now in evidence—that she had gone to see Brock Pernice, that he had watched TV at home, and that his cat scratched him. So was his second story, that Levin had scratched him in a quarrel at 86th Street and Lexington—no, 86th and Park—and then had departed with a blond stranger. And so was his final, supposedly truthful, videotape statement.

The judge rejected Litman's contention that all three versions heard by the police were illegal evidence because his client had been held incommunicado without a lawyer. Bell spelled out his reasoning in a thirty-two-page decision that called Chambers' divergent statements fully voluntary.

The suspect's Miranda rights had been read to him four separate times—once as soon as he was brought to the precinct—yet he never took the opportunity to phone a lawyer or either of his parents. Chambers never said he already had a lawyer; nor did he mention Putzel's name. He had "knowingly and voluntarily waived his constitutional rights," said Bell.

Fairstein could now hope to demonstrate to a jury that the defendant was a practiced liar. Litman, however, still had two consolations. He had managed to duck putting Chambers' cocaine and burglary history on the record. And every day's newspaper coverage during the three-month suppression hearings had included at least some reprise of Chambers' "rough sex" scenario.

The scoreboard in major judicial decisions was now 3–1 in Fairstein's favor. Litman won bail for Chambers. Fairstein won the diary battle. She got Chambers' videotape played in public and was now in position to expose his bag of lies.

Now there was a massive task at hand for the prosecutor, the defense counsel, and the judge. It was time to select a jury for the "Preppy Murder Trial."

Somehow they had to find twelve men or women in Manhattan who did not have a fixed opinion about the Chambers case.

9

THE JURY SELECTION

When Linda Fairstein talked about Jack Litman, she made the point that "our passions are very different." At no time was that more evident than when they began selecting jurors on October 21, 1987, for the murder trial of Robert Emmet Chambers.

Their lawyering passions now were rooted in circumstances. Their differences were interesting, and some were surprising.

While Fairstein was a thoroughly modern woman with a deep personal interest in reforms advancing the cause of women's rights, she now had good reason professionally to yearn for the bad old days.

"Twelve good men and true"—that was the ideal of the Anglo-Saxon jury selection process from its origins in the Middle Ages. And the earliest English juries of the twelfth century, in addition to being all male, were prized for being well informed. They were men with personal knowledge of the case in question.

Fairstein wanted well-informed men to judge Chambers, men who had read beyond the sex headlines, who understood the kind of violence that had killed Jennifer Levin and would not need the unknowable facts in order to reach a verdict of guilty.

Litman wanted what he later described as "virgin jurors" who knew nothing and craved guidance. With circumstantial evidence the primary case against Chambers, they could thus be prey to the reasonable doubt instilled by a jury swayer like Litman.

He had lost his own virginity as a juror in a make-believe murder trial on a stage at Stuyvesant High about twenty-five years ago.

"I was very much involved in the high school play *Twelve Angry Men*," Litman told me. "Ironically I played the Lee J. Cobb part, the last holdout for guilty. All the kids signed my high school yearbook either 'guilty' or 'not guilty.' I guess I was moved by that to some extent," he said, reminiscing about his decision to become a lawyer.

As a third-year law student at Harvard, he was assigned to the state's public defender program in Massachusetts and tried twenty-two cases as defense counsel. But Litman really got his start, in a way, as a holdout for guilty.

So now there were two ironies. Litman wanted virgin jurors with no holdout for guilty—his own first role. And Linda Fairstein, who was devoted to the progress of women, wanted as few women as possible on the Chambers jury.

Her hopes for a well-informed jury panel were doomed by both the nature and the depth of what now amounted to fourteen months of publicity deluge in the Central Park case. Judge Bell made it clear early in that October voir dire that any prospective juror over burdened with newspaper information would be excused.

They departed in droves, to Fairstein's regret. She mourned the twelfth-century jury standards that in any normal case might still have applied to some degree in 1987.

"The standard is not if you've read about the case, you can't be a juror," she said. "Most judges would say: 'That was the newspapers, this is the trial.' And they would say: 'Yes, Your Honor.' "

But Bell was adamant. Although he eventually softened in order to fill the last few seats on the panel, Bell excused most heavy readers for several weeks. To the relief of Litman and Chambers, the judge turned thumbs down "if people had read about the burglaries, if they had read about the drugs, if they knew about his background," Fairstein said. "So every well-informed person was excused."

The prosecutor had two reasons for prejudice against women jurors. One was based on their occasional glandular response to the handsome young defendant. The other derived from a curious tendency of many women jurors to turn against the victims in rape cases.

From long experience as chief of the DA's Sex Crimes Unit, Fairstein knew that some women jurors would judge Jennifer Levin harshly.

"I used to start trials and the defense attorneys would try to kick women off, assuming there was this natural sympathy with the victim," Fairstein told me. "I used to end up with all-male juries who would convict like that." She snapped her fingers.

"I started to learn . . . women who don't have any kind of feminist perspective are much harder on victims of sex crimes and obviously sex-related incidents like this than men are. Women tend to put themselves above other women, blame the other woman."

It shows up in voir dire as a sort of cultural blip.

"You heard it in this case: 'Well, I never did things like that. My daughters wouldn't go to bars. Nice girls

lon't do that—and maybe she didn't deserve what
happened to her, but she was looking for trouble.'

"Women are much worse on judging other women's
behavior than men are. That's been my experience
with sex crimes."

In this case, some women confronted her directly
with the other abiding problem of all concerned in the
Chambers case: his looks.

"There's just a vacancy in his face," Fairstein said,
"but it never ceases to amaze me the number of
teenagers and even twenty-five-year-olds who were
basing their opinions on how good-looking he was and
how he couldn't do something like that."

One prospective juror was a "very attractive young
black woman who worked for a bank." As she sat at
the voir dire table, with Chambers sitting three feet
away, Fairstein got an almost electric shock.

"She interrupted her response to a question of mine
and turned to him and said: 'You're even better-look-
ing in person than you are in photographs.'

"That's on the record," Fairstein said. "That's the
kind of thing that terrified us."

Had the young black woman ever thought "someone
who looks like that couldn't have committed the violent, horrible crime that he's charged with?" Fairstein
asked her.

"No, I haven't," the woman replied. But she was
too risky.

Fairstein considered it a severe loss. The prosecution was searching for black jurors to serve at the
Chambers trial.

"We wanted more minorities. We knew that if anybody . . . that the problem was going to be people
looking at this case and saying, 'He's only twenty-
one. Let's compromise somewhere.' And it would be
the whites who would do that."

A white juror faced with a charge of intentional

murder might decide that "it's an intent formed in a short period of time, and this kid shouldn't pay with his whole life for it," said Fairstein.

Prospective black jurors "had many times in their lives—in their neighborhoods—seen guys go away for long periods of time for the same thing."

The prosecutor, as a public official, was relatively circumspect about the profile of her ideal juror. The defense counsel, very much his own boss, could spell out precisely what Robert Chambers needed.

"People who didn't want to hang him going in, obviously," Litman told me later. "People who were young, who could understand this type of sexuality that Robert had described on the videotape, where a young man is playing essentially a role that is typically ascribed to the female. That is, he becomes the sexual object. He becomes sort of passive, sort of suffers it to occur until he must react when the pain gets to where it was. It's a very unusual role for a man. To put an older person in that situation—just in a stereotypic way—I thought would be difficult.

"I wanted people who were virgin jurors, who had not served on a jury before in criminal cases. And I wanted people who were, in the main, intelligent and educated because I like to think that some of the arguments I made, especially in this case, are going to be addressed more to their reason than the prosecutor." He said he knew Fairstein would "talk about Jennifer as a human being" and about "how a life was lost." He knew.

"And I wanted to tap in more to their curiosity and their intelligence. . . . There were some interesting issues in the case that required a certain sophistication. That was, in general, the kind of jurors I was looking for. . . ."

Litman also asked Judge Bell for a private individual voir dire of each prospective juror.

While not unprecedented, it was highly unusual for a murder trial that had generated so many fixed opinions. To find twelve objective New Yorkers for the Chambers jury—even twelve who sounded objective—would eventually require two months of voir dire.

A pool of 539 prospective jurors were called between October and December. Of that pool, 486 would be interviewed for the job.

The usual group method, with several candidates listening in, would not be viable here. Litman did not want prospective jurors overhearing the kind of opinion a twenty-seven-year-old woman law student uttered to her fellow pool members about Chambers:

"The little creep should fry!"

Bell threatened to hold the law student in contempt of court. "Didn't you realize that this is the American system of justice?" the judge thundered. "And another thing. We don't fry people in this state anymore."

Of the first batch of one hundred candidates, fifty-three were dismissed for discussing the case among themselves. Bell didn't say how he knew, but their replacements got a stern judicial warning.

Fairstein did not oppose individual voir dire. She had her own reservations about hostility to Jennifer Levin among jurors in groups. One had used the word "slutty." And it would be delicate work eliciting responses to "the T question" about Chambers' tale of squeezed testicles.

But it was most valuable to Litman to be able to question each prospective juror in a small room with one table, the judge, a court reporter, a law secretary, two sets of attorneys, a court stenographer, court officers, two media pool reporters, and Chambers.

Cramped, but since Chambers would not speak in court, Litman could use the voir dire to display his client to the jurors.

"I let his humanity and his individuality and his personality be there only by his physical presence," said Litman. "They sat there for an hour at a time with Robert Chambers sitting right there. I had to rely on that because I could not run the risk that these other things, about which so much negativity had been written in the newspapers, could come out at the trial."

Chambers' presence meant little to Fairstein. "There was a lot of light conversation around the room," she said, "but not like me and Bobby chatting."

Litman credited Bell for allowing individual voir dire. He viewed it as a huge breakthrough. Without it Litman told me, "I don't think we would have had a chance in this case."

And beyond rubbing elbows with Robert, jurors could respond in privacy to "very pointed, probing questions," said Litman.

Like the T question.

Women were asked: "Are you aware of the pain caused when a man's testicles are squeezed?" The men got a slightly different version: "You know, don't you, the pain that is caused when a man's testicles are squeezed?" Some just crossed their legs once or twice and nodded.

"If some individual causes you pain, do you believe you have a right to strike back or hit back? To defend yourself?" A male juror agreed emphatically. "Should a man react differently if it's a woman?" Litman asked. One man guessed the pain felt by Chambers was like the pain of being hit in the groin by a baseball.

Newsday columnist Linda Miller complained that nobody asked the jurors: "Are you aware of the pain of being strangled?"

Fairstein made it clear from the outset that jurors

would not need to read Chambers' mind to find him guilty of murder.

"There are things we don't have to prove, and one of those things is his motive. The state does not require us to get inside his head," she told one man. Litman asked him to focus on motive, provable or not: "You would certainly want to know the 'why'?" The man nodded.

"A fair and impartial jury"—that was the promise. But the heavy publicity had taken its toll. Just one of the first thirty-nine candidates had heard nothing about the case. Most said they had made up their minds from all they had read. At least one denounced Litman's blame-the-victim tactics to his face. A woman told him, "I have to admit I have negative feelings towards your client."

A few claimed to have changed their opinions of guilty and said they wanted to know more about the case. All were excused.

"You got a disproportionate amount of young people who, I think, were eager to be on it," Fairstein said. "The problem with a case like this is that it attracts people who want to sell their story and would know that there is a celebrity factor in being involved in this."

After the first day of voir dire, Robert Chambers expressed sympathy for the parade of candidates. "I feel bad for them, that they have to go through that," he told the pool reporters.

By chance, the first candidate questioned said he knew a sister of John Zaccaro, Jr., the fill-in bartender at Dorrian's on the night of tragedy. He also said he thought Chambers was guilty of murder. Good-bye.

But a gray-haired woman with glasses thought there might be "extenuating circumstances" in Chambers' favor. "I have three sons of my own," she said, "and

I could only project and put one of them in his place.''
Good-bye.

Litman questioned the young black woman bank
employee about her knowledge of sexual styles and
whether she had a boyfriend.

"Did you hear that Jennifer Levin was sexually
aggressive?" Litman asked.

"No."

"Do you believe it's possible for a woman to be
sexually aggressive?"

"I know a lot of girls who are sexually aggressive,'
she replied. Good-bye.

Voir dire questions ran the gamut. So did the answers. A standard query about religious beliefs
prompted one woman to volunteer that, like Shirley
MacLaine, she believed in reincarnation. "I brough
up her name," she said, "because to me that is par
of religion."

"Do you think Jennifer Levin is now some othe
form of life?" Fairstein asked.

"Do I have to answer that?" the woman asked. She
was excused.

One man in his fifties, asked about his relatives,
confided that he had not seen one son for more tha
twenty years. How come? "I don't know, he's a hippie
or something," said the father. "One day he told m
he was going to the mountains, and I haven't seen hin
since."

Litman advised one candidate to beware of news
paper stories. "Some of what you read in the press i
true," Litman said generously. "Most of it is not."

Pool reporters rotated in the voir dire room, two a
a time. The deal was that none of the candidate
actually selected for the Chambers jury would b
identified in print during the trial. Amazingly, the li
was kept on for five months.

By December 18 there were twelve jurors seated and four alternates.

The lucky dozen included four women and eight men. One of the women and two men were black. Of four alternates, one was a black man, another was an Asian woman. None of the women was over thirty-eight. Only three male jurors approached middle age.

Litman said the jury's average age was thirty-four. The forelady was a dazzling twenty-eight-year-old redhead named Cavanaugh.

"I had terrible concerns about the forelady," Fairstein said later. "[She] doesn't necessarily run the jury—but the fact that she was young, that she was Irish Catholic, that she was the oldest of five and had at least one brother, maybe two, in the same age range. Plus she's very different in life-style from Jennifer. She made a point in voir dire of saying that she never did the bar scene. And I could see that kind of almost disdain for the Jennifer life-style playing.

"She seemed on one hand tough as nails and very mature, and I believed that she could be fair. But I would never, had I not been already so low on challenges, taken her as a forelady in this case because it was just too obvious a chance to say: 'There but for the grace of God goes somebody in my family.' "

Bell told the jury the Chambers trial would start January 4 and last "six to eight weeks."

He was only off by a month.

Here is the hardy band of twelve jurors that spent three months judging Robert Chambers. Neither their names nor any other information about them, with minor exceptions, was known until it was all over.

#1 DEBRA CAVANAUGH, 28: Thick, long, curly auburn hair, small heart-shaped face, delicate features, petite frame. A fashion buyer, well dressed, wore only black, white, and rust colors. Obviously Irish but said she had no empathy for Chambers. For Levin? "Not at first, but yes." The forelady had a job awaiting her in London beginning March 1, 1988. She was very late.

#2 MIKE OGNIBENE, 30: Short, big-shouldered money-market analyst for foreign bank branch, also part-time assistant wrestling coach at Stuyvesant High—Jack Litman's alma mater. In voir dire Judge Bell said he liked the sport of professional wrestling. Ognibene said that was not a sport. Cocky.

#3 GERARD MOSCONI, 28: Biggest juror, 190-pound six-footer, owned computer graphics firm, described self as right-wing Republican. "The book in my briefcase is on the development of U.S. nuclear and thermonuclear warfare. I like aerospace technology." Too busy to read newspapers.

"All I knew was that they had met in a bar, they went to Central Park together, and some kind of sexual activity was going on, and she ended up dead. That's all I knew.

"The judge almost didn't believe me. He said, 'Really, you haven't read anything? What about the *Village Voice?* What about *New York* magazine?' I said, 'Look, Your Honor, nothing, zero.'

"Somebody else told me this was the Chambers case. . . . I said, 'Who's Chambers?' And they said, 'You know, Central Park.' And I said, 'Oh, okay.'

"They called me back a week or two later and said, 'Come in.' I expected a second interview. But they hauled myself and number four and five into the back room and said: 'Okay, stand against the wall. Raise your right hand and do you swear to decide this in a fair manner,' something to that effect. 'Okay, you're sworn, you can leave.' I said to the captain of the guard, 'What's going on? Are we on the case now, or is this like the second cut?' He said, 'No, you guys are jurors.'

"It was so alien to us. None of us really had any training. Very few of us were on trials before. [He never had been.]

"I was going skiing over Christmas and New Year's, so I was saying: 'Look, guys. When are you going to start? Give me an idea because I want to go skiing.' Finally they said, 'Go ahead, you can go, we're not going to start until January fourth.' And I was getting back on the third. So I went skiing, came back, and reported in January fourth."

#4 SHELLY FORMAN, late 40s: Sales exec in suit and tie, lived in same East Side high rise as defendant's current flame, Shawn Kovell. Maybe same floor. Told someone in the jury room. Probably told judge.

#5 ROBERT NICKEY, early 50s: Harlem mortician, dressed like one, snoozed occasionally in jury box. Wide awake when Mike Sheehan testified about defendant's lies. Lives half year in Florida, was in West Palm Beach when Chambers case broke. Knew nothing.

#6 JEANETTE, mid-30s: Only juror to keep identity secret after trial. West Indian origin, always dressed up, usually wore long hair piled up. Feisty, with a mind of her own. Has six-year-old daughter. Missed her during deliberations.

#7 GINNY HOESL, late 20s: Short blond hair, a bit chunky, got married December 18, joined husband in London four months later. Very serious in jury box but, others said, lots of fun.

#8 WAYNE GASTON, early 30s: Tall thin black man, worked as subway motorman. Charged racism and tried to bolt deliberations. Tried to sell his diary about Chambers jury duty after trial.

#9 COLE WALLACE, 31: Blond, slim, casually dressed in sweatshirt and Levi's jeans. Grew up in small town in Maine, attended University of Minnesota, works for Citibank now. Au courant, but knew nothing of Jennifer Levin's fate.

"My father had died that spring, so I went home almost every weekend, and in Maine you don't hear anything about anything. I tend to read just *The Wall Street Journal* and *The New York Times,* and I didn't even have the time for that then. And I just—there's so much murder and mayhem, I live in crack center down here—so I tend to stay away from it."

#10 ELIOT KORNHAUSER, early 30s: Medium-sized adman, likened lengthy voir dire to "Limboland." Started new job as trial began. "I read the newspaper coverage . . . I also as a former member of the press in college was well aware that you shouldn't believe everything you read."

#11 ELIZABETH BAUCH, 32: Light brown hair, very short and chesty in nice blouse and slacks. Smith College, Columbia grad school, wrote anthropology dissertation (on Peruvian labor problems) during trial. Took Ph.D. orals a month after trial. Small-town Iowa feminist from family of lawyers. She knew the drill in voir dire.

"They asked if I'd heard about the case. And I'd heard a lot. I'd heard the panty story obviously. I'd heard about the diary. I'd heard about underage drinking. I'd heard about the drugs. And I'd heard about the burglaries. All right? I'd heard a lot. I read papers 'd read the *Mademoiselle* piece. I read with interest but not absorption.''

They were down to no challenges? "I don't know. I think they still had one. I have one uncle who's a judge and was county prosecutor in Iowa. I have another uncle who was a county prosecutor. My dad is a lawyer. He doesn't do trials. My brother is a lawyer, he doesn't do trials. I've been going to courthouses since I was a very small girl.

"What else did they ask me? The standard questions. 'Have you been the victim of a crime?' Who in New York hasn't? . . . 'Would you be biased towards the prosecution because you have two former DAs in your family?' 'Do you think you can be fair and impartial?' Yes. I've had two days to think about it, and I really think I would be because I understood the gravity of it.

"I was sworn in December ninth. You know, the standard. 'Do you understand intent?' They defined intent. 'Do you understand burden of proof doesn't mean absolute proof?' Reasonable doubt is not a statistical measurement, it's reasonable doubt. Yes, yes, yes, yes. I must have given all the right answers because they couldn't dismiss me for cause or something. I don't know. I don't know why they kept me. I don't know.

"I kept hoping that they'd fill the box before they got to me. First of all, I was planning on getting out of it. I can't do this, I have this dissertation to do. This is a bad time, so I'm going to try and get out of it by asking the first judge I see.

"Of course, you only see clerks initially. Okay, when I get to the courtroom, I'm just going to explain to the judge, 'Excuse me, I have other things to do.' And then Robert Chambers walked in and I went, 'Oh, my God. This is major stuff.'

"He didn't antagonize me. . . . If I had been afraid

of him, I don't think I could have been on the jury. If
I had gotten a sense of anger during jury selection, I
don't think I could have been on that jury.''

#12 GUY GRAVENSON, late 40s: Greenwich Village
theorist battled nearly everyone in jury room, tried to
quit deliberations by claiming high blood pressure.
The last angry man.

Litman had a laundry list to clean up before the trial
could begin—for that matter, before most of the jurors
were seated.

"Several things, Your Honor, which I believe the
court must resolve, or at least give us guidance on
before we start," Litman said, "if we do. . . ."

The Justice for Jennifer buttons worn by members
of the Levin family had to go.

Of course, said Judge Bell.

Litman wanted to bar the Guardian Angels, a semi-
vigilante street brigade, from the courtroom. Its lead-
er's wife, the beauteous Lisa Sliwa, had a deep interest
in victims' rights and loved to raise hell. She brought
her muscled Red Beret legion to the suppression hearings.

Bell would not bar the Guardian Angels, but he
made them check their berets.

Next, Litman said he might want to double the
number of challenges he could make during jury selection because "three-feet high of prejudicial material
has surfaced in this case."

Decision reserved. Litman never did ask formally
for extra challenges.

A number of scientific experts were listed as potential prosecution witnesses. Litman wondered what
kind of evidence they would offer. He warned that
further pretrial hearings might be needed, for example

f newfangled scientific tests were used to analyze the bloodstains on Levin's denim jacket.

Decision reserved.

Litman now revived his suppression strategy. Its target was the Levin family's accusation that Chambers had robbed Jennifer of $70 her family said she was carrying that night and her rhinestone stud earrings.

The prosecution had photographs of Levin wearing earrings at Dorrian's just before she left with Chambers. And bartender John Zaccaro, Jr., was ready to testify that she told him there was "a lot of cash in her jacket" before he stashed it behind the bar.

No earrings or cash were found on her body. Her earrings were worth little but resembled diamonds. The cash seemed worth mentioning whether or not the DA claimed robbery by Chambers.

Thomas Kendris, co-prosecutor with Fairstein, fought hard to persuade Bell that Chambers could have killed Levin while robbing her. One theory was that she had caught him rifling her jacket.

"The most rational and reasonable argument that explains the missing money and the missing jewelry is that the defendant took them," Kendris insisted.

"It's a spurious allegation," Litman countered. "If they want to charge such a thing, they could have charged felony murder." Some thought prosecution would have been significantly easier if Morgenthau had charged felony murder, but proving it would have been a longshot.

Decision reserved.

Litman wanted a specific understanding about drug testimony. There must be no mention of Chambers' cocaine history, nor even of his two attempts at rehabilitation, Litman argued.

Fairstein had a witness who said he had smoked a marijuana joint with Robert outside Dorrian's that

night. She had other witnesses who would testify that
Chambers' "state of mind that night was hostility
depression, and anger."

When Litman pressed for a ruling on what he called
this "armchair psychology," Bell delivered. Prosecution witnesses could describe seeing Chambers smoke
a joint but could not evaluate his mood. Discussion of
his drug use beyond that one marijuana episode was
forbidden.

"I am concerned about putting into issue the background and reputation of the defendant," Bell said
That kind of testimony was prejudicial. Chambers was
on trial for murder, nothing else.

One December day a gossipy note ran in the *New
York Post*. Chambers was seen bringing his new cat
Gizmo, to the ASPCA for declawing. Whatever be-
came of Rasta?

Dorrian's Red Hand drew a ten-day suspension of
its liquor license and a $1,000 fine for serving minors
three months after the Levin tragedy. Jack Dorrian
charged persecution for having helped finance Chambers' bail bond.

New York State had just begun allowing cameras at
some trials, but Bell barred them from this one. Sex
testimony with cameras present would be an "inappropriate experiment," the judge said, and it might
intimidate four young women ready to testify.

With opening statements scheduled to begin on
Monday, January 4, Bell cranked out his final pair of
major decisions.

Both rulings went Litman's way, drawing him an
even 3–3 in key judicial decisions going into the trial.

First the judge scrapped any testimony that Chambers had robbed Levin. No claims of cash or jewelry
missing from her body could be mentioned at the trial

Bell even ordered the doctoring of Jennifer Levin

photos taken at Dorrian's on the night of the killing. Her earrings were clearly in place in the photos, but the jury would not see them. The earlobe would be taped.

While it was a setback for the prosecution and a shock to the Levins, the worst was yet to come.

It came on New Year's Eve, when Bell quietly issued a stunning decision that killed any mention to the jury that the defendant had told two sets of detailed lies to detectives at the Central Park precinct before his arrest for murder.

The judge was reversing his own October 16 decision granting prosecutors the right to use Chambers' bag of lies as evidence. It could have shed doubt on the truth of his videotape statement.

Chambers' long-awaited trial was due to start in just four days, but few New Yorkers and fewer news editors felt the impact of Bell's ruling. Most were completely oblivious that Thursday, on the brink of a huge four-day New Year's weekend that would even include a small wedding—my own.

But in the office of Chambers' prosecutor that day, Bell's ruling hit with the force of a bomb. Linda Fairstein's case had to be reconstructed almost overnight.

She learned that a November 24 decision by the New York Court of Appeals had restated some rules about self-incriminating statements made by suspects.

Prosecutors would have to notify defense counsel within fifteen days of arraignment about precise details of each such statement to be used as evidence, said the appellate court. Until then the fifteen-day deadline had been waived by judges who determined that a delay would not violate the defendant's rights.

The jury's awareness of the precise details of each Chambers lie at the precinct would prejudice his case, thus violating his constitutional right against self-incrimination. And while the November appellate ruling was not made retroactive, Judge Bell knew retroactivity could be imposed later. It could provide an appealable issue. It could trigger retrial of the Chambers case. Bell was unwilling to take that risk.

Only the five lies that Chambers briefly acknowledged on videotape would come before the jury. And four of the five were in essence the same lie:

1) A cat had scratched his face.
2) He had not been with Levin that night at all.
3) He had not left Dorrian's with her.
4) She had left him on 86th Street.
5) He knew nothing about her death.

Linda Fairstein remembered a long and depressing New Year's Eve.

"We had to regroup that afternoon and that night, working until very late . . . because of the time it took to understand the ruling. We really were quite stunned by the idea that every word in a ten-hour period, every detail of every lie, had to be noticed individually."

She never said much more than that about her disappointment. She didn't go public with it at all. But at four P.M. that holiday eve, Fairstein phoned her husband of seven months, lawyer Justin Feldman. He heard the dismay in her voice.

Tall, gray-haired, and courtly, Justin was at home when Linda got there just before the first midnight of 1988.

He had stopped at Tiffany's and bought her a New Year's Eve gift. She found it on her pillow.

10

THE TRIAL—Part I

On January 4, the first Monday of 1988, the Manhattan Criminal Court Building at 100 Centre Street buzzed in anticipation of its most kinky trial in, oh, several weeks.

It was tagged the "Preppy Murder Trial" to boost television news ratings and tabloid circulation. But by now Robert Emmet Chambers almost looked the part.

His appearance had changed in sixteen months. No longer was he the sullen teenage dropout who was led from the Central Park precinct in sweatpants and handcuffs to be charged with deliberately murdering Jennifer Levin.

When he walked into the crowded thirteenth-floor courtroom now, Chambers was a clean-cut young man of twenty-one wearing a dark suit and tie and a detached air, as though he were a character witness at someone else's trial.

Linda Fairstein, preparing to deliver her opening argument to the Chambers jury, was offended by his fake image.

"The whole—the misnomer that was put on it from day one—the 'Preppy'—he's no more a preppy than . . ." she fumed to me later. "He's a junkie, a thief who was thrown out of high school at sixteen for stealing a teacher's wallet and was institutionalized for drug detox, and he was stealing constantly after that—I have documentary proof.

"The kid is not a preppy, but once that headline came out . . . if he'd looked like Quasimodo, it wouldn't have been a big case."

Chambers' face was pastier and pudgier now. He seemed to have lost weight; the dark suit hung loosely.

As he sat down and slumped at the defense table between Jack Litman and Assistant Counsel Roger Stavis, thrusting his long frame under the table, the six-four defendant presented an absurdly low profile. He would stay in that position for most of the next three months, appearing a half head shorter than the five-nine Litman on his left and smaller next to the six-two Stavis.

Fairstein spent fifty minutes stating the case of the *People* v. *Robert Chambers* in her opening argument. She concluded by urging the jurors not to be fooled by Chambers' account of eighteen-year-old Jennifer Levin's accidental death during rough sex.

"Don't make the same mistake Jennifer Levin made. Don't trust this defendant," Fairstein said. "Don't believe his story."

Chambers stared into space for those fifty minutes. "He couldn't have showed less emotion if he had been made of wood," wrote *Newsday*'s Dennis Duggan.

Members of the Levin family sat behind a thirty-inch high barrier in the fifth row to the left of the spectators' aisle. They wore black clothing with dark glasses, but Steven Levin's full red beard seemed to glare angrily. He was graying at the temples.

On the right of the aisle, in the third row directly

behind Chambers, his parents and friends sat stoically. While there were no priests visible, the *Times* had run a quote that morning from Chambers' bail supervisor, Monsignor Thomas Leonard. He said:

"We would all hope that the trial will ascertain the degree of Robert's responsibility, and perhaps the degree of Jennifer's as well."

Litman was on his feet early with a motion that Chambers' videotape be shown to the jury as part of his seventy-minute opening argument. Fairstein's objection—"We have the right to determine when and how the evidence will be presented in this case"—was upheld by Judge Bell. He also denied Litman's motion to drop the alternate murder charge of depraved indifference.

Bell allowed Fairstein to introduce Chambers' unrepentant snarl to his father at the precinct: "That fucking bitch—why didn't she leave me alone?" But the judge reiterated his New Year's Eve decision to suppress the suspect's early series of lies to the police.

The heavy media coverage would focus on the major conflicts between Fairstein and Litman in their opening arguments. The issues included Chambers' motive, the significance of his lies, his rough sex scenario, the cause of Levin's wounds, and Chambers' behavior after her death.

But the most controversial question—was it an accident or was it murder?—dominated everyone's thoughts. The twelve jurors would have to answer it. The two lawyers now set out to persuade them.

On motive, Fairstein assured them that the law didn't require them to divine why Chambers killed Levin. The motive for what she called his "heinous crime" might remain "locked away in his mind," she said. Fairstein offered a theory—that they had quarreled over his indifference and that "his dislike turned to rage." Her only proof was Levin's "beaten and bruised" body—the "best evidence" of a violent struggle.

Litman countered: "Proving a motive is as important as proving evidence. Why would he want to kill her? They left Dorrian's in full view of the people in the bar. Why would he kill her, then stay there in view of the people who came by? 'Why' can't be proved. But it is a critical factor in deciding the criminal intent to kill."

On Chambers' lies, Fairstein said he tailored his story to fit when detectives pointed out inconsistencies. She argued that this showed Chambers to be "a quick and consummate liar" and rendered his final videotape statement worthless.

Litman said Chambers' cat scratch lie and his 86th Street lie "weren't cocky lies—they were obvious, silly lies" told by a frightened boy. He called his videotape version "unvarnished and untutored," thus addressing suspicions that such an original story had to be coached. For twelve hours "his only contact was with the police," observed Litman, not counting the cat.

On the rough sex issue, Fairstein called Chambers' scenario of masturbation and squeezed testicles a "complete fiction" designed to make Levin look "wild, kinky, or sexually unusual." Here Fairstein took a risk, possibly based on the fact that Chambers apparently was virile at nineteen and no semen was found.

But the prosecutor did not make that point. Her point was: "There was no sex that morning—only violence, only death."

The press and the public were dubious. After sixteen months of Chambers' rough sex scenario, Levin was branded as an insatiable wench flaunting her sexual liberation.

Litman told the jurors they would hear about Levin's "aggressive pursuit" of Chambers not from him, but from her own friends, who had been quoted in *Mademoiselle* and *New York* magazine. Litman questioned her friends about what they said in those interviews.

He told them how his client had struck out "in a frenzy" when he dealt the fatal blow "to ward off excruciating pain."

Then Litman retraced Chambers' entire rough sex scenario in case the jurors hadn't heard it. "She scratched his face, then sweet-talked him, sucking, then biting his fingers," Litman began. "He should have left then, but didn't."

The word "sucking" was new, albeit in a relatively innocent usage. Not even Chambers, so adept at innuendo, had used it. His four-page written statement said she kissed his fingers before biting them. He hadn't mentioned either action on videotape.

My thought was that Litman used "sucking" to deflect attention from something not even he could explain: why didn't deep finger bites—to the fat layer—propel Chambers out of the park? Why then let Levin handcuff him with her panties and squat on his face and torso? Was he showing his disinterest?

"She started to dig her fingers into his chest. Then she really hurt him, squeezing his testes," Litman went on. "He asked her to stop. She continued. He wriggled one arm free. In a frenzy, he reached up to grab Jennifer Levin to make her stop. He leaned up on his right hand while she still squeezed him. He grabbed and pulled back as hard as he could. She inevitably struggled with the pain and pressure against her neck, and he eventually flipped her over his shoulder."

That word "eventually" popped up in Ray Kerrison's column in the *New York Post*, so I knew at least two of us heard it. It didn't sound very "instantaneous"—Litman's usual word for Levin's death. But when I got a look at the trial transcript, there it was on page 164—''he eventually flipped her.'' I wondered how much time ''eventually'' really covered.

But true or false, the way Litman summed up the fatally erotic moment seemed to win wider acceptance than Fairstein's equally plausible ''no sex.'' Public conditioning does wonders.

On Levin's wounds, Fairstein said photographs of her badly scraped neck and chin and puffed left eye would show that Jennifer could not have died from a quick choke hold and flip. ''Her body is not going to lie to you,'' Fairstein told the jury.

Litman asked why Levin's clothes weren't ripped if there was a violent struggle. He said forensic experts would show that neck reflexes can react to a choke hold ''instantaneously''—that was his operative word—and can mean asphyxiation in ''less than fifteen seconds.''

On Chambers' response to Levin's death, Fairstein suggested that he first tried to make it look like a sexual assault by hiking Jennifer's miniskirt above her hips, her blouse and bra to her neck—although her own top medical witness would offer a conflicting theory. Fairstein noted that instead of summoning help, Chambers sat watching a biker discover the body, then ''coolly and calmly'' lingered to watch the cops buzz around.

''Cool and calm'' sounded unlikely in the circumstances, but that's what jogger Susan Bird had recalled. Litman told the jury Chambers was simply in a ''daze.'' Why else stick around? Hmmm.

Who was most to blame for Levin's death? Fairstein properly blamed Chambers' universally deceptive good looks. ''He was a dropout with no school to go to nor a job—only a facade of his looks to make him interesting to Jennifer Levin.'' Her parents, a row behind me, wept.

Litman surprised many who anticipated his standard blame-the-victim ploy, but others had no trouble recognizing it despite a new twist.

"No one here is faulting Jennifer Levin for aggressively pursuing or sexually pursuing Robert Chambers," Litman said unctuously. "Everyone in this courtroom would like to turn back the clock, but it cannot be done. This was a tragic accident—but not a heinous crime."

When Fairstein commented on the Levin family's suffering, Litman waited until the jurors were in recess before he objected.

"The deceased and her family should have no presence at this trial," Litman informed the judge. "The prosecution is weaving a picture of a wonderful Jennifer Levin as if only wonderful people have rights."

When the jurors returned, Bell lectured them. "You cannot have sympathy for the victim or the defendant. You must be neutral and decide only on evidence allowed in court and the exhibits agreed to. That's the yardstick you must use."

The defendant needed no sympathy, though. Bell's humanity was being crushed by a rigid criminal justice code.

That was Monday. For the next two days Litman stayed home with hoarseness and flu. He returned Thursday to cross-examine Pat Reilly, the cyclist who had found the body. Her story has been told in these pages. So has Litman's cat-and-mouse cross of the Nightwatch and Crime Scene Unit detectives who ineptly made hash of so much physical evidence within one hundred feet of Levin's body.

But some interesting postscripts came after the trial when I asked Fairstein and Litman about Reilly's runaway brown car, Sergeant Michalek's roped-off tire tracks, and other loose ends.

FAIRSTEIN: Jack Litman had at one time made a big point of telling us that he was going to possibly use a theory that Robert had hurt Jennifer badly and had left her, not knowing she was alive. And the brown car left the roadway and somebody got out of the brown car and finished her off. What does this mean? This means a brown car pulls up next to her and—choose any ethnic group that isn't on the jury—three Eskimos get out and beat the living daylights out of her. She's already in bad shape, and that's what killed her. And he was really going to go with this.

That caused us to speak to forty people who had seen the brown car at Ninetieth Street, enter the park, go down—we were working on things like that. We had the picture of the tire tracks, a complete red herring, but we couldn't ignore them. We thought he was going to use them in bigger doses than he did.

LITMAN: I'm not saying it was a car that drove up and dropped the body. Clearly not. Nor am I saying that it's a car that drove up and someone came out and killed Jennifer Levin. But it clearly could have been a car that drove up and ran over to the body and turned the body over. The way the body was found is not the way Robert Chambers left the body.

Clearly in my view someone else got to the body first and certainly had seen the body and just—run over to the body and said, "Hey, lady, are you okay?" And clearly a car could have done that.

The prosecution's theory is that it was a police car, you heard the testimony. The police officer [Michalek] saw the police car come up and turned his head for a second, turned back, the car's not there, and then he says to someone else, "Let's take photographs of it because who knows."

What can I say about that? I'm just trying to point out, as you do with a variety of things in a trial, that you just cannot accept at face value a person's testimony. But I didn't pursue that at great length. I'm not saying that the person who drove up in the car, if in fact a person drove up in a car, was a killer. That's not what I'm suggesting at all.

But that the body was moved, that someone carefully picked up the jacket and put it on the arm. I don't think Robert Chambers did that, I think someone else did that.

The defense side also had to overprepare for testimony on the ground disturbance near the crabapple tree, which was characterized by both Michalek and Detective Ferro as "drag marks."

LITMAN: Linda Fairstein, when she started the case, was going to put on the witness stand an expert who was going to say that the body was dragged from the second tree to the first tree. She abandoned that completely. As the witnesses are taking the witness stand, there's no way I know this. Indeed, at the sidebars the judge said, "You really shouldn't use the word 'dragged.' Are you going to have someone later who's going to actually be able to say this?"

"Oh yes," said the prosecutor. "We're going to produce a witness to that effect. We're going to produce an expert." So obviously I have to attack those police officers, a) because I don't think they're telling it the way it was, and b) because they are the predicate to this supposed expert.

The expert doesn't come up and people say, "Well, why did you attack the cops so much on an issue that didn't become an issue?" Why? Because by attacking them so much, showing that they were not credible, I stopped the prosecution from in fact making an issue of that which was all over the court papers that they told the judge they were going to make an issue of it.

We attacked some of this thing with the jacket. They were going to call experts to say this was definitely a gag, it was used to stifle her screams. Well, you didn't hear that at the trial. Why didn't you hear it? Maybe in part—maybe in part because of the cross-examination of some of the witnesses.

Watching Litman's courtroom technique with the cops who botched the park investigation, as demonstrated earlier, it was clear why he wanted to be a defense lawyer. Dueling with authoritative or privileged witnesses on cross-examination is his meat.

He doesn't talk party politics, but when I asked him why he became a defense attorney, Litman began by saying:

"I remember as a kid going to a rally in Union Square for the Rosenbergs in 1953, trying to protest— not trying to, but in fact protesting their, at that time, their impending execution."

At Harvard, "I had a double major in both theoretical math and French literature. And I had graduate full scholarships in both, but I didn't want to sit around working on theorems or just doing exigeses of literary pieces, I wanted to work with people. I guess I came awake to that my last year in college. I worked with disturbed youth, like being a Big Brother kind of thing—that kind of stuff.

"I wanted to work one on one with human beings, and I was taught by my parents to help people less fortunate than you, and that's the only reason I went to law school, was to become a criminal lawyer."

After graduation, Litman said, "I was offered a job by one of the best criminal lawyers in New York, Harris Steinberg, no longer alive. He said, 'Jack, you know, you can do very well here. The problem is you're a young guy, and when the clients come in and retain me, they're not going to give me their money for you to try the case. So if you want immediate courtroom experience, but not be inundated with cases, but be able to work and work very intensively on a case, you'd be much better off going with the prosecutor's office than being deluged at Legal Aid. And also, if you make a mistake, it's easier for the body politic to absorb it than for an individual.'

"So he suggested I cut my teeth on some serious trials in the DA's office. So I spent about five and a half years in the DA's office [under the late Frank Hogan in Manhattan]. I was given a lot of responsibility and handled very many major cases, and then I left and opened up my own firm."

The Chambers jurors respected Litman no matter which way they voted, juror Robert Nickey told me.

"When he got ready to cross-examine, one of us would whisper to the other one: 'It's showtime.'

"This is all professional, I understand that. It was part of his way of cross-examining a person. We would occasionally get annoyed, but we realized that he was just doing his job, as simple as that.

"To me it was a show. He was a hell of a lawyer. I got to say if I ever need a lawyer—of course, I can't afford him—but he's the one."

Betsy Shankin, who was closest to Jennifer Levin among the Dorrian's crowd, took the witness stand January 14.

Litman had repeatedly demonstrated in cross-examining police witnesses that Levin's nails were unbroken, raising doubt about her violent struggle with Chambers.

Fairstein, on direct examination, asks Betsy about Jennifer's fingernails. "She had beautiful nails, beautifully kept. Her nails were extremely strong," Shankin said.

Litman objected.

Judge Bell sustained it and told the jury: "Strike the words 'extremely strong' from your minds."

Shankin went on to testify that she bit her own nails. She said she used to refer to Levin as "Wilma Flintstone Fingers" because Levin rarely used nail hardener.

During a bench conference, Betsy started to eat something. Bell told her: "I know you're a youngster, but you can't eat in court."

Fairstein asked where Shankin went after Levin and Chambers left Dorrian's at 4:30 A.M. that August 26. She took her boyfriend Paul Delaney home and spent the night with him, Betsy said. The next night she was at the Central Park precinct for several hours of questioning and left about twelve-thirty in the morning, "with a police escort," she said. "They took me to Dorrian's."

Shankin identified a photograph as one taken at Dorrian's of Jennifer and two other girls. They all had their heads cocked, smiling broadly. The denim jacket hung from Jennifer's shoulder. Ellen Levin started to cry when she saw the photograph passing among the jurors. It was mounted briefly on an easel next to Shankin. She started to cry, too.

Chambers didn't look at it. Litman asked Shankin who took the picture and what time at night. She said: "I don't know."

Fairstein produced a torn piece of paper, which Shankin identified as half of a counterfeit dollar bill. She and Jen found it while going to work one day as they were paying the taxi driver. They ripped it in half.

FAIRSTEIN: Do you know where the other half is?

Litman objected. Bell overruled.

SHANKIN (*voice trembling*): In her coffin.

Litman was furious. Bell looked aghast. The Levin family broke into tears. Dan Levin exclaimed.

Bell admonished the jury: "You heard the answer to

the last question, and I must admonish you that you cannot let sympathy or prejudice affect your minds in any form or fashion. I realize that the answer may have caused you to feel some sympathy. If you do, then you're not doing your duty. You were chosen because you are men and women who could listen to the evidence, sift the evidence to determine who's telling the truth. Cast it from your minds. Decide on relevant material evidence. I believe you can and will do it.''

When Betsy Shankin faced cross-examination by Litman, she wore a black turtleneck sweater with the sleeves pushed up, pleated gray pants with a black belt. Her hair was pulled back on top so it didn't get into her face and she had earrings on. She also looked very wary.

But Litman surprised her by saying, "Good morning," and questioning her gently. His cross-examination of Shankin seemed easy—too easy, according to courthouse regulars. Mike Pearl offered the theory that Fairstein brought out all the bad things herself in hopes of softening them, but that might have backfired, allowing Litman to go easy. He could have looked like the heavy, beating up on an innocent teenage girl. Some jurors seemed to be expecting that, heads swiveling from Litman to Shankin and back again. They looked like spectators at a tennis match.

Instead, Litman was gentle. This was not his cup of cross. It only seemed rough when he began asking questions about Jennifer's diet pills. The press rows erupted in astonished whispers. Even the most stoical court observers agreed it was wrong if the over-the-counter diet pills could be brought up but Chambers' cocaine habit not mentioned.

In any case, Litman made it abundantly clear to the jury that this was Betsy Shankin, her best friend, testifying to Levin's sexual passion for Chambers and her pursuit of him.

Q: Sometime early in the morning Jennifer asked you to intercede with Robert, to speak to her outside. You refused initially?

A: Yes.

Q: Jennifer pursued you and asked you again, and you agreed?

A: Yes.

Q: When Robert and Jennifer left, you thought they were going to spend the night together?

A: Yes.

Q: And she looked happy? She was smiling?

A: At me she was.

Q: She understood what you said when you said, "I know what you're going to do"?

A: Yes.

Q: On the night of the twenty sixth, Jennifer told you about the sex they had together—didn't she also say something about Robert being handsome and sexy? Remember?

A: Yes.

Q: Do you remember Jennifer telling you she wanted to spend the night with Chambers?

A: No.

Q: Do you remember words to that effect?

A: No.

Q: But you knew what it was when you said to Jennifer, "I know what you're going to do?"

A: Yes.

Q: What you repeated of what she said about sex with him was her exact language?

A: Yeah, pretty much.

Alex LaGatta took the stand January 19. She told Fairstein on direct that she had seen Jennifer take an over-the-counter diet pill, Fibertrim, but not that night or all that weekend.

Fairstein evidently wanted to show that Levin wasn't the only teenager in her crowd acquainted with sex. LaGatta testified that when she left Dorrian's at two A.M. with Robbie Banker, she told Jennifer.

Q: You told her you were leaving with someone?

A: Yes, I told her I was leaving with Robbie. I didn't think he would stay all night.

Q: Did she think that?

A: No, she thought—

Litman objected. Bell cited rules of evidence.

A: Because she knew my parents would be furious. She knew my father was home.

Photos from Dorrian's were passed to the jury. "Don't even speculate about the piece of paper you see in one corner," said Bell. He was referring to tape over Jennifer's earlobe.

Following are excerpts from Litman's cross of LaGatta. He zeroed in on Levin's passion for Chambers. But he also took a stab at salvaging Chambers' lie about Levin going to see Brock Pernice. And he extracted LaGatta's published quote suggesting that Chambers was only a sex object to Levin.

Q: How many articles or books have you been interviewed for?

A: Two, one for *Mademoiselle* and one by Linda Wolfe.

Q: Jennifer was going to college in the Boston area?

A: Yes, so was Brock.

Q: She was supposed to go back to the Hamptons the next day with Brock, wasn't she?

A: No.

Q: Do you remember discussing with Jennifer if Chambers was good-looking?

A: Yes, we both agreed he was good-looking.

Q: Did she say he was good sexually?

A: Yes.

Q: Did she tell you that she didn't like him as a person?

A: Yes, she did.

Q: Did Jennifer tell you that she said to Chambers, "You're the best lay I've had all summer. I want to sleep with you again"? [The *Mademoiselle* quote.]

A: No, that's incorrect.

Q: Did Jennifer say, "You're the best sex I ever had"?

A: Something like that, not exactly those words.

Q: Did she tell you that she wanted to sleep with him that night?

A: No, she didn't say that.

Q: Did she also tell you that she told him, "I'd like to have sex with you again"?

A: I don't remember.

Q: Do you remember at the grand jury a few days later saying that? *(Shows her transcript.)* Now that you've refreshed your recollection that after Jennifer Levin told you that she told Robert that, she also said to you that she wanted to have sex with him again?

A: I just don't remember her saying it. I did say it to the grand jury.

Q: I ask you again if you remember Jennifer Levin telling you that she wanted to have sex with Robert again?

A: I just don't recall.

Q: At Dorrian's, when Jennifer Levin mentioned her conversation with Chambers, she said that Rob said to her: "You shouldn't have said that"?

A: You shouldn't have said that to me.

Edwina Early testified January 21. Litman's cross:

Q: Did you tell the police that Jennifer Levin was "definitely drunk" that night?

A: Yes I did.

Q: From what you saw and heard?

A: From what I saw.

Q: Did you go back to Dorrian's after going to the precinct?

A: Yes.

Larissa Thomson, the same day. Litman's cross:

Q: Jennifer told you that sex with Robert was the best sex, better than other times?

A: Yes.

Q: She told you that she wanted to spend the night with him?

A: Yes.

Q: You knew it was sexual?

A: Yes.

Q: Would you describe her as physically assertive?

A: Yes.

Q: She went after what she wanted?

A: Yes.

Q: Didn't you tell someone that she was determined to spend the night with Chambers?

A: It seemed that way.

Detective Frank Connelly, same day. Litman established an interesting fact that didn't come out on direct.

Q: Did you tell Phyllis Chambers that he would be home sometime soon?

A: I didn't, Detective Genova did.

BENCH CONFERENCE: Litman pointed out that Detective McEntee's testimony on Chambers' lie about the cat scratching his chest and stomach was not one of the five lies allowed in evidence. Only the lie about the cat scratching his face was allowed.

Bell offered to instruct the jury when he struck it from the record.

LITMAN: "I don't want you to remind the jury of it. What I want you to do is simply strike it from the record."

Detective Michael McEntee took the witness stand February 1 for four tough days. The first afternoon featured the playing of Chambers' video statement for the jury. The time came when Litman decided to show that Levin's panties were indeed stretched by Chambers' wrists, just as the defendant said. It provided some comedy relief.

He asked if Levin's dirty white panties, which McEntee found in the park, were stretched out. McEntee said he didn't know, he didn't know how big they were new, how many times they'd been worn or how many times they'd been washed. Litman produced LaGatta's identical new panties and had McEntee hold both pair together. They agreed the dirty panties were about an inch wider in the waist than the new ones.

Litman wanted McEntee to stand up—which he did—and put his hands behind him. Some members of the jury started to giggle. Judge Bell's mouth dropped open. Fairstein leaped to her feet, shouting, "Objection!" Bell sustained, told McEntee to sit down, and looked at Litman as if he were crazy.

Litman paraded both pairs of underpants in front of the jury so they could see the size difference.

Resuming his cross, Litman later wondered why McEntee didn't make Saracco aware he had found the panties. The ADA told Chambers no panties were found. Detective Sheehan concurred. Chambers said the panties must be there.

McEntee finally admitted he didn't want to interrupt

Saracco. He said Saracco was busy expressing his incredulity to Chambers.

Fairstein, on redirect, asked McEntee about Chambers' claim that he was in a "daze" after the fatal accident.

Q: Do you recall him talking about the woman with a bike, the ambulance arriving, the police officers taking pictures?

A: Yes, I do.

Q: Wouldn't you say that's a pretty observant daze?

Litman objected. Sarcasm was his thing. Bell sustained.

Q: Do you recall him on the video saying he lied to—

Litman objected. Fairstein showed him the videotape transcript and started reading aloud. Litman objected to a partial reading and said if she was going to use it, she should read the whole answer. A long bench conference ensued. Bell admonished the jurors to "disregard any statements about the stretching of the panties by anyone."

Litman recrossed McEntee. He asked him about the dirt on the panties in a sarcastic tone, casting doubt that McEntee could really remember that the back of the panties had more dirt than the front. He got McEntee to admit that he put 2200 hours on the arrest report, but that Chambers was not officially arrested until after midnight. McEntee said ten o'clock was the time he felt Chambers "was no longer free to leave the stationhouse."

During the next series of questions, Litman paced and yelled, sarcastically questioning what McEntee had said, repeatedly. When he questioned McEntee further about the note saying he had found panties, Litman said, "According to you," such a note was written. McEntee admitted the ten P.M. figure was on paper and that Chambers was not told he was under arrest at that time.

Litman moved on, asking in a more subdued tone if homicide cases weren't special. McEntee said all cases were important.

Q: Did you talk to the media on August 26?

A: I got some phone calls, yes.

Some cases, Litman had shown, were more important than others.

Litman wanted to show that his videotape interrogators tried to trick Chambers on the "missing" panties. He leaned on Mickey McEntee.

Q: Did you and the other detectives think it was a good ploy not to tell Chambers that the panties were found?

A: I can't testify as to what others were thinking. It was not part of any plan of mine not to tell him.

Q: Do you know where the note you wrote is now?

A: The note I wrote to Detective Sheehan?

Q: The note you say you wrote.

A: I don't know where it is.

Detective Michael Sheehan, the burly homicide detective, took the stand for three days through February 8. Litman's cross established that he helped Fairstein prepare her case. Chambers' video transcript ran fifty-nine pages. His statement written by Sheehan was four pages. Litman suggested that Sheehan left a lot out.

Q: There's no doubt that as you took this statement, Robert Chambers said he didn't intend to kill Jennifer Levin, not even to hurt her, simply to stop causing him pain. Do you agree that this is not in this statement?

A: I don't recall, but I'll accept what you say that it's not in there.

Q: And . . . he told you that after she tied up his hands with her panties, she pushed him to the ground—that's not written down.

A: That's correct.

Q: And he told you he was not taking her seriously when she tied him up, but you didn't write that down, did you?

A: True, but I've already testified to that.

Q: What I'm asking about—when he told you that before he was tied up, she would freak out and then apologize and be nice again—didn't he say that?

A: I don't recall.

Litman gives Sheehan a copy of his testimony.

Q: Do you agree that during the taking of the written statement, he'd say she freaked out and then apologized and that is not in the written statement, do you concede that?

A: I have to concede that, I'm taking your word for it.

Q: You saw him crying, right?

A: Yes, he filled up with tears.

Q: How many detectives were in the room with Chambers during the day—would you agree that it was eight to ten detectives?

A: Yes, that's right.

Q: Isn't eight to ten unusual?

A: Each case is different, but maybe it is.

Litman questioned Sheehan about Chambers' final statement.

Q: Voices were raised during the videotaping, both Chambers' and Saracco's?

A: Yes, sure.

Q: Would you say Saracco used a sarcastic tone?

A: Yes.

Q: Do you remember Saracco asking Chambers

about being tied up and then turning and asking, 'Detective, were any panties found in the park?'

A: He turned to me, not to Detective McEntee, who was on his right. I was sitting directly behind Saracco on his left shoulder.

Litman interrupts. Sheehan says, "Excuse me, Counselor," then finishes.

Q: You said that no panties were found by us?

A: That's right. I didn't find them with my partner.

Q: You're going to tell us that McEntee gave you something.

A: That's what I'm going to say.

Q: What happened?

A: He nudged me with his left elbow and gave me a note that said panties had been found. I placed it on the table next to Saracco's left hand.

Sheehan had arrived at the crime scene after nine A.M. and found more dirt on Levin's body than seen in earlier photos. Litman wanted to show that the cops mishandled the body.

Q: This is very important. When you got there, did you turn the body face down?

A: No.

Q: It didn't happen?

A: No.

Q: You testified that it had lots of dirt on the face, forehead, eyes, nose, ears, is that correct?

A: Yes.

Litman showed Sheehan photos taken before he got to the park and handed him a magnifying glass. "Use this if necessary, Detective," he said, playing Sherlock Holmes.

Q: Look at the photo, and you will notice clearly the dirt on the knee area but not see any on the face, forehead, eyes, ears—isn't that right?

A: There's not as much.

Q: You said she was covered with dirt?

A: Yes.

Q: You don't see any dirt on her face in these pictures, do you?

A: Not as much as I saw then.

Q: Someone turned her face down after this picture was taken?

A: I don't know that, sir.

Now Litman cross-examined Sheehan on his damage check of Chambers' genitals after midnight videotaping.

Q: You asked him to drop his sweatpants, and they went to his ankles?

A: Not that far.

Q: How far did they drop?

A: To my best recollection, not below the knee.

Q: Did you make a thorough inspection of the area?

A: I don't know what you mean.

Q: You looked at it.

A: Yes, I didn't see any trauma or scratch marks.

Q: Isn't it a fact that you looked very peripherally, if at all?

A: I didn't dwell on the area, no.

On February 17, Litman cross-examined two Central Park joggers. The first was Susan Bird, who had testified that Chambers was not "dazed" but watching the cops intently when she spoke with him at the crime scene. Litman explored her love life. He had done his homework, but his bid to discredit her went nowhere.

Next was Dr. Allen Garber, who'd jogged past the elm tree at 5:15 A.M. and told police the next day he saw "something sexual going on"—someone on top in a "rocking" motion, another person on the bottom. He now changed his story. He said he saw someone shaking what looked like a "lifeless body"—and saw it twice within sixteen minutes.

Litman went to work.

Q: It was closer to twenty minutes before you came back to that spot, wasn't it?

A: No.

Q: That's what you told the prosecutor?

A: If that's what you say I said, but it was a little less—sixteen, fifteen minutes.

Q: You told police that something sexual was going on, didn't you?

A: That's correct.

Q: Two people in the same spot, and the person on the bottom was not moving?

A: The person on the bottom was moved by the person on top.

Q: You're not mistaken about the location of your observation, are you?

A: No.

Q: Are you equally sure what you saw the first time and what you saw the second time?

A: I'm absolutely sure.

Q: On August 26, 1986, you were a doctor?

A: Yes.

Q: You saw what appeared to be a lifeless body?

A: Yes.

Q: And you didn't stop to help, isn't that true?

A: Yes, it is.

Q: On August 27, the events of the day before were fresh in your mind, weren't they?

A: Yes.

Q: Fresher than they are now?

A: Yes.

11

THE TRIAL—Part II

At first glance, it didn't look fair.

On the stand was Dr. Maria Luz Alandy, the pathologist who had worked at the city morgue only a month when she did the autopsy on Jennifer Levin. Cross-examining Alandy was Jack T. Litman, the clever scourge of unprepared witnesses.

Alandy spoke with a Filipino-Spanish accent in conversation, hesitating occasionally to find the right word. When talking about medical issues she was fluent and precise, the accent less pronounced. But she was still a rookie, not yet certified as a forensic pathologist, and Alandy looked vulnerable with her curly hair and round cheeks.

Her first courtroom clash with Litman on February 9 proved that appearances could be deceiving.

Litman had tried in vain to block admission of dozens of pre-autopsy morgue photographs. The natural settling of blood had made Levin's neck and chin wounds seem "more extensive," he maintained.

"Not exactly," Alandy said. "More prominent, not more extensive."

Her unflappable self-assurance was important. Alandy was the first of a series of prosecution doctors who would offer the jury "a reasonable degree of medical certainty" (a phrase included in every significant question) about the evidence in the case—opinions to be challenged by defense experts.

Fairstein had already lost two witnesses. The testimony of an EMS technician who recalled hearing Chambers say, "I hit something very hard"—explaining his fractured right pinkie knuckle—was barred as because it fell under the rules of medical confidentiality. A saliva expert offering a new method to analyze stains on Levin's denim jacket was barred because the method was too new. A lengthy closed hearing on saliva analysis produced nothing beyond the accurate spelling of "salivary amylase monoclonal antibody."

Litman had cast the medical witnesses early as the key to the trial's outcome. It began with Alandy, and by standing up to him on "more prominent" wounds, she gained stature. It was needed when Alandy had to explain a foul-up at the morgue.

The moldy condition of Levin's white sleeveless blouse had been mentioned by detectives who first saw it in the park, rolled up but intact. Fairstein asked Alandy about its deterioration.

Explaining that the blouse got wet on the freshly scrubbed autopsy block and then stored in a sealed plastic bag, Alandy said: "The ideal container is more porous so moisture doesn't accumulate, but in the absence of anything else, we used plastic garbage bags."

Fungus ate holes in the blood-speckled rayon blouse, destroying it as evidence. When the plastic bag was opened two months later, the blood could not be analyzed. It was not entirely Alandy's fault, but she took the blame.

She spent the rest of her first day in court testifying to the pinpoint petechial hemorrhages in Levin's eyelids, the basis of Alandy's conclusion that Levin was strangled. The next day Fairstein questioned her about Levin's more visible injuries.

Alandy's answers formed a blueprint of the victim's struggle to survive.

Fingernail scratches on the cheek could have been caused by the killer or by Levin herself, said Alandy, "trying to ward off compression of the neck."

A cut like the one in Levin's mouth, "on the tissue between the upper lip and the teeth in front," was usually caused "by a punch when the teeth are clenched," Alandy said. "It is also consistent with gagging or any force exerted on the mouth."

Fairstein steered her witness to the chin and neck areas.

"There were abrasions on the chin region. A fan-shaped one that measured from side to side two and a half by two and a half inches. A laceration on the left side of the chin, and to the right another abrasion. There were more linear markings on the chin, similar to those on the cheek."

On the neck there were "multiple horizontal abrasions covering the entire area, six inches by two inches—a lot of abrasions," said the pathologist. She also saw tiny gold flecks, which she lifted from the abrasions with Scotch tape and put into an evidence envelope.

In the park, Alandy had noticed the same rectangular neck mark that detectives saw, "slightly on the right side of the midline of the neck," she told Fairstein. "It looked like the point of an arrow."

Chambers on videotape had described his wristwatch coming in contact with Levin's neck as he yanked her with his left arm. Detective Sheehan sent the gold-trimmed watch to the morgue.

"We took a picture with the watch at the base of the neck," Alandy testified, "because it looked like the arrow was part of a boxlike pattern that could have been consistent with the face of the watch." Alandy had said that at a grand jury hearing. But Fairstein now raised doubts.

Q: Was the watch consistent with the injuries?

A: No.

Q: Can you state with a reasonable degree of medical certainty if you believe the watch caused any injuries?

A: Yes.

Q: Did they?

A: No. Today I know that it was not the watch.

The rectangular mark did not match the watch face.

Alandy stood by the jury box pointing out Levin's many injuries as the jurors grimly inspected each pre-autopsy photo. She returned to the stand to describe the autopsy procedure, including the Y-shaped incision into Levin's chest. The lungs were heavy with water, "more marked in the lower lobes," consistent with asphyxial death.

The jurors saw no stereotypes of strangulation, like bulging eyes or protruding tongue, so Alandy told them about the damage caused by pressure on the throat. It had been visible when she removed the neck organs—windpipe (trachea), voice box (larynx), esophagus, and tongue.

There was hemorrhaging everywhere. A horizontal sectioning showed an intramuscular hemorrhage on the inside of the tongue tip.

When did it occur? Fairstein had to establish that Levin was strangled in a struggle while still alive—not "accidentally" killed when Chambers flipped her, not "finished off" by someone from a brown car in the scenario Litman threatened to introduce.

"I believe all the injuries were ant-mortem [before death]," Alandy said. "It is almost impossible to sustain a postmortem injury to the neck, especially due to handling of the body."

On videotape Chambers had said that when he yanked Levin's neck, "it seemed like an instant. It must have been seconds. I wasn't holding her or anything." Fairstein now attacked that claim.

Alandy said Levin was not only held, but may have broken free several times and been repeatedly choked.

Q: How long was the pressure maintained on the neck?

A: I think for a considerable period of time, at least twenty to thirty seconds, possibly more. It looks like it was not maintained only once, but sort of repeatedly—some of the abrasions are more prominent than others.

Alandy said the force used was "quite strong."

Fairstein began to ask if Alandy thought Levin's wounds were consistent with Chambers' story, but Litman aborted the question with an objection. A bench conference ended the day with an eye-catching vignette—Judge Bell wrapped his arm around his neck as if simulating a strangulation.

At midday the media had been given copies of Chambers' videotape despite both lawyers' protest that it would sensationalize the case. TV reporters in court left to edit the video for their six P.M. news shows. Jurors craned their necks, wondering about the exodus.

Absent from all autopsy testimony was the victim's family. It was too "gruesome," Steven Levin told a TV interviewer. He said he was tormented by the thought that his daughter "spent the last few minutes of her life with someone who didn't care about her or value her."

On Alandy's third day, Fairstein posed her aborted question again, this time hypothetically.

"Assume Robert Chambers and Jennifer Levin are in Central Park, that she is five feet seven, 135 pounds, and he is six feet four, 190 pounds, that he is lying on the ground with his hands tied behind him, that he reaches up with his left hand . . . Is it your opinion that the injuries to Jennifer Levin's body could have come about—"

Litman, leaping to his feet, shouted his objection. "She left out that he was wearing a long-sleeve white shirt, that he was acting in a frenzy of pain, that he yanked, pulled, and grabbed at her—there are a whole series of actions described by Mr. Chambers that she left out."

Bell overruled him.

"I object!" Litman raged. "It is not a proper question for this witness!"

Bell told Fairstein: "Ask your question."

Q: Are the injuries consistent with the cause of death described?

A: The injuries are not consistent with that story.

Fairstein sat down. At 10:47 A.M. Litman opened his cross-examination of Dr. Alandy. His early questions were very tricky. He began with the subject of Levin's boxlike neck marks, which Litman called "squarish."

Q: This squarish area was approximately one and a half inches square?

A: That is not approximately, but exactly.

Q: In the grand jury you said the face of the watch was consistent with what you saw, isn't that correct?

A: No. [She had said it "could have been" consistent.]

Q: As you sit there now, you're telling us that the watch never came in contact with the neck?

A: No.

Q: Are you saying that it never left an imprint on the neck, are you telling us that?

A: No. [Only that it wasn't consistent.]

Q: Would you agree that the abrasions across the neck of Jennifer Levin are due in part or in whole to folds in the clothing fabric drawn across the neck?

A: Some abrasions may be consistent with them.

Q: Would you agree that they might come from fabric such as the sleeve of a shirt?

A: Yes.

Q: Would you agree that such abrasions are consistent with a long-sleeve shirt?

A: No, not in this case, they're not consistent. (*Alandy held out her left arm and motioned to show that folds in a long sleeve were vertical; the abrasions on Levin's neck were horizontal.*)

Q: Would you agree that some marks are friction marks, caused by friction from fabric?

A: Some may be caused by friction, but it was a rough material, not necessarily cloth.

Her definitive answers bothered Litman. At one point he challenged her description of the tongue hemorrhage.

Q: You mentioned a hemorrhage inside the tongue.

A: Along the tongue, yes—the hemorrhage was in the muscle along the tip.

Q: You wrote in the autopsy report, "in the tip of the tongue."

A: Along the tip of the tongue. My English isn't too good. I meant along the inside tip.

Alandy would not be destroyed, but Litman kept trying.

Q: This is the first time you've ever testified in court in this type of strangulation case?

A: Yes.

Q: You have no problem saying it was compression of the neck?

A: Strangulation is compression of the neck.

To counter the prosecution's strangulation theory, Litman in his opening argument had suggested that Levin died of simple heart stoppage caused by pressure on a portion of the neck's carotid arteries known as the carotid sinus.

He now offered this theory to Alandy. She wasn't buying.

Q: In some degrees of compression, there frequently develops in death a phenomena called cardiac inhibition, do you agree?

A: I agree with everything you said but the word "frequently."

Q: In a case of asphyxia caused by compression of the neck, the cartoid sinus reflex can intervene at any time, can't it?

A: It can, that's right.

Q: It complicates the effect if the person is struggling, doesn't it?

A: Yes.

Q: Some abrasions were caused by the deceased moving against whatever fabric was held against the neck, weren't they?

A: Yes.

Q: That curtails the asphyxial period, doesn't it?

A: Yes, if you mean shorten.

Q: And emotion or tension heightens and facilitates that response, do you agree to that?

A: In some respects.

Q: The sort of emotion that can occur when one is surprised during some sort of sexual encounter?

A: Possibly.

Q: And the more the victim acts to free the airway, the shorter the survival period?

A: Yes.

Q: Doctor, it is not unusual for an arm around the neck, pulling back, to cause the kind of injuries you saw—is that correct?

A: That's right. If the armlock is applied for a considerable amount of time, yes—if it's just for an instant, no.

Litman attacked her estimated time of Levin's neck compression. Alandy conceded she told the grand jury Levin was strangled for fifteen to twenty seconds. Here she had testified it was at least twenty to thirty seconds—possibly more than a minute.

Q: In your view, those abrasions on the neck that you saw could not have been sustained in less than twenty seconds?

A: If you're saying nineteen and a half, maybe, but not two or three seconds versus twenty.

Q: You understand that reasonable pathologists, particularly in cases of asphyxia death, may differ with that estimate?

A: Oh, definitely, yes.

The last answer was what made the papers—along with Alandy having doubled the time span to thirty seconds or more. It looked like being strangled for fifteen seconds was nothing.

A four-day weekend intervened (Monday was Presidents Day) before Alandy returned for her final day on the witness stand.

Litman tried to sow as much doubt as he could before the prosecution's rookie pathologist departed. Returning to the squarish bruise, he asked: "Will you admit or deny some impressions on the neck came from the watch?"

"No, the watch had nothing to do with it," Alandy said.

"You're as sure of that as you are of everything

else, aren't you?" said Litman, ending his cross on a bitter note.

Fairstein tried to clear up a few things.

Q: You were asked questions by Mr. Litman about the carotid sinus reflex. Tell us about it.

A: The carotid sinus reflex can be a cause of death in neck compressions cases, but it is not frequent. In a situation where the neck is compressed, not all of us will suddenly die. Some people are more prone to unconsciousness, especially those over forty, mostly male, with undiagnosed heart or cardiac disease, people on drugs to correct arrhythmia or who show signs of psychotic behavior. In a young, normal person, carotid sinus reflex is not a normal cause of death.

Alandy also made the point that injuries like Levin's were almost completely inconsistent with such a diagnosis. "The absence of any external injuries is one of the hallmarks of carotid sinus reflex."

Finally, Alandy had testified that a blood alcohol level of .10 percent meant legal intoxication and that Levin's level was only .06 percent. Litman countered that a level of .05 percent was considered "under the influence." Fairstein now asked just what a .06 percent level meant.

"It was enough to reduce inhibitions and increase a feeling of self-confidence," Alandy said, "but not high enough to make someone irrational."

Litman returned to cite choke hold analyses by Dr. Ronald Kornblum—later to appear as Litman's witness. Alandy agreed that death could result from the kind of single-arm choke hold that Chambers described—but she insisted that was not how Jennifer Levin died. Choke hold deaths were very quick, with few bruises. Levin's death took at least twenty seconds, with massive bruising.

It was February 16 now, and it was over. For four

days, Maria Luz Alandy had more than held her own with Jack Litman.

The prosecution's next expert witness took only a few minutes on February 17. Detective Nicholas Petraco, a police laboratory expert on trace evidence, testified about the gold flecks on Levin's neck. Petraco identified them as mica found in the soil of Central Park. They were not from Chambers' watch.

On February 18, Larissa Thomson's photos of Jennifer's last party at Dorrian's were released to the press. One shot showed her earlobe taped, requiring a captioned explanation of her missing earrings. Litman denied that his client robbed Levin. Jennifer's sister, Danielle Roberts, twenty-three, gave birth to her first child, a daughter. The baby was named Samantha Jennifer.

Dr. Robert Shaler took the stand February 22, primarily to testify that Chambers' blood type was found in about half the bloodstains on Levin's denim jacket. That was the jacket Chambers denied knowing anything about in his videotape statement, insisting the jacket didn't matter—"the most important thing was just explaining to her that I wanted nothing to do with her, and that she was bothering me."

Another day, another doctor—Frederick Gutman, who in 1986 was the Metropolitan Hospital emergency room resident who examined Chambers' bites and scratches five hours after his arrest. Gutman testified that the bite mark on Chambers' right third finger was "deep enough to go through the surface of the skin to the fat layer." Gutman also looked at X rays of Chambers' fractured right pinkie knuckle—the one Chambers said he fell on while yanking Levin's neck. The question arose whether the bone break was a "boxer's fracture"—from a thrown punch. "I don't think so," said Dr. Gutman, admitting he was only a neurosurgeon. He was excused.

Dr. Werner Spitz, chief medical examiner of Detroit, had a gray crewcut, horn-rimmed glasses, and a heavy Austrian accent. He showed his impatience with the proceedings as soon as he mounted the witness stand on February 24.

A possession problem quickly became apparent. Whose witness was this? Litman argued that since he was the first to contact him in this case, Spitz shouldn't be allowed to testify for the prosecution. A procedural hearing was conducted with the jury absent. As Litman questioned Spitz, there was obviously no love lost. But some of their exchanges were low comedy.

Q: Do you remember your first contact with me?

A: I think so—vaguely.

Q: Is it fair to say that you and I spoke just before January 23, 1987?

A: I have a note—on my way out of my office, either Christmas Eve or New Year's Eve, the phone rang and I picked it up and you were on it.

Q: And we agreed that what I sent and discussed would be in confidence between us?

A: Yes, and I assure you it was.

Q: We had a conversation two days in a row, don't you recall them?

A: No. I have no recollection of speaking to you more than once. I don't think I'll forget that phone call for a long time.

Q: In that call, did I convey to you ideas, suppositions, I had about this case?

A: It was a shouting match, and you paid no attention to what I said. You tried to influence my opinions.

Q: Did I give you information not contained in the materials sent to you?

A: If you did, it was of such minor significance or no significance that I don't remember that you did.

Q: Did you tell me that if you were useful to me, that would be fine and I could call you back?

A: You asked me to send you a bill, and I said I was not going to. You said, "I want you to send a bill." Eventually I said: "Mr. Litman, I'm not going to send you a bill. I'm sending you back the pictures. If you want to call me again, do so." I did not want to be retained in this case by you.

Q: Do you remember my telling you things that Chambers had said?

A: Maybe, I don't recall. I felt bulldozed, and I completely turned you off. That may be your style of conversation, but when that happens, I turn off. I was on the phone, but I wasn't listening to what you were saying.

It went on and on. Fairstein finally objected: "This was supposed to be a short hearing." Judge Bell begged for a lunch recess, but Litman wasn't quite finished.

Q: Is it your recollection that I was telling you about this case?

A: No, what you were telling me was how my opinion was wrong and it should be different.

Litman flushed bright red at least three times while questioning Spitz but managed to keep his temper in check.

Spitz was cleared to testify that afternoon.

Ellen Levin held a walnut in her palm. It was encrusted with fake pearls and shellacked. Once she showed it to her former husband, seated next to her, and he patted her shoulder. A few months later Ellen told Larry King on his CNN talk show that the walnut was made by a friend when Jennifer was little. Jennifer carried it as a good-luck charm.

"I eventually got it back," Ellen Levin said sadly. Jennifer did not carry it to Central Park.

Spitz told the jury he was educated in Europe and Israel, took part in investigating both Kennedy assassinations, and had performed sixty thousand autopsies in thirty-five years, many thousands of them involving asphyxial death. He assured the jury that Levin died of strangulation, based on his review of the autopsy and the damage to her neck.

Spitz also had an opinion about the exact manner of her death. "I noticed two patterns that could have been inflicted in only one way," he said, "and this is how she died."

He held up a bright pink blouse, which he said was identical except for its color with the one worn by Levin that night—the same material, same embroidery, same style, same manufacturer.

"Your Honor, I would like to have a volunteer to show how this works," Spitz said, startling the courtroom.

Fairstein volunteered, but Bell preferred using court officer James O'Neill. Litman objected.

"I can't do it on myself," Spitz said. "I have to have someone else hold it. I only have two hands. Someone has to hold the blouse. I tried to do it in front of a mirror, and I'm too awkward. You have to hold the blouse, then take the blouse the way it was taken at the time of death and twist it the way it was twisted to cause the patterns."

Bell was intrigued. "You're saying with a reasonable degree of medical certainty that the blouse was twisted?"

"That's right," Spitz said. "I need to have the blouse held with the straps taut as if it were worn to show how the damage was inflicted." He showed the jury a photo of Levin's neck bruises.

"The first pattern is on the right side of the neck—a diagonal line—with another diagonal on the left side of the neck, the two patterns which are arrow-shaped. The blouse was pulled up and twisted in a fist—and at one point the decedent was able to pull it down briefly."

He used more vivid language later, saying: "She pulled out of the noose." The blouse became "the noose."

Back on the witness stand, Spitz started to explain. "During the struggle—"

That was too much for Litman. The judge told Spitz to confine himself to the blouse-as-noose theory. And moments later, Spitz's demonstration of his theory became the prosecution's first detailed scenario of how Jennifer Levin had died.

James O'Neill assisted. The young blond court officer's distinctive haircut had earned him the pressroom nickname "Duran Duran," after a celebrated rock group, and now he was onstage.

O'Neill held Spitz's pink blouse by the shoulders, in front of him.

Spitz grabbed the front of the blouse in his fist. Suddenly he twisted it hard and bunched it at O'Neill's throat in one swift motion. His knuckles scraped O'Neill's chin.

The courtroom crowd gasped. Chambers looked exasperated, spreading his hands in disbelief. Steve and Ellen Levin walked out briefly.

"I didn't know about the blouse," said Jennifer's mother. "There's a lot I'm hearing for the first time. It keeps getting worse and worse. We're filled with emotion. There's only so much you can take."

Spitz vehemently disputed Chambers' shirt-sleeve scenario. "It was not caused by a man's shirt," he said. "There are certain injuries with a structure that indicate the mechanism."

Fairstein then asked him about Chambers' watch.

"None of the injuries in the pictures are consistent with the watch," he said. "The area on the right side of the neck surrounded by squares was not caused by the face of the watch. The face would not leave marks—only the frame of the face might leave an injury and then only a faint line. The size doesn't match the face. The marks on the side of the neck were not caused by links in the bracelet," Spitz said, meaning the watchband.

Fairstein asked him about choke holds. "In a bar-arm choke hold," Spitz said, "one arm is across the neck and the other hand is used to pull that arm back. In a carotid hold, the forearm presses the carotid artery on one side, the biceps hold the other and the crook of the arm is open. This presses the carotid arteries—not the front of the neck.

"Under no circumstances was this caused by a choke hold. The pattern on her neck doesn't support it. The carotid hold wouldn't have left the injuries on the front of the neck."

And a bar-arm hold?

"A bar-arm hold might have caused some of the injuries in front, but not those on the side. And it would have broken the gristle on the front of the neck."

Spitz sounded authoritative. He confirmed Alandy's findings that all Levin's bruises were inflicted before death—and his estimate of the time of neck compression exceeded Alandy's.

"It is my opinion that the duration of the cause of death was several minutes," Spitz testified. "Most of us can hold our breath for a minute or so without a problem. If you swallow at the end of that time, you have another ten or fifteen seconds. People do this by reflex."

Fairstein asked him what was the shortest possible time Levin was strangled.

"Yes, the longest is several minutes," Werner Spitz repeated. "The shorter time would be caused by the tremendous commotion of fear and frenzy that she experienced. It shortens the period of oxygen depletion and makes everything happen faster, perhaps as little as thirty seconds."

Had he ever certified a death due to cardiac inhibition?

"No, I have not. No pathologist anywhere has ever seen a death by cardiac inhibition. It is not a pathological entity. Pathologists shy away from diagnoses that are not documentable. Cardiac inhibition is a hypothesis brought about to explain things inexplicable in 1896. Today we know better and look for documentable causes."

Litman didn't like that answer. A long bench conference interrupted Spitz. Objections weren't enough for Litman. I counted sixteen bench conferences consuming well over an hour. Three times, Litman demanded a mistrial. He complained that Fairstein presented Spitz as a "pseudogod," and Bell asked if Litman thought the witness had a "vendetta" against him.

This time Bell dismissed the jury for the rest of that Wednesday, announcing that Dr. Spitz would not be back on the stand until Monday. Everyone breathed a sigh of relief.

Dr. Robert Beasley, a surgeon who had written a book called *Hand Injuries*, now volunteered to testify without charge as the prosecution's twenty-fifth and final witness, to "tell the truth" about Chambers' fractured pinkie bone.

It resulted from a punch of "high velocity, high

impact, like that in fistfights—amateur fistfights," Beasley said. "Professional boxers don't sustain injuries of this kind. This is the classic picture of a wild swing of a forcible nature striking a hard object."

He said it was "absolutely impossible" that Chambers sustained such a fracture falling on his pinkie. "The momentum and the velocity aren't enough to sustain an injury in that manner."

Litman couldn't shake him.

February 29 was leap year day—the trial's ninth Monday, exceeding Bell's six-to-eight-week promise to jurors with Litman's defense case still unheard.

Spitz returned to the stand as promised—again disputing Chambers' story that he yanked Levin's neck from behind. Spitz insisted the assailant was in front of her.

"The noose was tightened from in front. The struggle was in front. There is no doubt in my mind that this was a frontal confrontation."

Fairstein then tried several times to ask Spitz why the blouse did not tear during the struggle. Each time, Litman objected for a long bench conference. Fairstein finally found the proper wording. She asked Spitz if the blouse did not rip because it was bunched against Levin's body, not pulled apart.

Spitz gave his shortest answer in two days: "Yes."

When asked how Levin's total injuries were sustained, he responded quickly—before Litman's inevitable objection. "There was a violent altercation culminating in strangulation using the victim's blouse as a noose," he said.

"I move," said Litman, "to strike the answer and approach the bench."

After twenty-five minutes of legal arguments, Bell informed the jury: "I'm going to strike the last answer of Dr. Spitz."

Fairstein then delivered the world's most self-assured pathologist to Jack Litman's tender mercies.

The master of cross-examination began by seemingly searching for some common ground with Dr. Werner Spitz.

Q: Do you think the *Essentials of Forensic Medicine* is an authoritative text?

A: Certain parts of it are authoritative. In others, I consider the book unreliable. It is British. I rely on American books. They're better organized.

Q: How about Dr. Ronald Kornblum as an authority for a pathologist?

A: Yes. Dr. Kornblum trained in a place where I was head of the training program.

That drew appreciative chuckles. But Litman, as usual, had done his homework. He cited two British doctor-authors and asked if they were experts.

A: I never had the honor of meeting them.

Q: Did you lie under oath when you swore in Connecticut on July 12, 1977, and you said you knew them personally. Did you lie under oath?

A: I assume I testified. I never lie.

Q: You never lie except when it is convenient?

A: May I explain?

Q: No, you may not.

Litman then reminded the jury again of the strangulation stereotypes not present in Levin's autopsy.

Q: Do you agree that in many asphyxia victims the face is puffy, the eyeballs protrude, the tongue may hang out, there may be bleeding from the nose and/or ears?

A: It may happen.

Q: It didn't happen here?

A: Not puffy, the face was dusky.

Q: Eyes weren't bulging?

A: The left eye was bulging.

Q: You said that was the result of a trauma?

A: It was probably the result of a trauma, but I don't know what else.

Q: There was no bleeding from the nose or ears?

A: That's correct.

After the trial, Litman told me that Spitz's demonstration of the twisted blouse as a murder weapon was the first he knew of it. But he showed no sign of intimidation by it.

Q: Did you demonstrate for the jury the manner in which, according to you, the blouse was tightened like a rope?

A: Yes.

Q: It was grabbed in front, in the area of the buttons?

A: Yes.

Q: When it was grabbed in front, was it grabbed from both the top and the bottom at the same time?

A: I don't understand what you mean by the same time.

Draping Spitz's pink blouse over his own shoulders, Litman demonstrated.

Q: Grabbed like this at the same time?

A: I think it was like that.

Q: Was the thumb on the top and the rest of the fingers beneath, or reverse with the thumb on the bottom?

A: May I see the blouse? I think the thumb was inside.

Q: Meaning the four other fingers were on top?

A: Yes.

Q: With what hand was it grabbed?

A: I have no idea.

Q: Was it grabbed with one hand or two hands?

A: I don't know. I surmise it was grabbed with one hand, but I don't have any anatomical evidence for that.

Q: How many times was it turned?

A: Once each—there were two such manipulations.

Q: After it was turned once, Miss Levin moved the blouse down?

A: Yes.

Q: Then it was turned a second time?

A: Yes.

Q: When it was turned once, how long did the blouse remain tightened around her neck?

A: I don't know.

Q: Did it last for more than a minute?

A: I don't know.

Q: Did it last for more than two minutes?

A: I don't know. I can only tell you how long it lasted overall.

Q: Overall, your testimony was that it was tightened like a noose for several minutes, right?

A: Yes.

Q: Does several minutes mean four or five minutes to you?

A: Several minutes means until death.

Q: What does the word "several" mean—two, three, four, five, six?

A: More than two.

Q: When you look at that, you can't tell us which of those two manipulations lasted for more than a minute?

A: No, I can't.

Q: One of them had to, didn't it?

A: Yes.

Q: Which one?

A: I don't know.

Q: When the blouse was tightened, the person doing the turning and Miss Levin were essentially face to face?

A: Yes.

Q: When the blouse was turned taut around the neck and face to face, was Miss Levin standing up?

A: I don't know.

Q: Was Miss Levin kneeling?

A: I don't know.

Q: Was she on her back on the ground?

A: She may have been, but I don't know for sure. There is nothing anatomical on which to base what exact position she was.

Q: With respect to the second manipulation, the tightening of a noose taut around the neck, were they standing up then?

A: I have nothing concrete to base an answer on.

Q: It resulted from the blouse being turned tight like a rope?

A: That's correct—and the pressure in front of her.

Q: The back of the blouse was in its normal position at the time of the first manipulation?

A: I don't know that.

Q: Are you telling us anything was done to the back of the blouse when it was grabbed in front and twisted?

A: I don't know that.

Q: In respect to the second manipulation, anything done to the back of the blouse then?

A: I don't know.

Q: A person on her back on the ground, struggling for the better part of two minutes, you would see something on the shoulder blades, wouldn't you?

A: Maybe you would and maybe you wouldn't.

Q: But you don't see anything in this case, isn't that right?

A: That's right.

Having shown that Spitz didn't know everything, Litman now grilled him on choke hold studies by several pathologists. This was to focus the jury on the defense's core argument—that Levin died instantaneously from a nerve reflex that stopped her heart.

Spitz conceded only that the average time before loss of consciousness for a group of big Seattle policemen in one choke hold study was 7.5 seconds. For him, a huge concession.

Litman's three-and-a-half-hour cross-examination was a thing of thunder and lightning fueled by the mutual dislike of two opinionated men. Whatever one proposed, the other would oppose on principle. Linda Fairstein saw two of a kind.

Spitz was frustrated by questions requiring a yes-or-no answer, and when he tried to cheat with a detailed answer, Litman would slap him down with a curt "Just answer the question, Doctor—yes or no." Sometimes Litman would have the poor judge do that.

Spitz's Austrian accent gave him extra force. Litman would occasionally play off that, peppering his questions with a soft "If you would be so kind" or "If you please." Then he would let fly with a zinger.

It was like an opera. And for the climactic scene of the day, Litman challenged Spitz's noose theory.

Q: It is your view that this is a case of ligature strangulation, correct?

A: If you consider the blouse a ligature, yes.

Q: You consider the blouse a ligature, correct?

A: That's correct.

Q: It is a ligature when something encircles the neck and leaves what is called a ligature furrow, isn't that right?

A: It could be that.

Q: You don't find a ligature furrow in this case, do you?

A: That's correct, it's not typical of the run-of-the-mill ligatures. It was clothing used like a rope, but it's not a rope.

Q: There are no marks on the back?

A: Correct.

Q: There are no marks on the side?

A: Correct.

Q: Do we agree that a ligature furrow is left by pressure and not by friction?

A: In the case of strangulation, it is usual that it is left by pressure and friction. In the case of hanging, it's a different matter.

Q: What part of the blouse was on the back of the neck?

A: The back by the label had been moved about.

Q: This is the part of the blouse that encircled the neck, the back of it?

A: I'm not sure.

Q: I'm asking what part of the blouse was taut against the neck?

A: I can't tell.

Q: But you're sure the blouse formed a ligature, aren't you?

A: Yes. It left no mark on the back, so we can't be sure.

Q: Then tell us which part of the blouse was pressed against the sides of the neck?

A: It left no mark on the sides, so we can't be sure.

Shouting and gesturing, Litman threw down the gauntlet.

"I'm challenging you, Doctor, to tell us how the blouse was tightened into a rope around her neck! Can you or can't you tell us which part was against the side of her neck?"

A: I can't tell you.

Q: The fact is that you can't do it, can you?

A: If you want, I'll demonstrate to you right now—on yourself!!

Litman looked at Spitz contemptuously. Spitz was half crouched, shaking a finger at him furiously.

Litman said, "Tomorrow, we'll get someone of the same height and wearing the same blouse, and you can demonstrate and show the jury that it can't be done!"

Fairstein cried, "Objection! I tried to do that, and Mr. Litman objected. He's just grandstanding in front of the jury!"

"I'll take someone from the audience for a demonstration right now," replied Litman.

Bell decided to hold the demonstration the next day.

When the judge entered at 10:10 A.M. on March 1, Fairstein was livid. She complained that Litman was running the trial.

That riled Bell. "No one takes over Judge Bell's courtroom," he said. "I am running this court. I'm not going to run roughshod over a lawyer, but I have the power of contempt, and I will use it unsparingly on anyone. Mr. Litman is not running this court, I am."

He paused and peered at Litman. "Mr. Litman, you seem to be staring at me in an arrogant manner," he said.

Litman turned away. The tension at the Chambers trial was getting thicker.

Litman needed a model to demonstrate that Spitz's noose theory couldn't work. Judge Bell volunteered his secretary, then realized she would have to give her height and weight in open court. Litman summoned Elizabeth Weinfeld, twenty-one, who was seated with the Chambers family. Slender, with short curly hair, she wore wire-rimmed glasses, a long black oversize T-shirt, black racing tights, and black sneakers. Litman gave her another pink blouse identical to Jennifer's.

Chambers showed one of his few signs of animation, still expressionless but sitting turned toward the jury, chin in hand, watching intently.

Spitz approached Weinfeld. Facing the jury box, he seized the front of her pink blouse—supplied by Litman, who now began a running commentary.

"Is it fair to say, Doctor, that you've grabbed the front of the blouse with your fist, your thumb over the bottom of the blouse and the other four fingers at the neckline, and now you're raising your fist and twisting the blouse into a knot? Where is your other hand? Oh, it's holding up the back of the blouse, is that what happened, Doctor?"

Fairstein objected, and Bell tried to restore order. "Doctor, tell us what you're doing," said the judge. "Did he leave anything out of his description?"

Spitz seized the blouse again. Litman spoke immediately.

Q: Did you pick up the blouse with your thumb at the bottom and your fingers at the top?

A: Yes.

Litman resumed his disruption. "The doctor has the blouse in front, holding the blouse in the back. Can the young lady turn around so the jury can see how he's holding the blouse up in the back? Now the doctor is letting go of the back of the blouse. Now the doctor is turning his hand. He asked the young lady to hold her hands bent at the elbow upward. She's holding the blouse just inside the shoulder straps with the knuckles outward."

The judge advised the jury that Litman was providing a verbal record needed for the trial transcript. Fairstein objected. "If the doctor can't make his own verbal record, then Mr. Litman can add to it," she said. "But Mr. Litman is testifying."

Litman continued verbalizing. With each interruption Spitz dropped his hand, then started over. As Litman talked, his hands fluttered around Spitz, waving in front of his face, pushing the model, getting in the way. "The doctor has folded the blouse forward, his thumb now on top. The doctor now pushed up the blouse at the back."

Bell explained, "He has his hand basically in the middle of the blouse in the back."

To the model, Spitz said, "What I'd like you to do is sometime try to remove what I'm doing—use your neck to stop it."

Elizabeth Weinfeld stood with arms straight at her side, neck stretched. Spitz twisted the blouse in his right fist, jamming it against her throat while his left hand cupped her head. Litman talked.

Q: What is making contact—between the lady's neck and the blouse—is his hand. Am I describing it correctly?

A: No, you're not.

Q: That, Doctor, is a noose twisted taut around her neck like a rope?

A: You're speaking out of context.

Q: Did you tell Miss Fairstein yesterday that was how the blouse was twisted, like a rope?

A: Yes—and like clothing, Mr. Litman.

Q: I'm asking you what part of the blouse was taut against the back of Jennifer Levin's neck. You said absolutely that's the way it happened.

A: Correct—and I'll say it again.

During a recess, Ellen Levin told me she'd have volunteered as the model victim if the model male assailant were six-four and 190.

Fairstein took center stage that afternoon and asked: "Now may we do a demonstration with someone from my office, Your Honor?"

Replied Bell: "Bring your person forward."

Christina Callahan came forward. She was twenty-two and worked as a trial preparation assistant in Fairstein's office. Callahan bore a startling resemblance to Jennifer Levin.

Fairstein pulled out the same pink blouse Spitz used on O'Neill. Litman argued about the comparative sizes of Weinfeld's pink blouse and Callahan's. "The only size I can find in Callahan's blouse is a 'W,' " Litman said incredulously.

It was actually an "M." Litman had it upside down. "Obviously, Mr. Litman doesn't know much about women's clothing sizes," Fairstein said. "This is a medium, the same as the blouse that he used." There was laughter in the courtroom.

Callahan donned the pink blouse over her red turtleneck outfit and stood near the jury. Her long hair was tied back in a ponytail. Spitz approached her—and this time he did all the talking for the transcript.

"The blouse is pushed up in front along the bottom line and raised to the neck area. The blouse in back is also up. The fist with the blouse in it is raised to below the chin. Her chin came down, the fist was turned, rubbing the knuckles against the chin. The noose was tightened and pushed inward. The hands of the victim attempted to pull away the hand of the assailant."

Callahan's demonstration was more graphic than Weinfeld's. As Spitz twisted and pushed the knot of fabric into her neck, Callahan's chin lowered as if involuntarily. Her face reddened, her eyes began to tear, and she seemed to be choking. Jurors gasped. Bell said anxiously: "Doctor . . ."

Spitz let go and pulled down the collar of Callahan's red turtleneck, pointing out the marks left by his "noose." There were more gasps from the jurors as they saw the beginning of the same marks seen on Levin's autopsy photographs.

Spitz walked to the jury box and held up an autopsy photograph of Levin's neck, pointing with his capped pen.

"There's a V, and there's a pattern of embroidery. When she pulled it down with her fingers, a second V was made. One of the lines of the arrowhead has in it little dark dots spaced equally from each other. That's what I'm showing the jury."

Fairstein asked Spitz to explain the significance of Callahan's lowered chin.

"In strangulation, the victim puts their head down to close the space of the neck. It's a defense mechanism, to make the space available for the fist that much smaller," he said. "The chin comes very close and rubbed against the fist, and that's what caused the abrasions on the edge of the chin.

Q: There were two forces at work causing the abrasions and other injuries?

A: Two forces, the rotary force and the pushing force in. Also, the pressure of the victim's hands in a confined area when the chin was lowered.

Q: Do you have an opinion . . . why the internal neck area showed a hemorrhage?

A: Within the voice box is the vocal cord. The area of hemorrhage corresponds to the area of contact of the front wall of the voice box to the back wall, caused by the crushing of the voice box by a fist.

Spitz said Levin's congested organs and neck muscle hemorrhages were both consistent with strangulation. Fairstein drew him out at length on the subject of choke holds—the Litman thesis.

Q: Do you have an opinion if the choke hold is released, does the subject recover?

A: If the choke hold is released, even if it is some time after a loss of consciousness, no permanent damage would ensue provided it was not a long time. Loss of consciousness alone is not a cause of permanent damage.

Q: Do you have an opinion . . . on whether cardiac inhibition played a role in this death?

A: No. The blouse was brought up, the blouse was twisted into the equivalent of a noose, it was crushed into her neck, twisted. Her chin was down to make the area smaller.

Litman called out, "Objection," to which Bell responded:

"Overruled, the doctor is just giving his opinion."

Q: Based on the pictures you've reviewed, do you have an opinion . . . on whether sudden death was involved at all?

A: No sudden death. There is absolute evidence of a prolonged, very intense struggle.

Fairstein sat down. Litman leaped up to cover many of the same questions on choke holds—one involving a professor named Knight.

Some of Spitz's answers:

• "I've heard of other cases involving sex and strangulation, but those are males only. Not male/female."

• "She may have been lying down—and more can be applied. She was subjected to a lot of force."

• "Can I know where that was published? It sounds inaccurate."

• "I don't know if this is Professor Knight's signature."

Litman was furious. He asked Spitz: "Have choke holds been used by police in Detroit in the last five years?" Bell sustained Fairstein's objection.

Q: Do you agree that a choke hold can yield fatal consequences in totally unpredictable ways?

A: No. I think it is predictable.

Q: Do you agree with Dr. [William] Reay that the choke hold is like a firearm in that every time the choke hold is used, just as every time a gun is fired, it is potentially lethal?

A: In a broad sense, I agree, but it would have to be worded differently.

Q: In Reay's experiments, they found that unconsciousness could take as little as seven and a half seconds, didn't they?

A: Yes.

Q: And that the minimum time was six seconds to occlude the carotid arteries?

A: Yes.

Q: In one case, it was only 3.2 seconds?

A: I don't recall. (Glanced at piece of paper.) Yes.

Q: The fastest time for occlusion was 3.2 seconds, the next fastest time was only 4.1, isn't that right?

A: Yes.

Q: And Dr. Reay concluded that it might be the carotid sinus reflex kicking in?

A: Maybe.

Q: Maybe for you, but that is what he concluded?

A: He also concluded maybe.

Q: He also concluded that the carotid sinus reflex depends on the stimulation of the carotid sinus independent of occlusion of the carotid artery, didn't he?

A: You read me that question this morning.

Fairstein called out, "Please, can we control Mr. Litman?"

"I'm not going to control Mr. Litman unless I get an objection," replied Bell. "If you don't object, I'm not going to do anything. Mr. Litman makes objections, and I rule. If you don't object, I'm going to sit here and do nothing."

Q: You've done some experiments yourself, haven't you, Doctor?

Fairstein objected loudly. But Bell, who had lost a certain amount of concentration, asked: "What is it you're asking? I couldn't hear the question. Why is Miss Fairstein so upset?"

LITMAN: "I am entitled under the law—"

"Don't tell me what you're allowed under the law," Bell interrupted. "I know the law as well as you do, Mr. Litman."

There was another bench conference, from 3:35 to

3:50 P.M. Then Litman returned with this question for Spitz:

"In Detroit, did you sell pituitary glands from dead bodies to outside institutions and not put the money collected into the Wayne County coffers, but instead to a private foundation of which you are the president?"

Bell sustained the objection. Dr. Werner Spitz stepped down at 3:53 P.M., never to be forgotten at 100 Centre Street.

Judge Bell then ordered the six-four 190-pound defendant to walk over to the jury and stand there. Chambers looked at Litman, who nodded. Chambers stood vacantly at the jury box for a few seconds, then turned, went back to his chair, and slumped under the table.

But for the first time in two months, the jurors had gotten a close-up look at his imposing size.

At four P.M. on March 1, the prosecution rested its case. The defense would open its case the next morning. But before he left the courtroom, Litman moved to have the murder charges dismissed. He maintained that the prosecution had not produced enough evidence to convict Robert Chambers.

Bell said: "I deny the motion. We'll let the jury decide the facts."

12

THE TRIAL—Part III

Five witnesses would testify in Robert Chambers' defense. Despite twenty-five prosecution witnesses, the disparity did not faze Jack Litman. He had adroitly cross-examined all twenty-five, some at great length, and his demands for bench conferences created incessant delays.

"I thought the prosecution dragged," Litman later told me with a straight face. "There were several other witnesses I was contemplating calling. I made a tactical decision not to do that. I thought the jury was restless."

On March 2 Judge Bell was arranging a visit to Central Park for the jurors so they could see the crime scene they had heard about for two months. While awaiting the visit, Litman put up three witnesses.

Dr. Howard Balensweig, an orthopedic surgeon, assessed Chambers' broken pinkie knuckle. He had retired from surgery in 1974 with a heart condition, said Balensweig, but still testified, often in negligence cases. This was his first criminal case.

Beasley had called Chambers' injury a classic "boxer's fracture" from a high-impact punch. Balensweig deemed that "very unlikely." He called Chambers' account "perfectly consistent" with his spiral fracture, caused by the knuckle hitting something hard "in a rolling motion." Balensweig's conclusion: "The hand was open. When the fingers are open, you get rotational injury."

Dr. James Ebert, a photo analyst from New Mexico, measured Levin's neck scratches in a blow-up. He found them consistent within a millimeter to the links of Chambers' Seiko watchband. And Levin's squarish neck bruise was imprinted by something "very similar" to Chambers' watch, Ebert testified. But he admitted he had viewed Chambers' videotape before analyzing any photos.

Stephen Saracco, the prosecutor who questioned Chambers on videotape, was subpoenaed by Litman to testify about why he twice told the suspect that no panties were found despite McEntee's note that he had found panties at the crime scene. Litman zeroed in on the note. Saracco insisted: "Whether anyone had a note in the room, I don't know. I'm saying definitely that I did not read any note, if there was such a note."

The visit to Central Park, the jurors' first, came on Friday, March 4. It was a cold, raw day under an overcast sky.

The court buses arrived at 11:30 A.M. Judge Bell led lawyers and acolytes on a tour, using his umbrella as a pointer, tromping the muddy grove where Jennifer Levin was found. Chambers watched for a few minutes, from fifty feet west of the elm, until Litman told him to sit in a police car. Eerily, amid more than one-hundred journalists and lawmen, the only sounds came from police radios.

The jurors left their bus at 11:52. They were back on board by noon. They had spent eight minutes huddled near the fatal elm.

"It was worthless," juror Gerry Mosconi griped to me a few weeks later. "Did we look like blithering idiots up there, or didn't we? Every time I tried to move away, the guards sheepdogged us back together. We couldn't go up where Garber's stuff supposedly happened. We couldn't go back and see what Reilly had seen. And we weren't allowed to talk whatsoever. In fact, we got the mistaken impression that we weren't allowed to talk on the bus, so it was an awful forty-five minutes. We were angels as jurors go."

Litman's key witness appeared on March 7. Dr. Ronald Kornblum, chief medical examiner in Los Angeles, had written a book on accidental choke hold deaths inflicted by policemen. He built Chambers' choke hold case point by point. Here are excerpts of his question-and-answer session with Litman, organized by topic for added clarity.

Point One: The cause of Levin's death was asphyxia triggered by a choke hold from behind. Her internal neck injuries were not severe enough to indicate prolonged strangulation.

"An arm was placed around her neck, and she was flipped over," said Kornblum. "It's not a ligature strangulation." The small hemorrhage in her cervical spine was evidence of "whiplash" from being flipped. "It is consistent with hyperflexion injuries to the neck. Hyperflexion means the neck is stretched down."

Q: Do you see the injuries to the esophagus and voice box as consistent with a choke hold?

A: Yes, local pressure causes those.

Q: Is a hemorrhage in the left vocal cord consistent?

A: Yes.

Q: Do you agree with Spitz about the crushing of the windpipe?

A: No, you'd expect to see hemorrhages in the larynx or thyroid, possibly a fracture. [Alandy saw hemorrhages.]

Litman re-created Spitz's noose scenario, again with model Elizabeth Weinfeld. He asked if the blouse could cause a ligature that tightens around the neck like a rope.

"I don't believe it can do that," Kornblum said. With the blouse in that position there would be no abrasions on the front of her neck. "There would be wounds that would get your attention in the armpits, going upward and toward the midline."

What would the victim do? "She would step backward, use her hands to push away or otherwise disengage his hands."

Can someone die from a ligature strangulation like the one described? "No."

Point Two: How long was pressure applied to the neck?

"The minimum was five to fifteen seconds, the maximum up to a minute," Kornblum said. Why not more? "Primarily because signs of asphyxia are minimal. The longer the compression of the neck, the more signs you see. There were a few petechial hemorrhages in the eyes, that was about all. There was no protruding tongue, no bulging eyes, nothing of that sort."

Point Three: With classic asphyxial signs minimal, Kornblum said, the choke hold may have triggered the carotid sinus reflex—a theory Spitz ridiculed. Litman revived it.

Q: Is there a way to tell if the carotid sinus reflex kicked in after death?

A: No, it doesn't leave any anatomical abnormality.

Q: Did the carotid sinus reflex intervene?

A: I can't tell.

Q: It may have?

A: Yes.

Point Four: Apart from neck injuries, Levin's bruises from both sides of her face down to both hips were caused by "a single fall," not a violent struggle. Kornblum also discounted violence by describing Chambers' wounds as "playful" scratches.

Levin's puffy left eye? "Consistent with the position—lying on the left side of her face, the fluid accumulates. . . ."

Q: Consistent with a punch to the eye by a closed fist of someone who is six feet four and 190 pounds?

A: No, an individual like that would cause greater injuries, probably a laceration [cut], and the entire eye would be involved, not just the outer half. It is not big enough for a fist wound.

The face injuries? "They are superficial injuries, small and irregular. They appear to be the kind of injury from a fall face-down on terrain with pebbles and branches. . . . The wound on the cheek appears to be from a small twig or branch. The one on the nose appears to be from a small pebble, also above the eye."

Q: Are they consistent with a fall?

A: Yes.

Q: About her injuries apart from those on the neck and chin . . . are they consistent with a violent struggle?

A: No. The wounds are superficial. They are not what you'd expect in a fight. The wound on the hip, I don't know why anyone would get hit in the hip area.

Q: What is the significance that none of her clothing was ripped . . . and that a bracelet of beads was not broken, that there are no injuries on her back, the back of her neck, or her head?

A: The same—it's not consistent with a violent struggle.

Q: What about her fingernails being unbroken?

A: They are all intact points against a violent struggle. In this situation . . . she would grab whatever she can grab, and that would break off or damage areas of the fingernails.

Q: Jennifer Levin had a lacerated frenulum. Do you have an opinion . . . whether a denim jacket was crushed into her mouth to cause the laceration?

A: I don't believe that happened. You would see other injuries to the lip. This is a rough, coarse material.

Q: Do you see anything consistent with a punch in the mouth:

A: No.

Q: A fat lip, anything?

A: Other than the torn frenulum, there appear to be no other injuries.

Point Five: The abrasions on Levin's neck came from Chambers' long shirt-sleeve.

"If you have an arm around the neck, the cloth wrinkles," Kornblum said. "When there's a crease, there's an abrasion."

Q: Are widespread abrasions consistent with a long-sleeved, Oxford-style shirt?

A: Yes. . . . The abrasion on the chin was caused by the fabric of whatever the individual was wearing. It is darker than on the neck because it is over bone, and that gives more resistance. She possibly moved her neck as well to add more friction.

Q: Is the dark area of abrasion consistent with knuckles of a closed fist pressed into the center of the chin?

A: No, it's not.

Q: Why not?

A: Primarily because it's continuous. If it was a fist, it would have places not abraded because of the space between knuckles.

What is missing from Dr. Kornblum's edited direct testimony here is the rhythm he established by restating part of nearly every question in his answers. Each point was thus made twice and Kornblum's authority built up all morning. After lunch he was challenged by Linda Fairstein. Here are excerpts from her cross-examination of Kornblum. Frequent interruptions by Litman are excised. Fairstein came fully prepared.

Q: In 1986 did you receive from Jack Litman Kodachrome slides from an autopsy, slides from Polaroids, pictures of Chambers, the pictures taken by Dr. Alandy in Central Park, the autopsy work sheet and report, and acetate tracings?

A: Yes.

Q: Did you see a transcript from the video?

A: Yes, at the meeting in March 1987.

Q: When did you see any of the clothing connected to this case?

A: In December 1987, I saw a blouse, bra, skirt, and jacket.

Q: When did you first see tissue slides from the autopsy and see the neck organs?

A: Yesterday.

Q: When did you reach an opinion on the case?

A: Last March [before seeing the clothes, anatomical slides, or neck organs].

Q: None of that made any difference in your opinion?

A: I'm not sure of the hemorrhage in the neck organs.

Q: Hemorrhages in the neck organs are more apparent than in the photos, aren't they?

A: Yes.

Q: You testified that the injuries to Jennifer Levin's face were consistent with a fall. Was that opinion reached from the autopsy photos?

A: I am more likely to go over all of the materials, not just photographs.

Q: Including Chambers' videotape statement?

A: My findings fit the story, basically.

Q: Your study, it was mostly involving police officers exercising restraint?

A: Yes.

Q: Are you aware of a similar instance of a choke hold by a man lying on his back?

A: None.

Q: How many choke hold victims in your study were women?

A: None.

Q: The injuries, externally and internally to the neck, are not negligible?

A: True.

Q: Those signs of asphyxial deaths you said were not present—were any of the findings *inconsistent* with asphyxial death?

A: No.

Q: Were they inconsistent with strangulation as the cause of death?

A: No.

Q: Petechial hemorrhages are the hallmarks of asphyxia, aren't they?

A: Yes.

Q: External injuries in asphyxial death vary greatly, don't they?

A: Yes.

Q: In your study, there is no pattern of injury to make a diagnosis of a choke hold, isn't that true?

A: Yes.

Q: What else do you need to make a diagnosis?

A: You need what happened, the total picture.

Fairstein brought out that in Kornblum's study of one bar-arm case, a twenty-five-year-old robbery suspect was kicked in the abdomen and beaten by nine cops. He still struggled and continued to fight—even though the bar-arm hold was applied four separate times for up to twenty-five seconds each.

Q: At the autopsy, there was one external abrasion, isn't that right?

A: Yes.

In a second bar-arm case studied by Kornblum, there were no external injuries on the neck. In a third case there were only two small abrasions, and in another case no injuries at all, Kornblum agreed. Nearly every question in this sequence drew a Litman objection and a five-minute bench conference, disrupting Fairstein's momentum. But she kept going.

Q: In all of the cases you studied, the subject and assailant were standing, weren't they?

A: Yes.

Q: And all involved a struggle of some duration, didn't they?

A: Yes. (*Litman: "Objection." Bell: "Overruled."*)

Q: What does the term "doing the chicken" mean, in terms of what phenomenon?

A: On the West Coast, it is a police term for someone held in a carotid choke hold who has seizures.

Q: You describe them as going into seizures, convulsions, experiencing intense pain, but most live, don't they?

A: Yes, they regain consciousness when they are released from the hold.

Q: Can you say if Jennifer Levin was in a carotid hold?

A: I can't say if it was a carotid or bar-arm.

Q: Were any of the assailants in your study on the ground?

A: Not that I recall.

Q: Did any have a hand pinned beneath them?

A: Not that I recall.

Q: The vocal cord suffered a hemorrhage in the Levin case, didn't it?

A: The vocal cord was hemorrhaged.

Q: That's not consistent with a carotid hold, is it?

A: Not normally consistent, yes.

Q: In your carotid studies, case number four, there were neither petechial hemorrhages or injuries to the neck, is that correct?

A: Right.

Q: In case number ten, there were no surface injuries to the neck? (*Litman:* "Objection." *Bell:* "Overruled.")

A: Yes.

Q: In case number twenty-two, neither petechial hemorrhages nor injuries to the neck were observed, isn't that true?

A: There were also no injuries to the neck in that case. The individual died six weeks later.

Q: In case number twenty-seven, there were no hemorrhages and no neck injuries?

A: Correct.

Q: In your book, you say the carotid sinus reflex is not completely understood, don't you?

A: Correct.

Q: That it doesn't always reduce the heart rate or blood pressure?

A: Correct, it's an individual response.

Q: In the book, 37 percent of those tested have no response?

A: Correct.

Q: The patients were normal, with no heart disease?

A: Yes.

Q: It's quite rare that a healthy person dies of carotid sinus reflex, isn't it?

A: Yes.

Q: Do you recall if adrenaline abolishes the effect of carotid sinus reflex?

A: Yes.

Q: In a struggle, isn't it likely that someone is pumping adrenaline?

A: If they have enough time—thirty seconds or less.

Q: This morning you said up to a minute?

A: Probably less than that, five to fifteen seconds is the minimum.

Q: It is your opinion that all marks on Jennifer Levin's neck were caused in five seconds?

A: Yes.

Q: In what manner?

A: Compression of the neck.

Q: How many applications of pressure were there?

A: I don't know. There appears to be one application because of the widespread abrasions from the sleeve of a garment.

Q: And because of the history you got from Jack Litman? (*Litman: "Objection." Bell: "Sustained, rephrase the question."*)

Q: The history you were given affects the length of time in your estimate?

A: The history I was given fits with my findings. The length of time comes from my experience and the experiments done with the Japanese judo experts and those done in Seattle.

Q: No one died in any of those experiments, isn't that right?

A: That's correct.

Q: Do you agree that the degree of injury depends on the force, and the length of time, the amount of force?

A: Yes.

Q: In thirty-three studies, surface injuries were not distinguished?

A: Yes.

Q: And no pattern of abrasions was found?

A: Yes.

Q: And where there were injuries to the skin, they were small and superficial?

A: Yes.

Q: And you said you were unable to make generalizations as to the size of injuries?

A: Yes. You can't predict in advance where or how serious the injuries will be.

Q: No pattern of injuries appeared?

A: Correct.

Q: The injuries to the tongue, what is their significance, in your opinion?

A: They came from biting the tongue during the compression of the neck.

Q: Do you recall how many choke hold cases had internal injuries to the tongue of those you studied?

A: Either five or six out of thirty-three.

Q: Did you write it could also be due to a blow in the mouth area?

A: Yes, but I said there should have been other external injuries.

Q: How about the abrasion on the side of the mouth?

A: That's consistent with a fall, not a blow.

Q: How many times did she fall?

A: Once.

Q: Could you list for the jury all the injuries that were due to a fall in your opinion?

A: The contusions on the right eye and forehead, on the bridge of the nose, the swollen left eye, and the small contusions on the hip.

Q: How about the injury to the left elbow?

A: I don't recall seeing that, but it would be consistent with pebbles.

Q: Have you been to the area where the body was found?

A: No.

Q: The contusions to the elbow came in the same fall?

A: Yes.

Q: And the contusions to the fingers?

A: The basis of those, I couldn't say.

Q: And the right hip—that was no more than one injury?

A: Yes, one fall.

Q: At the same time as the left hip?

A: Yes.

Q: There are also abrasions on the abdomen?

A: Yes, those are consistent with the same maneuver.

Q: In your opinion, did this fall happen before or after death?

A: During.

Q: She was not dead during the fall?

A: Exactly when death occurs is hazy. She could have been unconscious.

Q: Is it your opinion that if compression of the neck had been released when she was unconscious, she could have recovered? *(Litman: "Objection.")*

Q: If the pressure is released after unconsciousness, she could have regained it?

A: She could have theoretically. It's possible she could have been revived.

Q: All the injuries with the exception of those on the neck were caused in a single fall after the neck was compressed, is that your opinion?

A: Yes.

Q: I don't mean to be facetious, Doctor, but did she bounce?

A: She was probably flipped over, landing on her head, then her hip.

Q: How did one fall cause injuries on both sides of the face?

A: In that kind of terrain, it's possible to get those kinds of contusions.

Q: But she would remain face down?

A: Yes.

Q: And you would expect those pebbles would stick to her, wouldn't you?

A: You can see dirt on the face, but there are no pebbles, no.

After an adjournment for the day, Fairstein's cross of Dr. Kornblum was resumed on Tuesday morning, March 8.

Q: Are you familiar with Bernard Knight—that it takes fifteen to thirty seconds of unrelenting pressure to produce petechial hemorrhages?

A: Yes, but you can also get them in less time.

Q: In your thirty-three studies, there was not a single case of death when the hold was less than five seconds, was there?

A: In one case death was almost instantaneous, case #4.

Q: That was a struggle between several deputies and one prisoner, wasn't it?

A: Yes.

Q: And there were no injuries on the neck, no wounds, no hemorrhages, no signs of asphyxia—isn't that correct?

A: Yes.

Q: And you don't say how long the struggle had been?

A: No, my information was that it was only a few seconds.

Q: In the course of that struggle, there were blows to the abdomen, the back, and the neck?

A: Yes.

Q: Did you discuss your testimony with Mr. Litman yesterday?

A: In an offhand manner, that it went well, like that.

Q: It went well? Congratulations. *(Bell: "Strike that comment.")*

Q: Do you agree that the physical application of a choke hold from behind is different than being on your back and grabbing at a neck with one hand?

A: Yes.

Q: You used the word "playful" to describe the scratches on his face, didn't you?

A: Probably.

Q: Is "playful" a medical term or from the history of the case?

A: Primarily because I heard there were no broken fingernails on Jennifer Levin.

Q: Looking at the scratch marks on the face, do you stick to your medical diagnosis of "playful"?

A: It was not medical.

Q: Did the description have something to do with the Chambers version of what happened?

A: Plus the fact that there were no injuries to her nails.

A stunning cross-examination. Linda Fairstein had proven that healthy people do not die from one quick choke hold. *The New York Times,* in its wisdom, gave it three paragraphs. When I congratulated Fairstein she smiled and said: "The different approach. On cross-examination you can repeatedly go back and make arguments. You saw Jack on cross. The ground rules are different."

Litman chose not to call his other pathologist, Dr. Dominick DiMaio. "I didn't think I needed to," he said. "I think it would have just gilded the lily to put another medical examiner on to say essentially what

Kornblum had said. I thought Kornblum's demeanor was very good."

Litman's fifth and last witness was his assistant counsel, Roger Stavis. Stavis testified that Spitz had told them by phone that he saw no sign that Levin was punched. Spitz had told the jurors that Levin's left eye was punched. They learned from Fairstein's cross that Litman taped the phone calls without telling Spitz.

The defense rested on March 10. After a weekend off, the jury got another look at Chambers' videotape, followed by ten hours of lawyerly summations.

Fairstein was more fiery than usual, hammering at the defendant's credibility: "Robert Chambers is not guilty of murder because he lied," she said, "but his lying is why you can't believe his story." Deprived of suggesting a robbery motive, Fairstein offered an impotence theory in her closing argument.

Litman seemed subdued but still drummed his blame-her number: "It was Jennifer who was pursuing Robert for sex."

Newsday's cerebral columnist Murray Kempton murmured: "I don't think he likes women very much."

Judge Bell spent two hours defining the charges of intentional and depraved murder. Three lesser counts now were added—voluntary or involuntary manslaughter or criminally negligent homicide—for any jurors unconvinced of murder. Nobody wanted a hung jury.

The lucky dozen got the Chambers murder case at noon on St. Patrick's Day. They vanished into the jury room to deliberate a verdict. And they sat on the fence for nine tense days, keeping everyone close to the case on tenterhooks.

On day two, the jurors asked for a readback of Garber's testimony. Then they quietly returned to

Central Park for a longer look at the crime scene—an hour this time. Nobody spotted them except a couple of joggers, only mildly curious. A cop assured them it was a jury from Queens.

When the jurors got back, they began sending out little notes to Judge Bell. They wanted more read-backs—of some Alandy testimony, of other chunks of medical testimony, of the judge's charge. They screened the videotape four more times, in private now, but for an endless week there was no verdict.

It shaped up as a deadlock.

On day seven, juror Guy Gravenson sent out a note and pleaded high blood pressure. He wanted out. The next day it was Wayne Gaston. He called his fellow jurors racists. On day nine—the second Friday of deliberations—forelady Debra Cavanaugh asked if she could fly to London. She had a job waiting.

All that day, Bell and Fairstein and Litman were conspicuous by their absence. Behind closed doors, they were busy dealing with the jury revolt—and dealing for something else as well.

A deal.

13

THE PLEA BARGAIN

On wooden benches in the thirteenth-floor court-room, a few dozen trial regulars were yawning with boredom at 4:00 P.M. on that final Friday.

Rumors had been flying all day. The jury was hung. A plea bargain settlement was being hammered out by the lawyers.

I wandered out to the hallway. At 4:18 P.M. the Levin family emerged from an up elevator with Linda Fairstein. She caught my eye and gave a shrug and what looked like a resigned smile.

By 4:33 P.M. the full cast of characters was filing back into Judge Bell's courtroom. Chambers and his parents were there. So was Robert's current girlfriend, Shawn Kovell. So were his groupies—hard-looking teenage girls dubbed the Bobettes by the press corps and reveling in that identity.

The Levins retreated into an antechamber—Ellen, Steven, Arlene. When they came out at 4:48 P.M. both women showed signs of tears and wore fresh makeup. "What has happened to the word 'justice'?" asked

Arnold Domenitz, Jennifer's grandfather. "I literally feel sick."

The plea bargain whispers spread: manslaughter two. If so, that would mean involuntary—with no mandatory prison time.

By 5:05 P.M. Litman was on hand, along with his assistant Stavis and Pete Putzel—the lawyer defending Chambers' burglary indictment. Fairstein now came in with co-prosecutor Tom Kendris—and the ADA prosecuting the burglaries, Jean-Roland Coste.

At 5:07 Judge Bell made his entrance. The stage was set, and Litman had the first word on the plea bargain. The word was "guilty"—of first-degree manslaughter.

"At this time, in conjunction with a similar application made by Mr. Putzel on the indictment charging Robert Chambers with burglary, we withdraw the plea of not guilty and instead plead guilty to manslaughter in the first degree," Litman said. "On the three counts of burglary in the second degree, defendant pleads guilty to one count."

Mansalughter one. That meant voluntary. Chambers sat at the defense table unmoving except for his feet, which shuffled nonstop.

FAIRSTEIN said: "The plea is acceptable to the People."

LITMAN: "It is agreed that the sentence to be imposed will be an indeterminate one of not less than five years and not more than fifteen on both guilty pleas, to run concurrently. The pleas are full and satisfy the prosecution of all crimes it is alleged that Chambers has commited at any time until right now."

FAIRSTEIN: "We accept the plea and the conditions with the understanding that they cover outstanding acts and allegations of theft, but do not cover a murder we don't know about—not to imply that there are any."

JUDGE BELL TO CHAMBERS: "Do you plead guilty to manslaughter in the first degree?"

CHAMBERS: "Yes, Your Honor." He was now testifying.

Q: No one has threatened or coerced you into this plea, nor made you any promise of a sentence other than the five to fifteen years mentioned?

A: No, Your Honor.

Q: You understand that the plea is the same as a guilty verdict—that you don't have to plead guilty and that you can wait until the jury comes in with a verdict? *(Chambers nodded.)*

Q: You understand that when you plead guilty you are giving up your right to remain silent?

A: Yes.

Q: Do you plead guilty to manslaughter in the first degree?

A: Yes.

Q: Is it true, Mr. Chambers, that on August 26, 1986, you intended to cause serious physical injury to Jennifer Levin and thereby caused her death?

A: Looking back on everything, I'd have to say yes, but in my heart I didn't mean for anything to happen.

Fairstein interrupted: "We're asking about his mind and his hands, not his heart."

Bell repeated his question. "Yes, Your Honor," replied Chambers, shaking his head in denial. Bell asked it a third time. "Yes," Chambers said, this time without body motion.

Q: Is there any question in your mind about causing her death?

A: There's no question, Your Honor.

Q: While you're on your feet, I'm going into the second [burglary] indictment. Your lawyer indicated you're going to withdraw the not guilty plea and plead guilty to the first count?

A: Yes.

Chambers spoke in a low voice—barely audible during the "in my heart" passage. He looked very shaken and appeared to be crying at one point.

One apartment he burglarized was a doctor's residence at 1125 Park Avenue. When Bell questioned him about it, Chambers threw up both hands and slapped them against his sides, biting his lip and shaking his head while answering, "Yes."

He obviously resented having to accept five to fifteen years in state prison for a voluntary manslaughter and three burglaries.

After his formal sentencing was set for April 15, Chambers sighed and said: "I want to thank you for providing as fair a trial as you possibly could. I appreciate it for my family and for me."

Replied Bell: "You can spend tonight with your family and will surrender tomorrow [at ten A.M.]."

"Under police guard, Your Honor," Fairstein interjected.

"In front of his home, not inside," said Litman.

In the background, Shawn Kovell was crying on someone's shoulder.

The jury was the last to know. The lucky dozen didn't even guess what was up when court officers led them into the courtroom at 5:38 P.M.

"Madame Forewoman, have you reached a verdict yet?" the court clerk asked cruelly.

"No, we have not," Debra Cavanaugh said.

Only then did Bell announce cryptically: "This matter has been disposed of. Thank you for your services."

And that was it.

Cavanaugh and juror Elizabeth Bauch began to cry. The other ten jurors looked stunned. Bell said that while they had the right to speak to the press, they also could refuse. As they marched out, juror Michael

Ognibene shook hands with all four lawyers and with the stone-faced defendant.

District Attorney Morgenthau held a press conference in his office an hour later. "At least he admitted it," Morgenthau said of Chambers. The DA made it clear that even if a hung jury had meant three wasted months and a retrial, there would have been no deal without the Levins' okay. That incensed legal scholars. They disapproved of ceding power.

Ellen Levin sat at Morgenthau's left, behind a bouquet of microphones. "I don't think we could have withstood another trial," she said. "We couldn't have sustained that strain and tension for another year and a half."

Steven Levin sat between Ellen and Arlene. He said: "I was glad to see Robert Chambers stand up in court and say he intended to cause Jennifer Levin harm and did in fact kill her. That negates his entire story."

But Jennifer's grandfather said bitterly: "Don't ask me my opinion of the jurors."

As the trial regulars filed out of 100 Centre Street on the night of March 25, 1988, word spread that the Chambers jurors had never discussed any charge but murder two with intent—and that's what had hung them.

It sounded as if Jack Litman had played his cards very well, folding a weak hand. But there was much more yet to be told about the nine-day deadlock drama.

And some of the jurors wanted to talk.

14

THE JURY'S STORY

#1—DEBRA CAVANAUGH, forewoman

Her note to Judge Bell at noon said: "I have given to my limit. I am planning to leave the country this evening to be available for employment in England. . . . I will be out of the country within minutes." After Chambers' plea she taped a WCBS-TV spot, half-hidden on camera. You could hear her confusion.

"What the hell happened? I'm just so frustrated. I'm exhausted. We were all in a tiny room . . . it got tighter. Several different factions . . . it could have gone several different ways. We were all split up, at times screaming and yelling, maybe we were overly competent, maybe too smart. . . . It would have taken another week minimum, with this jury. Another week minimum."

#2—MICHAEL OGNIBENE

He and other jurors figured it was a mistrial until a court officer explained the plea bargain. His thoughts are distilled from TV spots, including a *Good Morning America* on March 28:

"There's a sense of relief that I never have to look back and say, 'I wonder if we made the right decision.' Mine was one of those changing votes. I'm not going to say where I ended up. It swung [on intentional murder] from 9–3 not guilty to 9–3 guilty to 7–5 not guilty. It was tough to be objective and not let subjective opinions interfere. The hardest part was understanding operation of the mind. The so-called medical experts couldn't agree on the length of time it would have taken to cause anything. We were stuck on was it a second, five seconds, fifteen?"

Why did he shake hands? "In competition of any form I've learned that it's fairness to shake the hand of your opponent—win, lose, or draw."

#3—GERARD MOSCONI
Interviewed by author on April 11.

Q: What happened in the jury room? Why did you not get off the first count?

A: We weren't allowed to get off the first count and consider the second count unless it was 12–0 not guilty on the first count. That's the way it was explained to us. Someone else talked to lawyers afterward, and they said we were absolutely right. You're not allowed to do that.

Q: How did you discuss things?

A: We tried to set down rules and parameters, and it usually fell apart. It would center on specific issues, and certain people would have feelings on special issues, and it would always degenerate into stopping and going around the table and getting to you and me, that sort of thing. We would split up into groups sometimes, not physically, but in arguments. Don't forget, it's been eleven weeks. We're pent up. We're dying to talk about this. It turns out everybody does, and we didn't! Everybody reads the newspaper and cheats, and we didn't! I'm thinking, Oh, boy, if only I'd known. We were dying to talk about it, so when we finally got in there, you have to expect the inevitable explosion. And there were twelve of those.

Q: The first readback you got was Garber's testimony?

A: We wanted to hear that before we went back to Central Park. He said he got a much better look the first time than when he circled around the reservoir and came back down. Now when you come back down, you have a clear field of view for quite a long time before you get past this point. He said he saw more details the first time, which doesn't make sense. He had less time to look at it. He wasn't expecting it, whereas coming back I don't care if it was sexual or not, he wasn't looking away. He was looking at it, and it was lighter, by twenty minutes. So how could he see less the second time? That was the problem that I had.

Garber spelled out that he told the [police] it was a rocking routine, and that turned into shaking a lifeless body. Now what kind of credibility can you lend someone who changes their story like that. Minimizing feelings of guilt—we don't need to get into anything like that. If anything, I gave credit on the Chambers side because his first testimony corroborates Chambers' story. I think that was a point in their favor.

Q: What did you think of the videotape?

A: I felt that it was points on the not guilty side. Given that he was there without a lawyer for that length of time, I find it incredible that he could make up a story that is that ridiculous that no one could shoot down. We've got how many investigators—medical experts, photogrammetrists, anything you want—how many tried for a year and a half to shoot holes in that silly story and they couldn't do it? Something there had to be true. I'm certain it isn't the whole truth. But parts of it had to be true.

Q: On murder with intent, which side were you on?

A: I was on the not guilty side. Yeah, maybe I felt he was guilty—but was he proven guilty? No. You can't convict someone because of a feeling. There has to be concrete proof, so we spent days and days and days trying to think what would prove intent to us. There was no motive for it. If he had known her a long time, yeah, it could have been a lover's quarrel. I can see passion erupting into that kind of violence, but he didn't really care about her that much. She was casual sex. Why? You might hit someone wrong and punch her in the throat, yeah, then I can see logic in that. I see no logic in him killing her intentionally.

Did you see any of the pictures? Even the people on my side think this is off the graph, but I don't think she looked that bad. He did not hit her. If he hit her, she would look far worse. If he punched her in the face once, she would be a mess. He's a big guy. I had his watch on and it dangled on my wrist, and I weigh 190, exactly what he did, but he's gotta be stronger than me. And if I hit a girl, I know that I would do much more damage. I've taken karate for years, so I know exactly what a blow will do to someone.

I think he was most likely trying to restrain her in some way. This is a possibility, but then you have to go with the defendant's possibilities—under the law. And he didn't realize that he had her in a potentially lethal move. We did various examples of what we thought happened. We tried out the scenarios for three days. In the position—if she were sitting on him like he described in the videotape, and he grabbed her— we tried it.

I was in most of the demonstrations because my weight was perfect. I was also the tallest. And we had one of the "not guilty" people playing Levin. And one guy pulled him down and said: 'Okay, now go limp.' This was to get at the fact that she must have gone limp at one point and stopped struggling. The guy on the bottom said, "All right, all right, now stop struggling, go limp." And the guy said, "I am limp, I've been limp."

If you're pinned back like that, you can't move much. They tied my hands up. I lay back on my wrists. My weight alone, forget about somebody sitting on me, my weight pinned my arms. When I moved to get up and try to reach up, it took a couple swipes. I had to pull back, and I did it without thinking, pulled the neck back and then got it into the crook. And I hurt my hand when I did. It couldn't have been all coincidence.

Q: How about depraved indifference?

A: I thought it was a ridiculous charge, impossible to prove.

Q: Were there people adamant for guilty?

A: Always about three people on guilty, three or four on not guilty. The people who felt he was guilty, felt he was guilty, and that was their argument. There were people who fluctuated back and forth—how can you vote someone guilty and yet be willing to switch your vote so many times? Obviously, there's reasonable doubt in your mind if you can vacillate like that. I never changed my vote, but I believed I was keeping an open mind. I had an opinion of what I thought happened when I went in there, and it's not the same opinion that I have now, so I obviously gave weight to what other people said.

Q: Why wouldn't he have gone into a fetal position and rolled her off if she was hurting his testicles?

A: When I thought about him lying there, she's ignoring him—I think it could very likely be that when she squeezed a little bit too hard, he got up, grabbed her, pulled her down.

Then she was in a position where she had to listen to what he was saying. I think he probably held her like that, right next to him, and just said: "Look, you have to pay attention. You hurt me too hard and I don't ever want you to do that again." And he let go, and she was dead.

That could very well have happened. There was nothing that was inconsistent with that. It's Chambers' story, almost. It's the medical evidence. And it is not intent to kill.

Q: How did his lingering at the crime scene strike you?

A: If he were looking to see what was going on and to improve his story, which—I mean, do you think that was an improved story, well thought out for ten hours? I don't. He would have sat farther away. He would have been inconspicuous. I don't buy that he's a clever liar. I mean, the cat scratched me—that's ridiculous. And the cat was declawed? That's not a clever liar. If he were clever, he would have just said, "She scratched me and I left the park. I left, who knows what happened to her?" And they could have never pinned it on him. That would have been a clever lie.

Q: Were you aware of the Levin family in court?

A: Very aware. Mr. Levin was very conscious of making us aware, coming in and slamming his coat down, storming out—I don't mean during the autopsy, I don't blame him for leaving then—but making comments and then walking out during some of the witnesses. I thought that was inappropriate behavior.

Q: What about some of Chambers' inconsistencies?

A: Well, can you tell me what you did yesterday and then write it down, and would there be no inconsistencies?

Q: He told a series of stories to police: first that he didn't leave with her and the cat scratched him; second that he lost her at Eighty-Sixth Street.

A: *(Long pause.)* Well, it sounds bad, but is it getting more and more of the truth out, or is it a more elaborate lie? How can you tell?

Q: He said contradictory things about Levin.

A: Maybe you won't sympathize with this, but I said: "Haven't you ever had a one-night stand and then talked to your friends about it, and they said, 'What did you think of her?' and I'd say, 'Well, I think she's very, very nice, and gee, she was a lot of fun.' But I really didn't want anything to do with her after that night." I thought that fit in very, very well. She was nice, she was real easy to talk to, we had fun that night, but did you want to keep seeing her? Hell, no.

Q: His fingers were badly bitten before she tied him up, according to him, and yet there's no blood on the panties.

A: We talked about that for a long time. When I had my hands back here, I had them in fists and pulled them out. There wouldn't be blood. That's inconclusive. And I think Spitz was off the graph. There's no way this [blouse noose] happened. If he did that, why isn't there more blood on the blouse? I know there's some, but why isn't there more if they are that deep gashes?

Q: Would the suppressed things have changed your opinion?

A: I don't know what wasn't allowed, so why don't you tell me, and I'll let you know?

Q: His cocaine habit he's been treated twice for.

A: That in itself, no. I'm nervous when people say "drug habit." I knew guys who used to smoke dope every morning before going to class in college.

Q: They're talking about heavy cocaine use and twice going for detox out of state.

A: That's different. I don't know. He went cold turkey at the trial. Nobody caught on that he was . . .

Q: Were you bothered by the testimony about the life-style of these kids?

A: No, we're not that old.

Q: One thing you didn't hear was that Jennifer was trying to help him get off drugs.

A: That I didn't know. One thing that got me was her friend saying that she didn't like him as a person. That besmirched her character more than Litman could have possibly done.

Q: It's like a guy saying the same thing?

A: Yeah, easy lay.

Q: He used to take credit cards from his girlfriends and run up the tabs on them. He was never forced to face up to anything. He got kicked out of one school, so they found him another. He never had to take responsibility for anything.

A: Are his parents divorced? They didn't talk during the trial. We noticed that. One day they spoke to one another, and we all went: "Hey, look at that."

Q: He had a history of stealing since he was sixteen.

A: Is that proven? I would say that would have to have an influence, but I don't know. Maybe I'm being defensive and saying, "Yeah, that doesn't make him a killer"—and it doesn't. I don't know if I could be that objective, so I'm glad I didn't know.

Q: Who did you think was the most credible witness?

A: The most credible—unbiased—probably Dr. Alandy. I think she was slightly prejudiced for the prosecution, but not overtly so. She wasn't like Spitz. She wasn't like Kornblum.

The police? Even the guilty people weren't using the police testimony. It came down to medical testimony.

#4—SHELLY FORMAN

Shelly Forman confided to other jurors that Chambers' girlfriend, Shawn Kovell, lives in his building. Cole Wallace said: "It was like, 'Okay, so what? How many times do they have dinner a week, Shelly?' I was going, kiddingly, 'I mean, do they have sex? Or does she just sit in the Chamberses' living room with her legs crossed like this?' Then I picked up a picture of Jennifer Levin and I said, 'Looking at this, how many times do you think she takes a stroll late at night in the park with him?' He got very upset."

"Wallace continued, "Now I find out, of course, the day before sentencing, that this is why he [Forman] had been called in right before the end of the trial about this." But nothing came of it.

#5—ROBERT NICKEY

Interviewed by author on April 3. Probably the only Chambers juror who ever did jury duty before. "Yes, three times. I've retired now."

Q: Why did everyone get stuck on murder with intent?

A: That was the first charge, and I strongly felt that it was intent. But some jurors said, "He's too nice-looking a fella to . . ." He's six feet four, the guy is handsome, you can't take that from him. But . . . in my mind it was intent. I looked at those pictures of her every day, sometimes for an hour at a time, and there was no doubt in my mind that it was intent. Looking at the pictures and watching the videotape. Put those two together, and there was no doubt in my mind. In my opinion, he had time to go home and sleep on that story. He really got it down, very neatly.

All the way to Central Park, I believe him—up until the part that he flipped . . . it just couldn't happen like that. The way the girl was sprawled out there, one leg folded up, the other one out, everything showing.

There's no way he could have done that from a flip over the shoulder. He certainly was strong enough to do that, but he says, "She was strong, she was very strong." That means maybe she fought for her life.

I couldn't get the jury to see that. There was a blond lady, a very nice lady from Iowa, and things like that don't happen out there—murder, crime. I was trying to tell her that most anything can happen in New York, and she just said, "I just can't believe he was intending to do that." She was a very emotional person. I think if we had hung around another day or two, she would have come around, but she couldn't see it.

He stood across the street and looked. That's where the police didn't do their job. I mean, if you are going to investigate a murder, you've got all these detectives walking around and you see some guy standing across the street, looks like someone would have said: "Hey, buddy, you seen anything?"

Q: Did any witnesses impress you?

A: A couple of them. Spitz wasn't one of them. I was impressed with Dr. Alandy's testimony. The jurors said, "Well, she doesn't have enough experience." Well, she'd only been in this country two years, but she had experience where she came from, and it's practically the same. A body's a body, an autopsy is an autopsy.

Q: Did visiting the park again help you?

A: I was just trying to figure how Dr. Garber could not recognize this man if he was only fifty feet away. And when he came back from his jogging trip, it was daybreak then. Well, I can understand that. In New York, you just don't stick your nose in other people's business. You see and you don't see.

#6—JEANETTE

Her name was the best-kept secret of the trial, but she was open about her views, jurors said. "She was the most vocal," said one. "It was always, 'Shut up, sit down, you don't know what you're talking about.' She made a couple of good points but constantly bickered with juror twelve—they had an ongoing feud. It was funny, and then it wasn't funny."

#7—GINNY HOESL

As one of the three jurors who held out against Murder Two, she told CBS News' "This Morning" that she thought they could have agreed to a lesser verdict on Chambers. "I don't think there was any chance, really, that he could have been acquitted on all the charges against him," Hoesl said. Other jurors quoted her as maintaining, "I don't have anything to hang my hat on for murder."

#8—WAYNE GASTON

He told a TV street reporter the night of Chambers' plea: "Manslaughter one was the lowest charge I could have gone to." Gaston's note to Judge Bell two days earlier, charging racism on the jury, helped polarize the deliberations.

Some jurors agreed with him, including at least two whites and the only other black man, Robert Nickey.

Liz Bauch was most upset. "I reacted very violently to it. I yelled at him, because I was one of the people who was voting to acquit. Wayne, when he said that, I walked into the ladies' room. I said, 'If the only way I can prove to you that I'm not a racist is to vote with you, it's not going to happen. Think what you want to think.' Robert came after me and said, 'Wayne didn't mean you.' Which I appreciated."

"I think the issue that was so eloquently put by Wayne was very right on," Cole Wallace said. "Day one or day two, he leaned over to me and said, 'You know, if this guy were black, we wouldn't be having these discussions.' And I have to admit, if you were black, if you were acne pock-faced, if you looked a little less dramatic, you can almost see an intent to kill.''

Eliot Kornhauser said of Gaston's note: "We asked him to read it out loud. I applauded it. I won't say racial prejudice, but maybe subconsciously in some cases. I think he might have had a point.''

Gerry Mosconi, who said he related to Nickey, didn't appreciate Gaston's note. ''I found it very disturbing. I thought about it. I don't think that that's the case. The person who was responsible for it was very aloof throughout the trial. I think he may have been prejudiced against Chambers. I was shocked by that, I didn't like it.''

#9—COLE WALLACE

Interviewed by the author on April 25. He demanded readbacks of medical testimony to make a point to his fellow jurors.

Q: What did you tell them?

A: Going in, I said I was upset by the way Litman continually interjected. I was alert to—what's going on here?—there's something wrong. You have all these days—what, fourteen days?—and when we finally get the time of how long it will take to read, it's down to two days when you take out all the junk. I would say: ''If you hear it from beginning to end without all of the histrionics and all of the acting, one full time, I think you'll see what I mean.''

Q: What else bothered you?

A: The pictures of where she landed. I said. ''Show me how she got that way.'' In the initial crime scene pictures, you know she had not been moved because the biker had seen her and identified them. So she had to be placed that way. I've been flipped probably ten times in the jury room. There's no way for her legs to have been that way. They tried every which way to make it possible, and they couldn't do it. That's where I start going, wait a minute—intent. If you can intentionally do that to someone and leave them that way—you've seen the photos? Then that's the ability to intentionally kill someone.

Q: What did you think of Chambers?

A: I saw a kid who was on the outside because his friends had all left. He wasn't going off to school. She was—they all were—and I remembered the anger I felt when I didn't get accepted to a school and everyone around me is going off. So I kind of understood about the intent—the anger that could lead to it. I don't think that he ever thought, Jennifer Levin, I'm going to kill you. I think it was just the world.

I see that he probably knew she had money, was used to using people, takes her to a vulnerable situation, whereupon let us say that they play around, and he says, "Jennifer, can you let me have a couple hundred dollars?" And suddenly the light bulb goes off—and this fairly aggressive, intelligent woman, she says, "You really are something else." And that's when, because he's crazed—and I understand his drug levels were pretty damn high—it just begins to ignite.

The only person who ever said there was sex involved is Robert Chambers. If you take that issue away . . .

Q: You believed Garber's explanation of his changing story?

A: Right, because he could have just stuck to that rocking story all the way and maintained a very low profile. People in the jury room are saying, "He wants the headlines." Great, he wants to ruin his life so he can get a quick headline—DOCTOR LETS LEVIN GIRL DIE. Real good.

Q: What did you think of the videotape?

A: You go right down the whole thing, the percentage of lies—I didn't know she was dead until I saw the

ambulance pull away, I didn't know she was dead until
the police came later that day, I didn't know she was
dead until I woke up and Alex LaGatta called. Statement after statement after statement. He lies when he
didn't have to lie. So that little click went off.

Remember "Where are the panties?" Remember
Mr. Litman going, "You mean, you've got this kid
here who's under interrogation and you have the panties and you don't say a word?" And I was thinking,
Yeah, that's a pretty slimy operation. And you listen
to the videotape, and there's a portion where he
says—you have to put your ear right up to the tube—
and you think he says, "Well, I know they've got
them. They say they have them." It sounds like he
must have overheard.

Q: The description of Jennifer as aggressive—a
turnoff?

A: No, because I wish—I wish that more—being
a—growing up being a somewhat shy kid, I guess I
always wished that a girl would come over to me and
say, "Hey, I really like you." It wasn't till college that
I learned that you just go say: "Hey, let's dance."
And you pull them out on the floor, and while the
music's going, you figure out if you like this person or
don't.

Q: You tried all the scenarios—Chambers, Spitz,
your own?

A: Yeah. The only scenario that didn't work was
Chambers'. Any other scenario worked. It's amazing
because you buy his story, and you try and make it
work, and it still wouldn't work.

Q: You and Nickey and Gaston were from beginning to end for intentional murder?

A: Right.

#10—ELIOT KORNHAUSER
Interviewed by author on April 29. He insisted
Judge Bell had told jurors they could move to the

second count "when and only when" they had disposed of intentional murder.

Q: What effect did that have?

A: We were petrified of doing something wrong. We did not want to be the cause of a mistrial, of any kind of embarrassment to ourselves, to the system.

Q: If the suppressed factors were known—any difference?

A: I would have to say yes, sure. In trying to prove intent to kill, those certainly are factors that would have given us a whole lot more insight into the operation of his mind.

Q: For example?

A: The burglaries. Some of us had known about them. I knew about them. At some point we tried to put together a profile of Chambers that might allow us a little bit into his mind. And some of the points we brought up were uneducated, jobless, virtually directionless. But it came down to the fact that none of those things about him were ever entered. There was no proof that what we felt and probably all believed was in fact a fact.

Q: Did the inconsistencies in the videotape matter?

A: The extent of them. I look at the videotape, it's almost a two-part story, his version and then the Saracco questions and answers. That's when the contradictions became so evident.

Q: Did you get any sense of Chambers in court?

A: Not at all. Eleven weeks, he showed no emotion, nothing. I mean, even the lighter moments, there were no smiles.

Q: Did the suggestion that he was impotent bother you?

A: Actually we gave credibility to that possibility. One juror made an excellent point about how the male ego is so delicate, and it's so important to think that it's virile, and certainly a nineteen-year-old guy is not going to admit not being able to get an erection. I think a lot of that stuff about stroking and the manner in which she was jerking him off, the squeezing of the testicles, might have been an attempt to stimulate him.

Q: Did the underage drinking and casual sex surprise you?

A: Staying out late drinking, I was certainly a part of that when I was eighteen or nineteen. The degree of sexual activity, although it really didn't come out, was implied. It was a little surprising. We all knew that she wasn't angelic. But again, what's wrong with wanting to make love with somebody?

Q: Your reaction to the photographs of Jennifer?

A: Horrifying. Horrifying. For a very, very, very personal reason, horrifying.

Q: What was that reason?

A: The first time I saw the pictures the first week, the first time I saw the pictures, I saw my sister. She's a lot older than eighteen now, but at some point in her life, probably real close to the age of eighteen, she had hair like that, same style. She had a very similar body, proportionately, at least. Jennifer was about four inches taller, but there was a striking resemblance.

Q: How did the defense witnesses strike you—Dr. Kornblum?

A: I had a problem not only with him, but with some of the other people who testified. Given the end and you're told to come up with the means. It's easier to get to Thirty-fourth Street and Park Avenue if you know exactly where Thirty-fourth Street and Park Avenue is.

#11—ELIZABETH (LIZ) BAUCH

Interviewed by author May 24. An Iowa lawyer's daughter.

Q: How did you feel about Chambers' guilty plea?

A: I was very glad it wasn't a mistrial and nobody else had to go through this again. I found out later it was the only plea he could take, and I felt better because a couple of people had said, "See, he admitted it. And you were wrong." And I was going, "Well, maybe I was wrong. Maybe he was really lucky, and I was being a bleeding heart." I don't think I'm a bleeding heart, but you're in such a fragile emotional state after nine days. . . .

Q: You thought a lot of Litman?

A: I never discredited the passion with which he defended that boy. I don't think anybody could have defended him better. I felt very early in the trial a sense of relief because I knew I would be able to convict Chambers without question if the evidence was there because he had such a good lawyer.

Q: Did you think he was guilty of anything?

A: I would have hung them on murder. I feel very strongly about that. Everybody was so sure the three of us were going to crack, and I was sure that I wasn't. I was absolutely, resolutely sure that it was one of the lesser charges.

Q: Anything about the trial that stuck in your mind?

A: The photographs were very—it's difficult to look at pictures of someone who has a name and a family. It's like you're on display, and they have no idea who the hell you are.

And the fact that there were just enough pieces of evidence to fit his story, much to my surprise. If there was any possibility realistically that this was not an intentional act of murder, that's why I voted the way I did. I thought the defense brought that out very clearly. That manslaughter is an accident, and I understood that.

Q: Did it matter not knowing all his lies?

A: No. If I were his mother, I might be able to spot when he's consciously making something up, but obviously if you're responsible for somebody's death morally, it's a tremendous shock. He was blaming her on the videotape. That was Chambers' voice, and that was his face. He was doing that. Not a noble thing, but then again, I can't convict somebody because I think they're not nice.

I was very willing to be persuaded by the evidence. If we had someone who saw him carrying her body, that would help a lot. It still might not necessarily clear up murder with intent for me. I don't know what would have proved it to me because I don't know what else there might have been. I don't know. And the law is very clear on that. If you don't know, you have to acquit.

Q: Do you have a stronger sense of Jennifer than of Robert?

A: Well, I'm a woman. I've been eighteen. I can remember good times when I've had nothing to drink and people would probably have assumed I was drunk because you're just so excited and so happy, especially when you're eighteen years old. Her friends took the stand. Both attorneys really made her presence felt. Fairstein brought out her attitude, the excitement, the anticipation, she made her alive. And then Jack did it, by describing how she would have struggled against the pressure on her neck. I mean, he didn't diminish her in any way, I thought, during the trial. My impression of Chambers came from his behavior in the courtroom. And the videotape. And the fact that Jennifer wanted to be with him. That was an aspect of his personality. God knows I've known kids that have had drug problems. I know a lot of adults that have problems with substance abuse. Whether to call it a weakness—it certainly isn't a plus. I thought he was a kid who'd had trouble. But just because someone uses cocaine doesn't make him a murderer. Something else has got to be there.

Q: Litman is very passionate about bad parenting.

A: I'd heard, after the trial, from someone who

knew one of the kids in that group who said that basically Jennifer had a reputation for being a little tramp. Those were the kid's words, not my words. And my reaction is that that sort of behavior in a girl who is only eighteen years old is a sign of something bad in her life. I mean, we've all known kids who've had phases of one sort or another, and this may have been her phase of looking for attention and looking for love, looking for some sort of acknowledgment that she was attractive. I don't know.

Q: Do you have a sense of what happened in the park?

A: Yes and no. I don't think she was attempting to hurt him. I think they were both drunk, and I think she may have done it—"playful" sounds so cheap. She wasn't trying to incapacitate him. I think she'd gotten too rough. You can hurt a partner without realizing that you're causing them that much discomfort.

Garber had seen two people in the same place fifteen to eighteen minutes apart. I think if he were beating on her for fifteen minutes, she would have had a lot more damage because he's a big guy. I don't think he punched her. I think there was some sort of sexual horseplay going on. I think they were both drunk. We heard about Levin's blood alcohol level. It's plausible to me that she would have done what he described. I don't think it's the weirdest thing I've ever heard of. I don't think it's unusual for people to fight and have sex. However, what happened—I'll never know.

Q: People ask, "Why couldn't you convict him? He was guilty."

A: Lay people don't know how to apply the law. When I was twelve years old a girl I had known in summer camp was raped and murdered. She was seventeen. It happened in another town, but Iowa is a small state and it was front-page news. I remember finding it out at breakfast, and my father was down in the kitchen with me. First of all the shock of knowing someone who had been a crime victim. I didn't know her well. She was older than I was, and she was always nice to the younger kids.

She was out bird-watching in the park. The man who did it was caught and convicted of second-degree homicide. In Iowa you have—malice aforethought is murder one, and I was very upset. I thought, Well, she was such a nice person. She didn't deserve this. It should be murder one. I was young, and my father explained to me very patiently that the charge has nothing to do with the worth of the victim.

#12—GUY GRAVENSON

His story comes from other jurors. Wallace said: "His theory was the bra theory. The blouse left marks, but the bra had the same spacing, and that creates new bruises on the back of the head, you see, so you've got this bra that is in a sense, total control, so you don't have that flinging. I buy every minute of it. On the other hand, if it didn't happen that way, so what? He was someone who just couldn't let go of— that's all he was interested in, proving his case, not working with people. He was second-degree depraved indifference. We never got around to it."

15

THE SENTENCING

Nineteen months ago to the day, almost to the exact hour, Robert Emmet Chambers had awakened in his bedroom at 11 East 90th Street, wondering if it was all just a bad dream.

As justice took its slow but inexorable turn, he lived in a fog of denial. Not once did Chambers face the reality that he had deliberately hurt Jennifer Levin enough to kill her.

On March 26, 1988, reality waited on the doorstep five stories below Phyllis Chambers' apartment at precisely ten A.M.

When her son emerged with Jack Litman, escorted by Detectives Mike Sheehan and Mickey McEntee, there was a surging crowd on the elegant block just off Central Park.

"Murderer! Murderer!" some of them began chanting. They had waited in a drizzle since dawn. Some seemed disillusioned that after all his defiant denials, Robert Chambers had copped a plea.

He watched them without a flicker of expression.

He wore a bulletproof vest under his white sweater and gray jacket. And while seeming dazed as usual, he shot one quick glance at the neighbors' faces pressed against windows high across the street.

As Chambers ducked into the rear seat of a black Cadillac DeVille with Litman at the wheel, a woman in the crowd told a reporter: "This is history. I want to get a close look."

Behind police barricades, twenty Guardian Angels in red berets waved placards denouncing Chambers' five-year minimum sentence. The neighbors had seen nothing like this. One placard said, *Jennifer Levin got death—Robert Chambers got a bargain!*

My husband and I watched it on television later. As Chambers rode off to jail in a Cadillac, I thought of his murky boyhood climb from Jackson Heights to Park Avenue and the Knickerbocker Greys. I wondered where the money came from and why his mother's loving ambition somehow spurred him from the $2300-a-month townhouse to Dorrian's Red Hand bar and Jennifer Levin.

There were many unanswerable questions. "I want you to know," Jennifer said, "that the sex I had with you was the best sex I ever had in my life." And Chambers told her: "You shouldn't have said that to me." What did that mean? Most men crave glowing sexual reviews. Who could explain such a rebuke?

Some questions didn't even seem to get asked.

What was Chambers searching for when jogger Chris Ferrer saw him rummaging through the leaves with his toe?

Why had Jennifer worn borrowed panties that night? Even teenagers traveling light usually manage their own underwear.

Where was the white long-sleeved Oxford-cloth shirt he wore that morning? Was it bloodstained? Why didn't the police find it?

Who contacted Jack Litman overnight? How and
when? I finally asked Litman that question myself. He
ducked it.

Chambers spent his first three weeks behind bars at
Rikers Island. An inmate told *The Post* that Chambers
admitted robbing Levin. That was a yawn. But when
Chambers appeared before Judge Bell on April 15 for
sentencing, a television camera recorded a strangely
revealing tableau.

Denial became an art form. Chambers began his
first public statement in twenty months by pronounc-
ing his trial "a trial with no winners" and calling the
courtroom "this circus arena." Jennifer was looking
down on it—"looking and wondering why it all happened," Chambers said, "and I don't know. I never
wished any of this to happen."

He also said he had never "wanted" it. He did not
say he never meant it, but Chambers' disavowal of his
guilty plea to voluntary manslaughter was clear
enough. It would become even clearer.

"I am sorry," he said for the first time. The Levin
family, seated behind him, had "gone through hell
because of my actions." He didn't look at them. Soon
he thanked all who had "kept the faith," his family
and friends. And then Chambers added:

"To Jennifer, nothing I can do or say will ever bring
her back. But I am sorry."

He did not say why. His guilty plea—that he had
intended causing the injuries which killed Levin—had
waived any right to silence. But Bell did not make
Chambers explain why he did it.

If such omissions seemed routine, what happened
next would explain why Chambers resisted apologiz-
ing for killing Jennifer Levin.

As Bell cited his pleas of guilty to voluntary manslaughter and burglary, Chambers began to shake his

head. During the judge's hour-long proceeding, Chambers shook his head eleven times.

Denial was unmistakable, but if any journalist mentioned it except for WNBC-TV's Magee Hickey, I missed it. A cop friend of mine, watching it on tape, was outraged. "I've never seen anybody get away with that," he said, "after copping a plea."

Chambers went to prison shaking his head. I shook mine and got out my tape recorder one more time.

JACK LITMAN
May 9, 1988

Q: How would you have prosecuted this case?
A: I think Linda lost a little bit by suggesting too many different variations and saying to the jury "any of them amounts to murder." . . . When she said, "Well, it could have been the noose as Spitz said, but even if you don't like Spitz, then there's this story and if you don't like that, then Dr. Alandy says this and if it didn't happen here, the jogger says it could have happened there." You lose a little bit too much.

She was afraid to say that his story is in the main accurate because she would have been buying into his claim that it happened during rough sex . . . But to fire off that there's this violent struggle and the variety of other things, none of which is really fully corroborated by the facts, I think was, if not a mistake, a strategic decision that I would not have made.

When she said the whole thing is an out-and-out lie, I don't think any of the jurors thought it was an out-and-out lie. When she said flat-out there was no sex at all—and then I thought fairly disingenuously on summation, "Well, what I meant by no sex is no sexual intercourse"—I don't think any of the jurors bought that argument.

I think she had to backtrack after those young ladies

in the bar testified that there may well have been some sexual activity in the park.

Q: They helped you?

A: I think Linda put them on the stand because she was fearful that if she didn't, I was going to. She needed them to show what time Robert left. Alex LaGatta was necessary to establish that the clothing was hers, and she claimed Jennifer had no bruises on her and only she could testify to that. So she had to call them. Yeah, they turned out to be "defense witnesses" insofar as they actually corroborated what Robert said—what Jennifer was saying about him, and pursuing him in the bar. That wasn't made up by Robert to besmirch Jennifer's reputation.

Linda made it appear as if Robert treated her like a sexual object. You heard testimony to the reverse— that Jennifer never liked Robert as a person but thought he was good in bed—and that comes from one of her best friends . . . It adds a lot when the prosecutor says that sex has nothing to do with this.

Q: How did the videotape affect your thinking about the case?

A: My job was to shore it up, to show that if there were failings in it, those failings are eminently human given his state of mind at the time, the shock, the effects of being in police custody for twelve hours. And to show that whereas a juror might find that Robert was not a thousand percent accurate, that his memory of events and his sincerity measure up very well when compared to the witnesses and the job that I intended to do on them in cross-examination.

Q: Did you consider dismissing the videotape because he was a 19-year-old under stress?

A: Coming up with my own tale? I could have fleshed out the story more. But I don't think it's that easy to dismiss because a lot of what is on the videotape obviously comes from Robert. It's not something that you can pin on the police as having said to him as he ruminated and then rehashed some of the details. Some of the visual imagery can only come from Robert. I think his story fits the facts better than any other you can conjure up. You've got to ask yourself under what circumstances can you put a choke-hold on a person from the rear without an intention to cause harm. And the story he tells, I think, is probably the only realistic one. It's very hard to conjure up another one.

Q: Why do you think the case got so big?

A: Certainly their youthfulness, their perceived station in life. And as my wife keeps reminding me about real estate in New York—location, location, location. The park and the museum probably had a lot to do with it. And the issues it raises about what's happening to a potential lost generation, and very significant questions it raises about parenting. That to me is a very, very important issue. That's one of the reasons I think there was so much venom laid at the doorstep of Robert and the defense in general, because it's easy for people to point a finger and say, he's guilty. Rather than deal with the inadequacies that we all have as parents, we shut that out and say he's a killer. He's bad. I think that's why the venom rose to the level it did.

Q: A lot of people were thrown by the comment during the diary hearings that Jennifer's rights ended with her death.

A: That's not a statement I made. I quoted from a case where a judge wrote an opinion that the right of privacy of an individual does not survive that individual's lifetime. People think that I made up the line. It's American law, not Jack Litman on the law, but what the law is in the United States.

Q: What about the organized attack on the blame-the-victim defense?

A: It is curious in a way, because if you change who the victim of the case is, you don't get that same type of publicity. In the Bernhard Goetz case, where most people were against the victims, there it's okay to sully the victims. It all depends on whose ox is gored. When I defend a woman who kills her husband because he had allegedly battered her, even though she shoots him while he's asleep, nobody raises an issue about that. There everyone is for the victim "besmirching" the husband's reputation because everyone says, "Well, it's true." It really depends to some extent on whose ox is gored.

In any case of self-defense the issue is: what provokes it. Usually people kill for a reason—what was the reason? Some reasons people believe in our times are acceptable, others aren't. But the same legal principles underlie all of the reasons. You either have a justification that the law allows—for example, defense of your own life—or you don't. Some people say if you're bigger and the other person's smaller, you shouldn't have it. That's ludicrous.

Q: Do you think Robert's looks affected his life?

A: That's a classic remark. If you put the shoe on the other foot, you hear that about a woman.

Q: Well, this whole case is about the fact that things were reversed.

A: I don't know about everything, but a lot of the stereotypes were reversed, yeah. Perhaps. Perhaps that's so. Certainly one tends to put one's best foot forward. If the best foot happens to be looks and you can get by on that without doing something else, you utilize it. You defer doing the kind of things that most other people have to do, which is applying yourself diligently to a task to get ahead. So perhaps that might have had some effect of deferring certain maturation. I don't really think so, but perhaps it did.

Q: There's certainly a pattern in his life that can be seen in women who are particularly attractive.

A: He was the sexual object. I'm sure you're right about that. I'm sure that's why the media liked it.

Q: Do you like Robert?

A: Yeah, I guess I've come to like him. If you were to think back to where you or I were at nineteen, making critical decisions about our education, the outlines of careers . . . Robert, up until this point, didn't do that. There was a certain degree of irresponsibility. What I saw at this trial was the maturation of a young man who really is a very good young man but who had to cut his eyeteeth of maturation in this kind of a crisis. But I think he came through it pretty well. I really do . . . There is no more criminality. There are no more drugs. The prosecutor may now say, "Oh, we've got all this other stuff." They claim to have all this other stuff. They don't.

Q: Do you identify with your clients to some extent?

A: I get involved with my clients. I have a responsibility to defend as zealously as I can, and I defend very zealously, as you know. And in the framework of helping them make important decisions, I try to help out.

I don't identify with clients. I'm not a youthful kid who spends time in bars. I never go to them. The kind of lifestyle that he and Jennifer led is just not my lifestyle at all, and never will be.

Q: You don't usually try murder cases. Would you do another one soon?

A: If it's interesting enough, perhaps I would.

Q: What made this one interesting to you?

A: Most people from a distance said this kid didn't have a chance going in. There were a lot of strategic calls. How much to supposedly go after her reputation. How to weave in the signs in Robert's statement and not use him as a witness—which takes away from me a lot because obviously I'd like to project him as an individual. I guess putting the whole thing together, there were so many myriad aspects of the case. Just picking a jury for nine and a half weeks is a significant challenge. When they see thirty members of the media every day in the courtroom it puts them under intense pressure—and how to give them the courage to stand up to that pressure. Because it's not pressure to acquit. It's public pressure to convict, and I think we were pretty successful in that. And I take a lot of heart from that.

LINDA FAIRSTEIN
March 31, 1988

Q: Gerald Lefcourt said this case was unique, sui generis, a situation that would never come up again.

A: In how it generated the social interest that it did, I do think this is a once-in-a-lifetime case, for some of the wrong reasons. I broke it down into three aspects that were equally fascinating

We interviewed more than a hundred kids—acquaintances of both, kids that were there that night, kids who weren't—from both address books. That investigation was fascinating. It is unusual that this kind of killing occurs with kids of these backgrounds in Central Park. If it had happened in Southampton, with the same players, it would have a different twist.

And medically it was fascinating. A shooting or a stabbing is such a simple, uncomplicated form of death. Strangulation is one of the most interesting—medically. We learned about asphyxial deaths and carotid sinus reflex and stimulation . . . I don't mean to make her an object but there is a uniqueness to it . . . Jack even argued prescribed medication could affect time of death in an asphyxial setting, which is true. He said the diary may show that. He wanted all the medical records, but it was gynecological information.

The legal part of the case, because Jack is such a good lawyer, the issues that he raised throughout—there was not a day that we didn't go up there practically that something would be thrown in that we just hadn't anticipated. Being forced, being challenged, to think like he did . . .

Q: Would you like to try another case against him?

A: Not next week.

Q: What was the effect of the New Year's Eve decision to suppress Chambers' series of lies?

A: My feeling in general has been that his different lies were not as vital a factor as we think in judging his guilt or innocence of murder. Jack in voir dire attributed it to fear—said Chambers was afraid to admit even that the death had been accidental and he had been in any way involved in it. I think other people—even other people here in my office—put more weight on the various stories than I did.

I wanted that, though.

Q: One of the jurors, Gerry Mosconi, said knowing the details would have made a difference.

A: That's interesting. I accept it.

Q: Was there any point in the trial that you thought was a turning point?

A: I really felt that after Alandy's four days on the stand, that murder was there. I felt this young woman was just so calm and competent. First of all her litany of what these injuries were, from top to bottom, inside and out, was overwhelming and she didn't ham it up, which was wonderful. On cross-examination Jack never touched her on medical issues. She stood up to him. When he started with "these are more extensive . . .", her manner was, "not extensive Mr. Litman, prominent."

I just felt, they may compromise, but it is a murder case.

I felt very good about that because every lawyer we talked to said "manslaughter," and Tom [Kendris] and I would come and look at the pictures and say "murder." But realistically, we expected manslaughter. That was a turning point because I didn't care what Jack did thereafter—I just felt this was a person who had done the autopsy and she just held up beautifully for four days.

She came down from I think the third day when Jack had questioned her and there's a line in the autopsy report where she'd described the hemorrhage along the tip of the tongue and Jack had said, "You said inside, not along." She came down, she was close to tears. She was summa cum laude at the University of San Tomas—a very bright woman—and she was very upset. She said, "You know what he did, it's a terrible thing. English is my second language." She really wanted me to go back on the last day and bring that out. I really felt that she had done so well that it was minimizing—here's this woman who is very bright and whose command of the language was excellent, and to make that kind of little mistake, and the picture is there showing where the hemorrhage is, and I refused to just belittle her by taking one thing that she'd done out of context in an eight-page report and four days on the stand and say: Don't you know the difference between inside and along? It was "along" the inside tip, that was what she left out.

But for me her testimony was the turning point.

Q: If you had to do it over, what would you do differently?

A: I was sure Dr. DiMaio [the ex-medical examiner on Litman's original witness list] would testify and I devoted a great deal of energy to preparing for him. I've got two file drawers of his autopsy reports in other strangulation cases. The day he viewed the body he never took a single measurement, never took a photograph, never examined the neck organs. Dr. Alandy and Dr. Gross said, "The organs are on the other table." He said: "I don't need to see that." I saved one of my best witnesses, Dr. Hirsch, for rebuttal of DiMaio. *Boom!* He wasn't called. Would I have front-loaded it the next time? Possibly.

I wanted Balensweig recalled. What Jack did was unconscionable, not telling me until ten o'clock the night before the name of a witness who's going to testify the next day. Then I get five phone calls when the guy's off the stand—three from lawyers I never heard of—saying the guy's a whore. And asking the judge to have him recalled and that was never ruled on. By that time, I had the transcript in my office, maybe three feet high, where Balensweig had perjured himself, the same way he did in this trial, by saying he had stopped practicing at New York Hospital because of a heart condition. He stopped practicing because they lifted his privileges in 1974, when his heart was pumping fine.

Q: How about the testimony of Jennifer's girl-friends?

A: The kids-in-the-bar issue. I had originally planned to call only Betsy Shankin and Alex LaGatta. Then Jack [in his opening argument] opened on: "You watch and see. She's not going to call those kids from the bar. Or she's not going to tell you what Jennifer was really like." Do I want to do it or do I want to hear it like they are defense witnesses—which I don't think they were? So I did it and everybody behind me is bitching: Jesus, get out of the bar and let's go on to the next thing.

Q: Is it something odd that she would choose to go to Central Park at that hour of the night?

A: I don't think she chose to. I think it was his

choice because he didn't want her at his house. I think she would have followed him anywhere, but according to her friends there's no reason to believe that she would ever have had sex with him in the park. They say she wouldn't let him push her to do something at a time and place that she didn't want to do it.

Q: Chambers used the term "pushy" to describe her.

A: Lieutenant Doyle made that point. Chambers said he had left Boston University, and Doyle asked him, "Did you like it there?" and he said, "No, it was too Jewish." That's part of what we weren't allowed to use. I think that's such an undercurrent. *Pushy*. We have his phone records. You can see the nights that he would be alone between four and five, there are phone calls to—it's a number like Weather, 4-7-6—[sic] "Hi, my name is Gidget. I'm sitting here with my breasts out . . ." I just have a vision of Robert Chambers lying in bed masturbating—and that she was just something for before he went home and did that.

Q: At the plea Chambers looked furious that he was being put through this humiliating spectacle.

A: He was. He was.

Q: Did he not know what was going to happen in court?

A: We were demanding conditions and it was a typical Jack move to stand up and say: "My client is going to plead guilty. These are the conditions." Like he wanted them. I mean, he was eating what we had shoved down his throat. He didn't want to plead on the burglaries, he wanted the whole burglary indictment dismissed. I said, "No, it's going to be a plea, the time can be concurrent, but he's got to plead. And no right to appeal." He told us that he was going to have Robert say, "What I said on the videotape, and then that I pulled more than I was aware I was doing." And I said no, I wanted a negation of the video, not just the same story so he can still say it's really an accident.

Robert until four o'clock was not prepared that he was going to have to say that he intended to harm. I can't prove it but I would bet you money—because Robert doesn't have a brain in his head—that Jack scripted that line . . . that compromise line that "Yes, looking back I intended to, but in my heart . . ." Scripted it as a legal way around it, that would hold up the legality of the plea, but it would give the kid and Jack a face-saving . . . I mean intent negates Jack's whole defense for two years, too.

I just blew up because it was not what was supposed to happen. I wasn't going to let that kid get out of there without saying "Yes, I intended to cause her serious physical injury."

Q: But it still leaves up in the air what actually happened.

A: That's in Robert's head. It's probably in Jack's head. And when we talked to the Levins about a plea they asked, "Do you think you can make him stand up and say what really happened?" But Jack would no more—it's Jack's story too. And Jack has lived with it seriously for two years. So there's not a prayer in the world that this kid is going to get up and tell a different story. It's just never going to happen.

EPILOGUE

No, he has not told a different story. But other stories of the tragedy in Central Park and its aftermath seem certain to emerge in the 1990s while Robert Chambers is in prison.

The notoriety of his three-month trial was blamed by Litman when he quoted a former state parole board chairman as saying Chambers would have "no chance" for release on parole until he has served at least ten years—double his minimum sentence.

But barely a month after Chambers was shipped upstate to prison cells at Fishkill and then Sing Sing and then Great Meadow, his name and face were back on Page One.

His face was fiendish this time. He held a doll in his hands and was twisting its head off.

It seemed that Chambers had starred in another videotape spectacular two weeks before his murder trial began—a home movie filmed with Shawn Kovell and three of her East Side girlfriends, just before Christmas 1987.

On the videotape they cavorted in their underwear with Chambers, passing around a marijuana joint and drinking beer while playing Ring-around-the-Rosie and mugging for the camera.

One scene on the fifty-minute tape stood out. When Chambers twisted off the doll's head he looked into the camera lens and said, "Oops, I think I killed it." On his face was an almost satanic grin.

At another point he looked at Shawn Kovell and said, "So I'll say you're lying. People will believe me."

Notoriety? The remorseless videotape ran nationally on Fox Television for two days to record ratings.

Linda Fairstein found public opinion crystallizing sharply against Chambers after people saw the doll video.

"The reaction I've been getting is that the fence-sitters are dropping off," she told me. "These are people, both professionally and personally, who know I'm the DA on the case. People who had not thought Robert was guilty of murder and who simply didn't think he was such a bad kid. Or who thought something had happened but not bad enough to be called murder. This seems to have put them over the edge."

Litman refused to discuss the doll video with me on the record. He sounded sincerely hurt, however, and the potential jeopardy to his courtroom success seemed to worry him.

There were still some apologists. Liz Bauch, the nice juror from Iowa who had vowed to hold out against Murder Two forever, said of the Chambers doll video: "It was a stupid thing to do, but those girls certainly weren't afraid of him."

Ellen Levin felt vindicated at some level. Calling the doll video "hideous," she told Larry King on his CNN talk-show that at least it showed the public "the nature of the beast that we're dealing with."

She thought she saw something new in Robert
Chambers since her daughter knew him. "There's a
scary kind of 'Village of the Damned' look in his
eyes," Ellen Levin said, "that I don't believe was
there before this happened. I think that whatever took
place in the park that night triggered . . . evilness, or
whatever you want to call it."

Shawn Kovell said she still thought Jennifer Levin's
death was an accident. "I know it was an accident,"
she said in a Fox TV interview after the doll video.
But, the reporter said, Chambers admitted it was
intentional. He had admitted it in court.

Shawn, nineteen, looked the reporter in the eye.
"Didn't you see him shaking his head, no?" she
asked. "He was forced to say that—for reasons."

I remember the photographs of 18-year-old Jennifer
Levin, sprawled at the base of the elm tree behind the
museum in Central Park.

It will always be the saddest story I have ever
covered. It is my hope that there will never be a
sequel.